# 外国专家科学讲堂

## Foreign Expert Science Classes

科学技术部国外人才研究中心  编著

中国出版集团有限公司

研究出版社

图书在版编目 (CIP) 数据

外国专家科学讲堂 / 科学技术部国外人才研究中心编著. -- 北京：
研究出版社，2023.9（2024.9 重印）

ISBN 978-7-5199-1516-2

Ⅰ.①外… Ⅱ.①本… Ⅲ.①科学知识－青少年读物

Ⅳ.①Z228.2

中国国家版本馆CIP数据核字(2023)第107285号


出 品 人：陈建军
出版统筹：丁　波
责任编辑：张　琨

**外国专家科学讲堂**

WAIGUO ZHUANJIA KEXUE JIANGTANG

科学技术部国外人才研究中心　编著

研究出版社 出版发行

（100006　北京市东城区灯市口大街100号华腾商务楼）
北京中科印刷有限公司印刷　新华书店经销
2023年9月第1版　2024年9月第2次印刷
开本：710毫米×1000毫米　1/16　印张：23.25
字数：220千字
ISBN 978-7-5199-1516-2　定价：68.00元
电话（010）64217619　64217652（发行部）

# 编委会成员名单

# 序 言

　　我非常高兴看到第二本关于"外国专家科学讲堂"的书出版。这本书的内容来自"外国专家科学讲堂"——外国科学家面向中国年轻学生（主要是10—15岁）的科普讲座。该讲座由科学技术部资助，科学技术部国外人才研究中心具体组织。全书共包括12篇文章，用中英双语的形式讲述与生命、生活中的科技、科技前沿有关的科普知识。

　　如果有人想了解科学技术为人类带来的福祉，他们只需看看人口预期寿命。150年前，人类的预期寿命约为35岁，如今在包括中国在内的许多国家，人类预期寿命已接近80岁。预期寿命大大提高，原因在于公共健康及卫生的改善，包括饮用水的清洁，农业水平提升带来的营养改善，药物和疫苗的开发等。药物和疫苗的开发治疗甚至预防了许多致命疾病。张其军、王义汉和储扎克的文章普及了一些必要的科学和工程学知识，基于这些知识，医生才能为我们开药方或是对身体进行扫描检查。詹姆斯·爱德华·阿亚拉的文章介绍了野生动物保护，吴晖锽和罗杰威介绍了可持续发展，李飞介绍了清洁能源。开恩在关于计算机科学和编程的文章中表示，计算机已经在我们的生活中扮演了不可或缺的角色。展望未来，计算机的影响将不断增加，正如郑子斌在关于人工智能的文章中所讨论的那样。穆罕默德·沙法和让–皮埃尔·索维奇在他们的文章中表示，与人工智能一样，纳米技术是另一个新兴领域，有望对我们生活的许多方面产生重大影响。

对我们从事科普工作的人来说，2022年是非常令人鼓舞的一年。中共中央办公厅和国务院办公厅印发了《关于新时代进一步加强科学技术普及工作的意见》（以下简称《意见》），以促进科普工作的发展。《意见》设计了激励框架，鼓励更多研究人员，包括年轻学者和老年研究人员，在传播科学知识方面发挥积极作用。

我很荣幸应邀参加了2022年上海科学节的上海科技传播大会。科技部副部长、国家外国专家局局长李萌在大会上讲话，他赞扬了在华外国科学家为中国科普事业作出的贡献，希望更多的外国科学家参与中国的科普工作，加强国际合作与交流，提高中国在该领域的国际影响力。《外国专家科学讲堂》的出版表明，这一进程已经开始。特别令人鼓舞的是，作者之一让–皮埃尔·索维奇教授是诺贝尔奖获得者，他与弗雷泽·斯托达特爵士和本·费林加教授因"分子机器的设计和合成"共同获得了2016年诺贝尔化学奖。

《意见》还提出了雄心勃勃的目标，将公民具备科学素质的比例从目前的11%提高到2025年的15%，到2035年提高至25%。"外国专家科学讲堂"将为实现这一目标作出重要贡献。因为它面向青少年，而当今的青少年就是未来的公民。年幼的孩子们天生就拥有好奇心。作为科普工作者，我们的任务不是创造好奇心，而是确保他们的好奇心不被应试教育的压力和约束所磨灭。本着这种精神，这本书并非简单地向学生灌输知识以告诉他们"学什么"，还指导他们"如何学习"，打开通往许多迷人新世界的大门，这将激发他们通过提出问题以了解更多知识。爱因斯坦经常强调不断质疑一切的重要性，因为创新和创造力源自提出正确的问题，而不是回答问题。

作为科普工作者，我们自然希望激励一些人走上科研道路从而成为科学家，但这只能是美好的愿望，成为科学家的永远是少数。尽管如此，每个人都能从参与科普活动中受益。与所有优秀的科普平台一样，这些文章介绍了分析问题的方法，即通过科学思考、不断怀疑和寻找数据从而得出结论。显然，科学家需要这些技能，但事实上其他人也同样需要。我们处在一个信息爆炸的时代，有些信息是可信的，但更多信息是不完整、不准确甚至是虚假的。我们应该基于逻辑思考和证据形成自己的观点，而不是被娱乐性网站或好朋友直率的观点所误导。培养年轻人的科学思维，将有助于提高公民具备科学素质的比例。

经常有人问我，为什么大学或研究所的科学家应该花时间和精力来做科普，而不仅仅是在实验室里完成他们的研究。我相信本书的作者们也同样面对过这个问题。市场上有许多科普活动的商业供应商，他们的工作人员通常来自媒体或类似背景，具备优秀的沟通能力和表现力。为什么不把科普工作交给科学家们呢？尽管他们可能需要一些技能使科普讲座不同于学术会议或给本科生的讲座，但我同意本书各位作者的观点，即科学家最适合担任各自学科的科普大使。这包括向决策者和纳税人即公众解释为什么我们的研究领域很重要（而且应该有充足的资金！），并培养未来的科学家。科学家们会密切关注所在领域的最新发展，可以提供很多教科书没有的最新信息。这还可以消除许多学生和公众心中的一种错误观念，即科学知识是固定不变的。事实上，情况并非如此：曾在1966年—1973年和1980年—1995年间，担任知名科学期刊《自然》编辑的约翰·马多克斯爵士被问及："《自然》发表的内容有多少是错误的？"他毫不犹豫地回答道："都是错误的！科学就是如此，新的知识会不断纠正旧知识。"我们这本书里，托马斯·斯坦哈姆的文章很好地说明了这一过程。他在文中描述了他和团队如何发现了一种已经灭绝的猫头鹰的骨骼化石，并证明它在白天活动而不是晚上。托马斯的同事李志恒博士指出："这个化石改变了我们对猫头鹰进化的了解。"科学中没有一成不变的东西，此事实应该是对年轻学生的极大鼓励，因为它表明，如果他们努力工作成为一名科学家，将会拥有很多机会，为发现并理解新的科学知识作出自己的贡献。

科学家做科普工作还有一个优势，那就是基于专业知识，他们有信心解决年轻人提出的许多富有想象力和发人深省的问题。其中一些问题会促使他们以一种全新的、不同的方式来看待自己的研究。实际上想方设法满足受众的好奇心，可能会提高他们自己对所研究对象的理解。因此，科学传播成为一种双赢的活动。

我相信，所有参加"外国专家科学讲堂"的科学家都会认为，参与这项活动不仅非常有趣，还能充实自己。除了为广大读者提供一个宝贵的科学交流平台外，我希望本书的出版能激励其他外国科学家参与此项活动，让我们能够读到本系列的更多图书。

戴伟（英国）

北京化工大学科普实验中心主任、教授

（张晓　译）

# PREFACE

It is a great pleasure to welcome the publication of the second volume of "Science Classes from Foreign Experts", consisting of 12 essays based on popular science talks given by foreign scientists to young (mainly in the age range 10–15) Chinese students. This project was organized by the Foreign Talent Research Center under the auspices of the Ministry of Science and Technology of the People's Republic of China (MOST). The bilingual (Chinese–English) essays describe some of the exciting developments in many frontier areas of science and technology, encompassing the fields of medicine, paleontology and zoology, the impact of technology on our everyday lives, computer science and nanotechnology.

If anyone needs evidence that science and technology have brought great benefits to humankind, they need look no further than the figures for life expectancy at birth. Only 150 years ago, this was around 35, whereas nowadays, in many countries—including China—it is close to 80. This approximate doubling of life expectancy resulted from improved public health and sanitation, ensuring clean drinking water, improvements in agriculture leading to better nutrition, and the development of medicines and vaccines, which enabled the treatment or even prevention of many, often fatal, diseases. The essays by James Zhang, Wang Yihan and Zachary Smith highlight some of the science and engineering that is necessary before a doctor can prescribe a drug for you or take an imaging scan of part of your body. Nowadays, however, rather than seeking a further doubling of life expectancy, improving the quality of life has become the target for most people. Several of the essays cover this issue from different viewpoints, including conservation (of seeds and wildlife, respectively, by Uromi Manage Goodale and James Ayala), sustainable and ecologically sound development, by Goh Hui-Huan and Paolo Genovese, and clean energy, by Rafael Nieto.As explained by Lo Leung Mimia Hoi Yan in her introduction to computer science and programming,computers already play an indispensable part in our lives. Looking to the future, their impact can only increase, as discussed by Alex Cheng in his essay on Artificial Intelligence (AI). Like AI, nanotechnology is another emerging field that promises to make significant impacts in many aspects of our lives, as reviewed in the essays by Muhammad Shafa and Jean-Pierre Sauvage.

2022 was a very encouraging year for those of us engaged in science popularization (outreach). The general offices of the Communist Party of China Central Committee and the State Council issued a set of "Guidelines" for facilitating and promoting the popularization of science and technology. These set out pathways and a framework of incentives to encourage more researchers—both young and old—to play an active role in disseminating scientific knowledge. I was honored to be invited to participate in the Shanghai Science and Technology Communication Conference, part of the 2022 Shanghai Science Festival.In his speech at this event, Li Meng, Vice-minister of MOST and Administrator of the State Administration of Foreign Experts Affairs, commended the efforts of foreign scientists to promote science popularization in China. He expressed the hope that more foreign scientists will participate in China's sci-tech communication work and strengthen international cooperation and exchanges and enhance international influence in this field. The publication of "Science Classes from Foreign Experts" shows that this process has already begun. It is particularly encouraging that one of the authors, Prof. Jean-Pierre Sauvage, is a Nobel Laureate, having shared the 2016 Nobel Prize in Chemistry" for the design and synthesis of molecular machines" with Prof. Sir Fraser Stoddart and Prof. Ben Feringa.

There are also ambitious targets in the "Guidelines" to raise the proportion of Chinese citizens with scientific literacy from the current level of ca. 11% to 15% in 2025 and then to 25% by 2035. "Science Classes from Foreign Experts" will make an important contribution to realizing this objective since the young people who are its target audience are the citizens of tomorrow. Young children are innately curious, so our task as science communicators is not to create curiosity but to keep it alive by ensuring it is not worn down by the pressures and constraints of an exam-oriented education system. In this spirit, these essays do not just tell students "What to learn" by simply feeding them with factual knowledge but also guide them in "How to learn".By opening the doors to many fascinating new worlds,they will inspire readers to want to find out more information by asking searching questions. Albert Einstein often stressed the importance of constantly questioning everything, because it is finding the right question—rather than the answer—which leads to innovation and creativity.

Although, as science communicators, we naturally hope to inspire some of our audience to go on to follow a path that leads to them becoming a scientist, with the best will in the world, this is always going to be a minority. However, all the audience members can benefit from participating in science popularization activities. These essays, like all good popular science platforms, provide an introduction to a way of analyzing problems by thinking scientifically, being constantly skeptical and looking for data to support conclusions. Scientists obviously need these skills but,in actual fact, so does everyone else. We are constantly bombarded with information, some of which is credible, but much more is incomplete, inaccurate, or even fake. Rather than being seduced by an all singing, all dancing website, or overwhelmed by a good friend's forthright opinions, we need to form our ideas based on logical thought and searching for evidence. Inculcating this way of thinking in our young audience will make an important contribution to raising the proportion of citizens with scientific literacy.

I am often asked—an experience I am sure is shared by the authors of these essays—why a scientist from a university or research institute should be willing to spend time and effort popularizing science rather than simply getting on with their research back in the lab. Since there are many commercial providers of popular scientific events, often using graduates from a media studies or similar background who have excellent communication and performing skills, why not leave the science popularization to them? Although scientists may need to develop the skills and tricks of the trade that make a popular science lecture different from a presentation at an academic conference or an undergraduate lecture, I agree with the authors of these essays that practicing scientists are best placed to act as ambassadors for our respective disciplines. This includes explaining to policymakers and the tax-paying public why our research area is important (and should be well-funded!) as well as cultivating a pipeline of future scientists. Scientists also closely follow the recent developments in their area and can provide up to date information going beyond what may be in the textbooks. This is not just important in itself but also tackles the misconception that many students and the general public have formed in their minds that scientific knowledge is fixed and immutable. In reality, this is very much not the case: when Sir John Maddox, the eminent former editor (1966–1973 and 1980–1995) of the prestigious scientific journal Nature was asked, "How much of what you publish in Nature is wrong?", he unhesitatingly replied, "All of it! That's what science is about—new knowledge constantly arriving to correct the old.".This process is nicely illustrated in the essay by Thomas Stidham, where he describes how he and his team discovered a fossil skeleton of an extinct owl and were able to show that it was active in the daytime, rather than at night.As his co-worker, Dr. Li Zhiheng noted, "This fossil skeleton turns what we thought we knew about the evolution of owls on its head.".The fact that nothing in science is set in stone should be a great encouragement to young students since it shows that if they work hard and become a scientist, they will have plenty of opportunities to find a niche and make their own contribution to new knowledge and understanding.

A further advantage that we, as practicing scientists, have as communicators is the confidence—based on our background knowledge and training—to tackle the many imaginative and thought provoking questions posed by our young audiences. Some of these questions can prompt us to look at our subject in a new or different way, and having to step back and find ways to satisfy the curiosity of an audience may actually improve our own understanding. Thus science communication becomes a win-win activity.

I am sure that all the scientists contributing to "Science Classes from Foreign Experts" will agree that their participation has been enriching from a personal viewpoint, and that it has also been great fun! As well as providing a valuable science communication platform for a wide audience, I hope its publication will inspire other foreign scientists to join the program so that we can look forward to reading further volumes in the series.

Prof. David G. Evans

Director of the Outreach Center

Beijing University of Chemical Technology

# CONTENTS 目录

# 第二章　生活中的科技
## Science and Technology in Life

### 第三章　科技前沿
**Frontier of Science and Technology**

# CHAPTER 1 第一章

## 生　命

### Life

# 病原微生物与人的战争

文／张其军［英］

　　微生物是先于人类存在几十亿年的原始级生物体。当人类进入农耕时代，生活方式从游散向群聚发展后，微生物特别是病原微生物在人群中的传播便成为可能。自有文字记载的近3000年来，人类经历了一场又一场代价惨重的"瘟疫"。直到140年前，科学家才从显微镜下辨认出这些曾令人类恐惧的"瘟疫元凶"竟是肉眼看不到的病原微生物。表1仅列出公元后几个著名的疫情事件，数以百万计的生命代价不亚于大型战争对人类的伤害。

表1. 人类历史中几宗重大传染病事件

| 发生年代 | 疫情名称 | 推测病原 | 死亡人数(万) |
|---|---|---|---|
| 165—180 | 安东尼瘟疫（欧洲） | 天花病毒 | 500—1000 |
| 541—549 | 查士丁尼瘟疫（欧洲） | 鼠疫杆菌 | 3000—5000 |
| 1334—1353 | 黑死病（欧洲） | 鼠疫杆菌 | 7500—20000 |
| 1520—1600 | 新世界天花（美洲） | 天花病毒 | 2500—5600 |
| 1817—1923 | 六次霍乱大流行 | 霍乱弧菌 | 500+ |
| 1855—1959 | 第三次鼠疫（全球） | 鼠疫杆菌 | 1200—1500 |
| 1918—1919 | 西班牙流感 | 甲型流感病毒（H1N1） | 5000—10000 |

（数据来源：互联网）

# ▌ 影响文明进程的病原微生物

病原微生物对人类的文明进程产生过重大影响。

## 重创希腊文明

最早有文字记载的瘟疫大流行发生在公元前430年的伯罗奔尼撒战争期间。染有病原的斯巴达人把"瘟疫"带进雅典，超过三分之二的雅典人因感染死亡。公元前五世纪是希腊文明最辉煌的时期，苏格拉底、柏拉图、亚里士多德、修昔底德等大思想家和大科学家就活跃在那个时代。希腊文明曾萌生了人类多个政体形式，包括寡头制、贵族制、君主制、共和制甚至民主制。然而这场至今尚未明确病原的疫情大爆发使希腊人遭到灭顶之灾，希腊文明受到重创。

## 致衰罗马帝国

人类第一次有记载的天花大流行（史称安东尼瘟疫）发生在史称罗马黄金时代的公元165年。瘟疫可能是由向西扩张的匈奴传染给罗马士兵后播散到整个罗马帝国的。持续了15年的疫情使至少500万罗马人死亡，连罗马皇帝马库斯·奥勒琉斯也未能幸免。这场瘟疫使鼎盛时期的罗马帝国元气大伤，政权陷入危机并很快进入分裂的东西罗马帝国时代。

公元541年曾爆发人类第一次有记载的鼠疫大流行。疫情源自于埃及，拜占庭帝国（即东罗马帝国）成为重灾区并波及整个地中海、欧洲及近东国家。这个以拜占庭国王名字命名的查士丁尼瘟疫导致数千万人丧生，约占当时世界人口的26%。这场瘟疫直接导致罗马帝国复兴计划破灭，东罗马帝国崩溃。

### 安格鲁–撒克逊人崛起

另一场在欧陆蔓延了近2个世纪的赛普里安瘟疫于公元444年传入西罗马帝国治下的不列颠岛。当时的不列颠岛经常受到来自北方的凯尔特人袭扰，瘟疫的蔓延使边防守军严重匮乏，大量的欧陆日耳曼人被征召戍边。罗马帝国崩溃后，更多的日耳曼人涌入空虚的不列颠岛。六个多世纪后，当诺曼人征服不列颠岛时，这些隶属日耳曼民族的安格鲁人，撒克逊人和朱特人已被称作"英国人"了。

### 欧洲人殖民美洲

1492年哥伦布发现新大陆后，欧洲人开始移民美洲。欧洲人带去的不仅是枪炮，还有令美洲土著人恐怖的各种病菌，包括鼠疫和天花。突如其来的病原微生物迅速在缺乏免疫力的土著人群中传播。数据显示，天花在当时欧洲大陆的致死率大约是30%，而从未接触过天花的土著人死亡率达到惊人的90%。瘟疫造成至少5600万美洲土著人死亡，为欧洲殖民者统治美洲大陆荡平了障碍。

### 康熙继承大位

瘟疫重创中国的事件也不胜枚举。东汉末年（推测为鼠疫）和明朝末年（鼠疫和天花）的两次大瘟疫均加速了两个王朝的覆灭。

然而疫情也可以从另一方面改变个人和国家的命运。当年满族人从北方进入中原时，最令他们恐惧的是瘟疫天花。清朝第一个皇帝顺治据说是染天花驾崩，据传其遗诏选定康熙的主要原因是康熙曾经染过天花，因而不会再染，有利皇权长期稳定。康熙在位的61年（编者注），是中国历史上最稳定和长足发展的时期之一。

## ▍ 人类抗击病原微生物的努力

长期以来人类为抗击"瘟疫"不断做出努力。

### 中国贡献

公元317年东晋医学家葛洪在其医书《肘后备急方》对天花有详细记载。对治疗狂犬病也具体到"乃杀所咬之犬，取脑敷之，后不复发"。书中治疗疟疾用的青蒿的制作方法曾对1700年后获得2015年诺贝尔医学奖的屠呦呦起到启发作用。另外，该书还提出用黄连治疗痢疾的方法。

清初医学家俞天池在《痧痘集解》中对明朝隆庆年间使用的人痘法预防天花有具体描述：把天花患者的痂疤剥离干燥后磨成粉，吹到未患病幼童的鼻孔里。康熙帝得过天花，深知天花之害。他于

1682年下令全国普及人痘接种法预防天花，《庭训格言》中记录了他对人痘法挽救无数人生命的喜悦心情。

中国的人痘法很快引发他国仿效。1721年英国的玛丽女士跟随担任大使的丈夫来到奥斯曼帝国，看到当地人使用中国的人痘法预防天花后决定给自己的两岁儿子接种并获得成功。随后，她向英王推荐了这个来自中国的天花预防术。

中国的人痘法预防天花开启了人类人工免疫的历史先河，尽管当时人们并不清楚天花的病因是什么。

### 疫苗的诞生

人痘法防治天花虽然效果明显，但接种的死亡率却高达2%，副作用也不小。

1796年英国医生爱德华·詹纳观察到挤奶女工感染牛天花后仅出现轻度症状。于是他设想能否利用牛的痘癍来预防天花。他把挤奶女工手上的痘癍渗液点染到花匠8岁儿子的手臂上，几周后该童出现轻度症状。之后他再直接用牛的天花痘癍渗液感染该童，居然未出现任何症状。他确信女工的痘癍使男童获得了抵御天花的能力。因拉丁语中把牛叫Vacca，于是他把牛痘接种的做法叫Vaccination。与人痘法相比，牛痘法更加安全。

然而牛痘接种法预防人天花却遭到众多非议和广泛抵制。直到1840年英国政府才正式通过使用牛痘法预防天花，13年后英国政府颁布政令强制民众接种牛痘，并动用警力监督执行。而这时詹纳医生已经去世30年了。两年后美国、德国也相继颁布了强制接种牛痘的法令。

牛痘成为人类首个广泛推广的安全疫苗。如今，Vaccination已成为疫苗接种的通用名词了。

### 巴斯德与人工疫苗

1876年德国医生罗伯特·科赫使用显微镜观察到炭疽杆菌，数年后先后分离出伤寒杆菌、结核分歧杆菌和霍乱弧菌等病原体。人们终于认识到那些曾令人恐惧的疫情元凶其实是这些肉眼无法看到的病原微生物。

天花疫苗的成功激发了原本是化学专家的法国人路易斯·巴斯德对病原微生物疫苗的开发兴趣。1879年巴斯德研究鸡霍乱疫苗。当助手把遗忘数周的霍乱菌液给鸡接种后发现接种死亡率远较使用新鲜霍乱菌液低。进一步实验证实久置的霍乱菌毒力虽然明显下降但依然能让鸡产生对霍乱菌的免疫力。这一发现启发了科学家对减毒疫苗的开发思路。之后的1881年巴斯德利用加温处理开发出炭疽杆菌减毒疫苗。

巴斯德实验发现狂犬病患者晾干后的脑脊髓组织可制作疫苗。有位叫约瑟夫的9岁男孩被疯狗咬伤后其家人找巴斯德求助。但狂犬病疫苗从未在人身上使用过。当医生确认约瑟夫必死无疑后，巴斯德决定尝试。令人惊喜的是，疫苗注射后患童居然没有出现狂犬病发作症状。此后，巴斯德用同样的方法救治了一位被咬得奄奄一息的15岁牧羊倌。在随后的两年里，上千名来自各地、被狂犬咬伤的患者都成功获救。

狂犬疫苗的成功使人们认识到疫苗可成为预防传染病的商业化产品，整个世界都为之振奋了！大量鼓励巴斯德继续研发的捐款接踵而来，这促使巴斯德研究所于1888年在巴黎建立。疫苗可人工产自实验室而非受染动物，人工疫苗的诞生开启了人类抗击病原微生物的历史新篇章，为人类传染病主动免疫计划打下基础。

回顾过往，我们发现1700年前东晋医学家葛洪在其著作《肘后备急方》中对狂犬病的阐述，与巴斯德治疗狂犬病的思路是如此相似。中国早于西方1000多年前就对天花、狂犬病、疟疾和痢疾等的治疗有相当丰富的经验总结，为什么现代医学没有在中国产生呢？

### 计划免疫工程

1796年疫苗出现前天花的平均死亡率约10%，牛痘疫苗使用后天花死亡率逐年下降，至1880年起伦敦的天花死亡率已接近为零。1900年英国对全体儿童正式实施天花疫苗接种计划，带动全球开启了人类计划免疫工程时代（图1）。

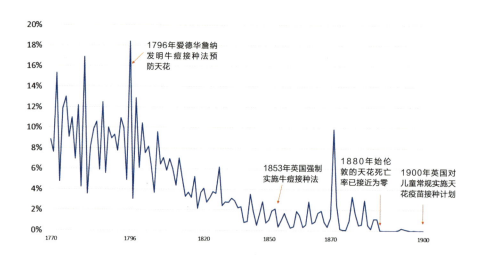

图1. 伦敦1770—1900年天花死亡率数据图。（数据来源：OWID 2017年资料）

1934年英国宣布消灭天花。1979年12月9日世界卫生组织宣布消灭天花。天花疫苗成为全球第一个，也是迄今唯一一个成功清除病毒危害的人类计划免疫项目。

目前全球陆续已有数十种病原微生物疫苗纳入儿童常规接种计划。有序的儿童免疫接种计划使无数人免于传染病的威胁，计划免疫工程为人类彻底战胜病原微生物疾病带来信心和希望。

### 青霉素与抗生素时代

人工疫苗通过主动激活人体免疫系统以抵御特定病原微生物的入侵，其所针对的多是传播性强、病死率高的病原微生物。而那些传播力较低但更为常见的细菌感染也严重威胁人类，曾经也缺乏有效治疗手段。

一个偶然让英国细菌学家弗莱明受到启发。1928年休假前他忘记关上实验室窗户，回来后发现金黄葡萄球菌菌落周边出现消融圈，他敏锐推断该金葡菌的繁殖可能受到了窗外飘进培养皿的霉菌抑制。他把这个发现写成论文却未引起反响。9年后二战爆发，前线急需抗菌药物。弗莱明的这篇论文被翻出查验。剑桥的弗劳瑞和钱恩团队成功提取了青霉菌素并通过临床试验证实了青霉素的出色抗菌效果。青霉素在二战中大显神威，成了受伤战士的救命神药。在以往的战争中，受伤官兵除了截肢基本没有其他救治办法。而一旦出现伤口感染多难逃一死。

青霉素迅速成为感染性疾病的治疗利器。弗莱明、弗劳瑞、钱恩三人共同获得了1945年诺贝尔生理或医学奖。

青霉素开启了人类抗生素时代！

随后人类针对不同的病原菌开发出一系列不同种类多代次不同抗生素。包括 β-内酰胺类（如青霉素类、头孢菌素类、新型 β-内酰胺类等），氨基糖苷类（如庆大霉素、阿米卡星、妥布霉素等），大环内酯类（如红霉素、克拉霉素、阿奇霉素等），四环素类，林可霉素类，多肽类（如多粘霉素、万古霉素等），喹诺酮类（诺佛沙星、环丙沙星等），磺胺类，抗结核药以及抗真菌药等。

1900年至今，全球人均寿命由不足30岁迅速上升到70岁左右与人类计划免疫的全面实施和各类抗生素的普及应用密切相关。疫苗和抗生素成为人类健康的保护神。

# 新挑战——抗生素耐药

## 抗生素的不当使用

青霉素强大的抗菌能力拉高了人们对抗生素的期待和依赖。相当多的人包括一些医务人员都把抗生素当作治疗首选，特别是原因不明的发热或感染。

由于致病源的即时检测手段有限，面对病情压力时，很多医生常用抗生素作"诊断性"治疗。据统计，能够引起发热等"感冒样症状"的病原不下300种。以抗生素为例，青霉素对病毒、霉菌以及抗菌谱以外的细菌几乎没有治疗作用。而抗生素过量或不当使用的现象十分普遍。

假以时日人们发现原来很容易控制的"感冒样症状"变得困难了，曾经颇为有效的抗生素效果明显下降甚至无效了。

## 病原微生物基因变异

世界卫生组织警告，全球每年超过70万人死于因抗生素耐药导致的无药可医。

作为自然进化的一部分，病原微生物的基因变异在繁殖过程中不断出现。当变异引致抗生素的效力下降甚至无效时，这个产生变异的菌株便成了耐药菌株。图2阐述了耐药菌株的发生和发展过程。假定细菌在开始是没有耐药性的，繁殖过程中因编码错误而产生基因突变，当使用抗生素治疗时，不耐药的菌株会被抗生素清除，而出现耐药突变的菌株则不会被清除。这些未被清除的菌株继续繁殖成优势菌群时，在治疗上便出现耐药现象。

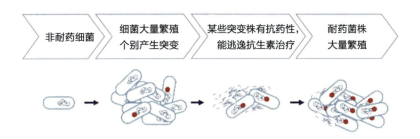

图2. 耐药菌株的发生和发展

抗生素耐药菌株可能在下列情形出现：1）抗生素使用不当或滥用，使耐药菌株成为优势菌群；2）抗生素未足量或未足期使用，使未除清的病原菌株有突变可能；3）食用使用过抗生素的家畜和家禽有可能感染耐药菌株；4）医院是耐药菌株滋生和存留的高风险区域，被动感染风险大；5）较差卫生环境中病原微生物滋生和突变机会大。

世界卫生组织报告，2013年全球抗结核菌药物耐药新增患者人数达到50万人。预计到2050年死于因结核菌耐药无法救治的病人将达到1000万人，而同期癌症的预计死亡人数却仅有800万，远远高于同期的糖尿病和交通事故死亡人数。难治性耐药菌株在人群中的播散其实如同另类形式的疫情，其隐形传播的特征应引起足够的重识。

# ▌ 新冠疫情大流行及反思

2023年5月4日世界卫生组织宣布新冠疫情不再构成"国际关注的突发公共卫生事件"，肆虐人类3年有余的新型冠状病毒大流行终于告一段落。

3年多来，全球确诊新冠病毒感染人数超过7.65亿人，确诊死亡病例超过692万人（WHO数据），成为西班牙流感大流行后100年里最大的疫情事件。世卫组织总干事谭德塞表示，新冠疫情大流行至少使2000万人死于新冠，是官方公布数字的三倍。3年的新冠疫情大流行无疑成了病原微生物与现代人类战争的现实版演练。

## 在未知病原微生物面前人类依然脆弱

人类对病原微生物的认知仅仅有百多年历史，且远未掌握针对疫情大流行的有效预防、诊断和控制手段。即便是最发达国家，对新冠疫情的应对表现也远不尽人意。世界卫生组织数据表明，GDP前20位国家新冠病毒肺炎确诊总数近6亿人，约占全球确诊患者总数的78%，而其人口总数的全球占比仅有58%。说明相对优越的经济和医疗条件并不足以构建阻止病毒传播的有效篱笆。现代人类在病原未知的疫情大流行面前，尚十分缺乏防治病原微生物的有效手段。

和历史上的"瘟疫大流行"一样，新冠病毒疫情也重创了全球经济。美联储数据表明，与2019年10月相比，2021年4月全球低收入国家GDP增长减少5.2%，中等收入国家减少8.7%，高收入国家减少6.4%；全球GDP增长减少的量相当于英国和法国2019年全年GDP之和，而全球经济的实际相关损失远远不止这个数。

### 新冠病毒的变异和疫情演化

国情不同，新冠病毒疫情在各国的传播也各有不同。但大致经历了由原始病毒株向变异株进化的不同阶段。图3.1和图3.2分别展示了自2020年1月至2022年11月底英美两国每百万人口新冠病毒疫情的每日新确诊人数和死亡人数的走势，图3.3展示了英国不同新冠病毒变异株的演进态势。

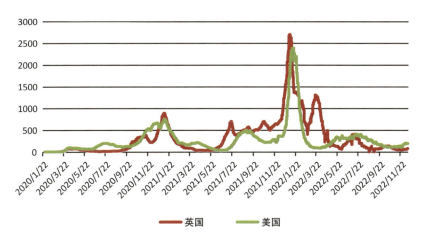

图3.1 2020年1月至2022年11月英美每百万人口新发病例走势图（数据来源：约翰·霍普金斯大学）

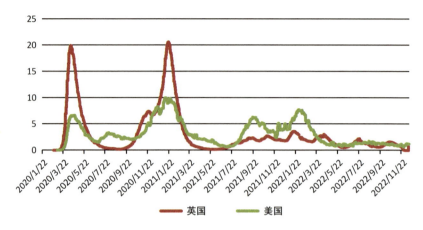

图3.2 2020年1月至2022年11月英美两国每百万人口新增死亡报告走势图（数据来源：约翰·霍普金斯大学）

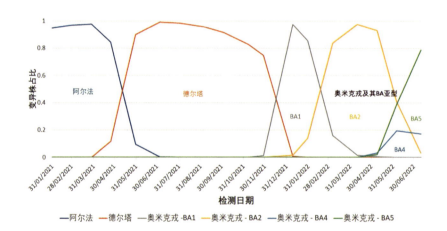

图3.3 2021年2月—2022年7月英国新冠病毒变异株占比走势图（数据来源：英国保健局）

　　不难发现，在2020年7月之前的原始病毒株阶段，英美两国虽然每日新增确诊病例数表现平缓，但每日新增死亡数却呈现高位。2020年11月进入阿尔法变异株期后，每日新增确诊病例英美出现小高峰，每日新增死亡病例对应出现较大峰值。2021年5月进入德尔塔病毒变异株期后，英美每日新增确诊病例和新增死亡病例再度走高，但与原始株和阿尔法株期比较已经明显趋缓。2021年12月进入奥密克戎变异期后，每日新增病例突然大幅增加，但每日新增死亡数变化不大。奥密克戎变异株很快出现新的亚型，其在每日新增确诊病例和新增死亡病例两方面逐渐趋于颓势。说明新冠病毒传播从奥密克戎变异株起进入高传播低死亡阶段，毒力大大减低。

　　同前述的细菌一样，病毒在繁衍过程中也会不断发生变异。与细菌不同的是病毒寄生在宿主细胞里，病毒的生存和进化与宿主细胞反应密切相关。在疫情初期陌生病毒会引发宿主细胞剧烈反应，临床死亡率和重症率较高。病毒株的自然变异或者呈现为宿主细胞的强烈反应（如阿尔法变异株），或者呈现为宿主细胞的一般反应（如德尔塔变异株）甚至温和反应（如奥密克戎变异株）。只有当宿主细胞对病毒呈现温和反应时，病毒便易于在宿主体内生存和繁殖。由于症状的隐蔽性，毒力较弱的病毒具有更强的生存能力和更隐蔽的传播能力，表现为传播速度倍增，但症状轻微。

　　英国保健局数据（图4）表明在阿尔法病毒株期间（2020年9月—2021年4月）新增住院患者基本都是重症，该期的死亡患者曾达到每天1000人以上，超过英国新冠疫情初期（2020年3月—2020年6月）的重症和死亡数。当疫情进入德尔塔病毒变异期（2021年7月—2021年12月）后，住院患者出现小高峰，临床虽然还以重症为主，但与阿尔法变异期相比重症患者数量已有明显下降，死亡率呈明显回落并维持在较低水平。2021年12月起奥密克戎变异株迅速占据优势，社会面病毒检测阳性确诊患者数量剧增，远远超出以往水平。虽然再度掀起数波次住院高峰期，与阿尔法和德尔塔变异株明显不同的是重症患者和死亡患者新增数量基本维持在较低水平。

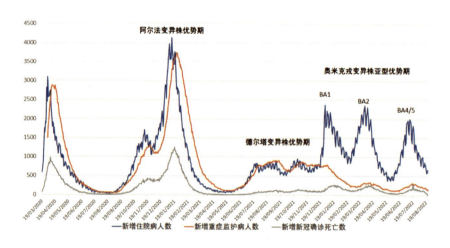

图4．2020年3月—2022年8月英国新冠病毒感染住院，重症和死亡新发病例走势图（数据来源：英国保健局）

### 新冠疫苗的保护作用

病毒的寄生特征给治疗带来困难。到目前为止人类尚无有效药物治疗病毒感染，接种疫苗是最佳的防御手段。疫苗接种所产生的抗体能够中和病毒从而实现预防病毒侵袭或者减少重症和死亡发生。然而在新冠疫情开始后的12个月内没有疫苗，唯一能做的只有对症处理，在实施较为宽松的管控政策的国家中，早期重症率和死亡率偏高是可预料到的。

以英国为例，2021年初新冠疫苗上市至2021年8月，英国境内的疫苗两针接种率已达80%以上；至2021年12月疫苗加强针的接种率也达到60%以上。

然而英国德尔塔变异株和奥密克戎变异株期新冠疫情新增死亡数的明显下降是因为病毒本身毒力下降还是因为疫苗接种后人体产生抗体后对病毒的中和作用，还有待更多的相关数据才能进行分析。

毋庸置疑的是，疫苗接种对于新冠病毒的防御具有重要作用。

图5. 英国2020年1月—2022年8月间新冠病毒再度感染患者新增病例数据（数据来源：英国保健局）

从英国保健局数据分析发现，在奥密克戎变异株流行期间出现相当数量的再次（甚至多次）新冠感染患者，再次感染新增病例数与奥密克戎变异株不同亚型感染曲线基本一致（图5），而再次感染现象在阿尔法和德尔塔变异株期几乎没有发现。这种现象反映出奥密克戎变异株已和前期变异株明显不同，或者说前期接种的疫苗已失去对奥密克戎变异株的防御效能。基因分析表明奥密克戎病毒株的变异位点已多达32以上，其对针对早期病毒版本制作的疫苗很可能存在免疫"逃逸"。显然，针对新冠病毒奥密克戎变异株的新疫苗接种是必要的。2022年11月英国对50岁以上人群实施了针对奥密克戎变异株疫苗的接种（第四针）。

表2. 主要国家新冠疫苗接种数据和新冠病毒感染确诊病人死亡率

| 国家 | 疫苗接种数/100人 | 疫苗2针接种数/100人 | 疫苗加强针/100人 | 确诊死亡率% |
|---|---|---|---|---|
| 印度 | 159.9 | 68.99 | 16.57 | 1.18 |
| 巴西 | 239.65 | 80.12 | 51.71 | 1.87 |
| 俄罗斯 | 127.7 | 54.54 | | 1.74 |
| 美国 | 171.21 | 65.51 | 31.39 | 1.08 |
| 英国 | 222.8 | 74.59 | 65.0 | 0.91 |
| 法国 | 234.5 | 78.98 | 60.61 | 0.42 |
| 德国 | 232.3 | 76.42 | 62.68 | 0.45 |
| 日本 | 302.96 | 81.72 | 68.28 | 0.22 |
| 中国 | 238.97 | 87.3 | 56.67 | 0.12 |
| 新西兰 | 254.08 | 84.69 | 56.39 | 0.12 |
| 韩国 | 251.9 | 82.97 | 75.3 | 0.11 |
| 新加坡 | 254.75 | 87.5 | 79.1 | 0.07 |

（WHO数据）

世界卫生组织统计数据（表2）表明新冠病毒疫苗的接种率与新冠病毒感染死亡率之间似有一定的关联性，疫苗接种率较低国家特别是第三针接种率较低国家其新冠病毒感染的死亡率相比略高。但十分明显的是，表中实行"清零政策"的四个国家或地区其新冠病毒感染病死率均处于较低水平。值得关注的是相对而言，韩国（非"清零政策"国）和新加坡两国拥有相对更低的新冠感染病死率。

**未来展望：挑战没有终点**

如同世间万物，微生物以其自有的生存需求不断与其他微生物，与动物，与植物，与人类间发生交集。数万年的生存发展，作为大自然食物链的一部分，人与微生物之间更多的还是相互依存的关系。然而如同人类自身基因突变能够引发癌症一样，微生物自身的基因突变也会把微生物变异成致病源伤害人体健康甚至导致疫情大流行。因此，人类与病原微生物之间的战争还会经常发生。

值得欣慰的是，尽管人类识别病原微生物的历史不足150年，疫苗和抗生素的出现让那些曾令人谈之色变的人类大部分病原微生物所引发的传染性疾病基本都已得到控制。但从应对新冠病毒大流行的结局和抗感染现实来看，人类还远未掌握病原微生物的发生发展规律，还没有具备保护人类免受病原微生物侵害的能力，在很多方面，依然有很大空间可以探索以增强抗击疫情的效果。

展望未来，提高人类抗击病原微生物的能力，需要从以下几个方面着力：

1）提高疫苗研制速度和临床安全应用机制，以最快速度遏制疫情传播，降低疫情早期死亡率；

2）在疫情早期果断实施"清零政策"，最大限度阻断病毒高危期传播；

3）科学实施"清零解除政策"，保护高危人群，最大限度巩固清零政策成果；

　　4）加快研制新型抗生素，科学管控抗生素使用；

　　5）以新思路研究病原微生物变异和耐抗生素机制。

**作者简介**

　　张其军，英籍华人。1985年毕业于西安交通大学医学系，出国前系北京大学第三医院主治医师，1997年获英国剑桥大学医学系博士学位。现为英国皇家医学会会士，皇家药学会科学家，中国科协特聘专家，世界华人医师协会理事，旅英华人高新科技商业协会会长。

# The Battle of Human against Pathogenic Microorganisms

By James Zhang (UK)

Microorganisms are primitive organisms that existed billions of years before humans. When human entered the farming era and the lifestyle developed from dispersal to clustering, the spread of microorganisms, especially pathogenic microorganisms, among the population became possible. In the nearly 3,000 years since there were written records, humanity has suffered many costly pandemics. Only until 147 years ago that scientists recognized from the microscope that these "pandemic culprits" that once terrified humans were pathogenic microorganisms invisible to the naked eye. Table 1 lists only a few famous pandemic events after AD.Just like the harm caused by large wars to human beings, those events have cost millions of lives.

Table 1. Several major pandemics events in human history

| Years | Pandemics/Epidemics | Pathogens | Death (M) |
|---|---|---|---|
| 165-180 | Antonine Plague | Smallpox | 5-10 |
| 541-549 | Plague of Justinian | Yersinia pestis | 30-50 |
| 1334-1353 | Black Death | Yersinia pestis | 75-200 |

Table (Continued)

| Years | Pandemics/Epidemics | Pathogens | Death (M) |
|---|---|---|---|
| 1520-1600 | New World Smallpox | Smallpox | 25-56 |
| 1817 -1923 | Six Cholera pandemics | Vibrio cholerae | 5+ |
| 1855-1959 | The Third Plague | Yersinia pestis | 12-15 |
| 1918-1919 | Spanish Flu | H1N1 Influenza A | 50-100 |

(Data source: Internet)

# Pathogenic Microorganisms Affecting the Progress of Civilization

Pathogenic microorganisms had significant impact on the progress of human civilization.

## Severely Damaging of the Greek Civilization

The earliest recorded plague pandemic occurred during the Peloponnesian War in 430 BC. The Spartans infected with the pathogen brought the "plague" into Athens, then, more than two-thirds of the Athenians died caused by the infection. It is known that the fifth century BC was the most glorious period of Greek civilization.Great thinkers and scientists such as Socrates, Plato, Aristotle, and Thucydides were active in that era. Greek civilization also gave birth to many forms of human government, including oligarchy, aristocracy, monarchy, republic and even democracy. However, the outbreak of the pandemic with unrecognized pathogen devastated the Greeks, which significantly damaged the Greek civilization.

## Declining the Roman Empire

The first recorded smallpox pandemic in humans (known as the Antonine plague in history) occurred in AD 165, the time known as in the period of Roman Golden Age in history. The plague may have been caused by the Huns who expanded westward to Roman soldiers and then spread to the entire Roman Empire. The epidemic that lasted for 15 years, killing at least 5 million Romans, and even the Roman Emperor Marcus Aurelius did not survived the pandemic. The plague severely damaged the vitality of the Roman Empire in its heyday, and the regime fell into crisis and soon entered the era of the divided Eastern and Western Roman Empires.

In 541 AD, the first recorded plague pandemic broke out in the human history. The epidemic originated in Egypt. The Byzantine Empire (i.e.the Eastern Roman Empire) became the hardest hit area. The pandemic then spread to the entire Mediterranean, Europe and the Near East. The Justinian plague, named after the Byzantine king, killed tens of millions of people, roughly 26 percent of the world's population at the time. This plague directly led to the faliure of the revival plan of the Roman Empire and the collapse of the Eastern Roman Empire.

## The Rising of the Anglo-Saxons

Another Cyprian plague, which existed in Europe for nearly two centuries, was spread to British Isles where was part of the Western Roman Empire in 444 AD. At that time, the British Isles were often harassed by the Celts from the north. The spread of the plague caused a

serious shortage of frontier defence troops, and many European Germanic people were conscripted to guard the border. After the collapse of the Roman Empire, a large number of Germanics moved to the empty British Isles. Six centuries later, when the Normans conquered the British Isles, the Germanic such as Anglos Saxons and Jutes were already called 'English'.

## The Europeans Colonizing America

After Columbus discovered the New World in 1492, Europeans began to immigrate to America. Europeans brought not only guns, but also various germs that terrified Native Americans, including plague and smallpox. The sudden emergence of pathogenic microorganisms spread rapidly among the indigenous populations who lacked immunity. Data showed that the fatality rate of smallpox in continental Europe at that time was about 30%, while the mortality rate of indigenous people who had never been exposed to smallpox reached a staggering 90%. The plague killed at least 56 million Native Americans and cleared the way for European colonists to rule the American continent.

## Kangxi Succeeded to the Throne

There are many incidents where pandemics hit the land of China. The two major pandemics at the end of the Eastern Han Dynasty (presumably plague) and the end of the Ming Dynasty (plague and smallpox) both accelerated the fall of the two dynasties.

However, pandemics can also change the destiny in another way.

When the Manchus entered the Central Plains from the north, what frightened them most was the smallpox. Shunzhi, the first emperor of the Qing Dynasty, is said to have died of smallpox. It is said that the main reason why Kangxi was selected as his successor was because Kangxi had been infected with smallpox and he would not be infected again, which was conducive to the long-term stability of the imperial power. The 60 years of Kangxi's reign was one of the most stable and rapidly growing periods in Chinese history.

## ▌ The Human Efforts in Combating Pathogenic Microorganisms

Human beings have never stopped their efforts in fighting against pandemics.

### China's Contribution

In 317 A.D.,HongGe, a medical practitioner in the East-Jin Dynasty, described smallpox in detail in his medical book "Elbow Reserve Emergency Prescription". The treatment of rabies is also specifically described as "kill the dog that bit people, take its brain and apply it to the lesion, and then the condition will have no recurrence". 1700 years after, the production method of Artemisia annua used to treat malaria was recorded in the book inspired Dr.Youyou Tu, which led her to win the 2015 Nobel Prize in Medicine. In addition, the book also described method to treat dysentery with Coptis chinensis.

Tianchi Yu, a medical practitioner in the early Qing Dynasty, described in detail of prevention method used in the Longqing period of the Ming Dynasty to prevent smallpox in his book *Skin Rash Deciphered*: peel off the scars of smallpox patients, grind them into powder, and blow them into the nostrils of the unaffected children. Emperor Kangxi had smallpox and deeply knew the harmfulness of smallpox. In 1682, he ordered the nationwide popularization of variola vaccination to prevent smallpox, and his "court motto" recorded his joy at the variolation method that saved countless lives.

China's anti-smallpox method had quickly triggered other countries to follow. In 1721, Ms. Mary of England came to the Ottoman Empire with her husband who was an ambassador. After seeing the local people using the Chinese method to prevent smallpox, she decided to vaccinate her two-year-old son, which was successful. Later, she recommended the smallpox prevention technique from China to the King of England.

China's smallpox prevention method had opened the history of human artificial immunity, although people did not know the cause of smallpox at that time.

## The Birth of the Vaccine

Although the Chinese variolation method is effective in preventing smallpox, the mortality rate was as high as 2%, and the side effects were serious as well.

In 1796, the British physician Edward Jenner observed that milkmaids who contracted smallpox in cattle showed only mild symptoms. He wondered if the pox scars of cattle could be used to prevent smallpox. He then stained the arm of a gardener's 8-year-old son with exudate from the acne scar on the milkmaid's hand, and the child developed mild symptoms a few weeks later. After that, he directly infected the child with smallpox exudate from cattle, and the child did not show any symptoms. He was convinced that the acne scars of the female workers gave the boys protection against smallpox. Because the cow was called Vacca in Latin, so he called the practice Vaccinations. Compared with the previous Chinese method, the vaccinia method is safer.

However, using vaccination against human smallpox had been criticized and widely resisted. It was not until 1840 that the British government officially passed the law of using the vaccinia to prevent smallpox. Thirteen years later, the British government issued a decree to force the public to vaccinate and used police to supervise the implementation. At that time, Edwards Jenner had been dead for 30 years. Two years after, the United States, Germany and other places also promulgated mandatory vaccination laws.

Vaccinia became the first widely promoted safe vaccine for humans. Today, Vaccination has become an official medical term.

## Pasteur and the Artificial Vaccines

In 1876, German doctor Robert Koch used a microscope to observe Bacillus anthracis, and several years later he isolated pathogens such as Salmonella typhi, Mycobacterium tuberculosis and Vibrio cholerae. People finally realized that the culprits of the once-frightening epidemics were those pathogenic microorganisms which were invisible to the naked eye.

The success of the smallpox vaccine inspired Louis Pasteur, a Frenchman who was originally an expert in chemistry, to develop vaccines against other pathogenic microorganisms. In 1879, Pasteur researched chicken cholera vaccine. When his assistant inoculated the cholera bacteria solution from infected chicken which had been accidentally left forgotten for several weeks to the healthy chicken, it was found that the mortality rate of the inoculation was much lower than that of using fresh cholera bacteria solution. Further experiments have confirmed that although the virulence of cholera bacteria has been significantly reduced for a long time, chickens can still develop immunity to cholera bacteria. This discovery inspired scientists to develop ideas for attenuated vaccines. In 1881, Pasteur developed an attenuated Bacillus anthracis vaccine using heating method.

Pasteur's experiments found that the dried brain and spinal cord tissues of rabies patients could be used to make vaccines. A9-year-old boy named Joseph was bitten by a mad dog, his family asked Pasteur for help. At that time, the rabies vaccine has never been used in humans. When doctors confirmed that Joseph could unlikely survive with the healthcare management at that time, Pasteur decided to give it a go. Surprisingly, the child did not show symptoms of rabies after the vaccination. Pasteur then used the same method to successfully treat a dying 15-year-old shepherd who was bitten by a dog. In the following two years, thousands of rabies bite patients from all over the world were successfully rescued.

The success of the rabies vaccine has made people realize that vaccines can become commercial products for the prevention of infectious diseases, and the whole world was excited about it! Substantial donations followed, encouraging Pasteur's continued research and development, which led to the founding of the Pasteur Institute in Paris in 1888. Vaccines can be artificially produced in laboratories instead of infected animals. The birth of artificial vaccines has opened a new chapter in the history of human combating pathogenic microorganisms and laid the foundation for active immunization programs for human infectious diseases.

Looking back 1700 years ago, Pasteu's concept in treating rabies was surprisingly similar to what described by Hong Ge, a medical practitioner in the East-Jin Dynasty of China. China had rich experience and accurate documentation summarizing the treatment of smallpox, rabies, malaria, and dysentery,which is more than 1,000 years earlier than the West. Why did the modern medicine not emerged from China?

## Programmed Immunization Project

Before the vaccine appeared in 1796, the average mortality rate of smallpox was above 10%. After the use of vaccinia vaccine, the mortality rate of smallpox decreased year by year. Since 1880, the mortality rate of smallpox in London had been closed to zero. In 1900, the United Kingdom officially implemented the smallpox vaccination program for all children, leading the world to enter the era of human immunization (fig.1).

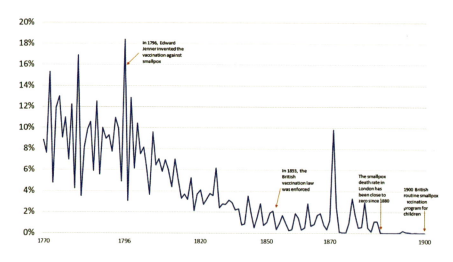

Figure 1. Smallpox mortality in London from 1770 to 1900. (Source: OWID 2017)

Smallpox was declared eradicated in Britain in 1934. On December 9,1979, the World Health Organization announced the eradication of smallpox globally. The smallpox vaccine has become the world's first and the only human program to successfully eradicate a pathogenic virus.

At present, dozens of pathogenic microorganism vaccines have been applied in the routine vaccination program for children in the world, which have saved countless people from the threat of infectious diseases. The success stories of vaccination have brought confidence and hope for human beings to completely defeat pathogenic microbial diseases in the future.

## Penicillin and the Age of Antibiotics

The artificial vaccines could activate human immune system to resist the invasion of specific pathogenic microorganisms with high contagious and high fatality rate. However,many bacterial infections even with lower transmission rate,could pose a serious threat to humans. In early 20th century, there was no effective treatment available for these infections.

In 1928, an accident inspired Fleming, a British bacteriologist. When he grew Staphylococcus aureus,he forgot to close the laboratory window before left for his holiday. When he came back, he found an ablation zone around the colonies of Staphylococcus aureus. He believed that the growth of Staphylococcus aureus might be inhibited by the mold floating into the petri dish from the window. He wrote up the discovery in a paper but received no response. Nine years later, when World War II broke out, antibacterial drugs were urgently needed on the front lines. Fleming's thesis was brought to attention again. The team of Florey and Chain in Cambridge successfully extracted penicillin form the cultured mold and confirmed the excellent antibacterial effect of penicillin through clinical trials. Penicillin showed its power in World War II and became a life-saving medicine for the wounded soldiers. Prior to this, there was basically no treatment available for the injured soldiers in wars, except amputation, and wound infections used to inevitably led to death.

Penicillin then quickly became a powerful tool in the treatment of infectious diseases. Fleming, Florey, and Chain shared the 1945 Nobel Prize in Physiology and Medicine.

Penicillin ushered in the era of human antibiotics!

To date, humans have developed a number of different antibiotic families for different types of pathogenic bacteria, which include β-lactams (such as penicillins, cephalosporins, new β-lactams, etc.), aminoglycosides (such as gentamicin, amikacin, tobramycin, etc.), macrocyclic Esters (such as erythromycin, clarithromycin, azithromycin, etc.), tetracyclines, lincomycins, polypeptides (such as polymyxin, vancomycin, etc.), quinolones (norfofloxacin, ciproterone, etc.) Floxacin, etc.), sulfonamides, anti-tuberculosis drugs and antifungal drugs, etc.

Since 1900, the average life expectancy in the world has risen rapidly from less than 30 years to about 70 years, which was closely related to the full implementation of human immunization programmes and the use of various antibiotics. Vaccines and antibiotics have become the guards of human health.

## A New Challenge-Antibiotic Resistance

### Inappropriate Usage of Antibiotics

The strong antibacterial ability of penicillin has raised people's expectations and dependence on antibiotics. A considerable number of people, including some healthcare workers, regard antibiotics as the first line choice of treatment for infections, especially those unexplained fever.

Due to the limitation of detecting the identity of pathologies at point of care, many doctors often use antibiotics as "diagnostic" treatment when faced with the situational pressure of the disease. According to statistics, there are no less than 300 pathogens that could cause "cold-like symptoms". However, penicillin has almost no therapeutic effect on viruses, molds and bacteria which are outside the antibacterial spectrum. The practice of overdose or inappropriate use of antibiotics has been very common.

Over time, people found that the 'cold-like symptoms' that were previously easy to control had become difficult, and the effectiveness of antibiotics that were once powerful decreased significantly or even became ineffective.

## Pathogenic Microorganism Genetic Variation

The World Health Organization warned that more than 700,000 people worldwide died each year due to antibiotic resistance.

As part of natural evolution, genetic variations of microorganisms continue to occur during the reproduction process. When a mutation causes antibiotics to be less effective or even ineffective, the mutated strain becomes drug-resistant. Figure 2 illustrates the occurrence and development of drug-resistant strains. It was assumed that bacteria do not have drug resistance at the beginning, but gene mutations keep occurring during replication, leading to the occurrence of resistance strings. When antibiotics were used, the non-resistant strains will be eliminated by antibiotics while strains with resistant mutations survive. When these resistant strains continue to multiply into dominant flora, the drug resistance occurs in treatment.

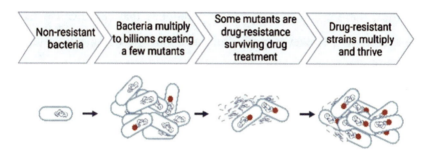

Figure.2. Development of drug-resistance strains. Genetic mutation creates drug-resistant bacteria.

Antibiotic-resistant strains may appear in the following situations: 1) Improper use or abuse of antibiotics which could allow the drug-resistant strains grown as to be the dominant strains; 2) Insufficient or insufficient use of antibiotics could give the pathogenic strains a chance to develop into the drug-resistant strains; 3) Livestock and poultry that had used antibiotics may be infected with drug-resistant strains; 4) Hospitals are high-risk areas for the breeding and retention of drug-resistant strains, and the risk of passive infection is high; 5) Pathogenic microorganisms could be easily breed and mutated in poor sanitation environments.

The World Health Organizationreported, the number of new patients with anti-tuberculosis drug resistance had reached 500,000 in a single year of 2013. It was predicted that by 2050, 10 million patients will die due to antimicrobial resistance, much higher than the number of deaths from diabetes and traffic accidents in the same period,while the estimated number of cancer deaths in the same period is only 8 million. The spread of the refractory drug-resistant strains in the population is a kind of epidemic, and its characteristics of invisible transmission should arouse sufficient awareness.

# ▌ COVID-19 Pandemic and Reflections

On May 4, 2023, the World Health Organization announced that the COVID19 has no longer constituted a "public health emergency of international concern". The pandemic that has ravaged mankind for more than three years has finally come to an end, even though the strains of SARS-CoV2 are still exist.

Over the past three years, more than 765 million people have been diagnosed with COVID-19 worldwide, and more than 6.92 million people died (WHO data), making it the largest pandemics in the past 100 years since the Spanish flu. WHO Director-General Tedros Adhanom Ghebreyesus said that the SARS-CoV2 has killed at least 20 million people so far in fact, which are three times of the official figure. The three-year COVID-19 pandemic has undoubtedly become a realistic version of the battle between pathogenic microorganisms and modern humans.

## Humans are Still Vulnerable to the Unknown Pathogenic Microorganisms

Human beings only have a history of150 years of understanding of pathogenic microorganisms, faraway from effective prevention and control the pandemics. Even the most developed countries have fared far less well in responding to the COVID-19 pandemic. According to data from the World Health Organization, the total number of confirmed cases of COVID19 in the top 20 countries of GDP ranking is nearly 600 million, accounting for more than 78% of the total number of confirmed patients in the world, while their total population is only 58% of the world. The infected numbers in the low income countries have probably not been fully counted.The fact suggests that relatively superior economic and medical conditions are not sufficient to build an effective fence to prevent the spread of the virus. Modern humans still lack effective means to prevent and control pathogenic microorganisms for a pandemic with unknown pathogens.

Like each of the pandemics in history, the COVID19 has also severely damaged the economy. According to data of the Federal Reserve, between April 2021 and October 2019,the GDP growth in low-income countries had decreased by 5.2%, that of middle-income countries had decreased by 8.7%, and that of high-income countries had decreased by 6.4%.The reduction in global GDP growth in the same period was equivalent to the sum of the whole GDP in 2019 of the United Kingdom and France.In fact, the actual associated losses of the global economy are far more than this figure.

## SARS CoV2 Variants and the Pandemic

The situation of each country is different, and the spread of the SARS-CoV2 in each country was also different. However, different stages of the evolution of the original virus strain could be classified. Figure.3.1 and Figure.3.2 respectively show the trend charts of the daily number of new confirmed cases and deaths per million people in the UK and the United States from January 2020 to the end of November 2022 (data resource: Johns Hopkins University) and the evolution of different dominant variants of the virus in the UK (Figure.3.3).

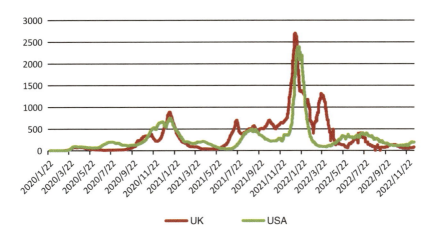

Figure 3.1　New cases (per million) in the UK and USA from January 2020 to November 2022 (Data source: Johns Hopkins University)

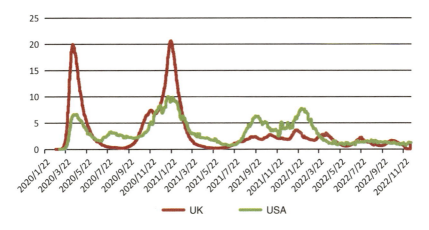

Figure 3.2　The trend chart of new deaths per million people in the UK and the US from January 2020 to November 2022 (Data source: Johns Hopkins University)

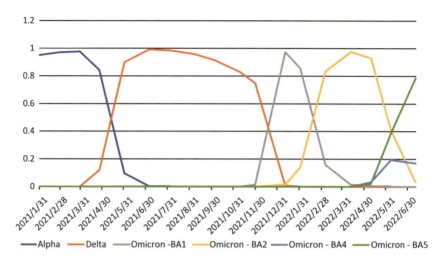

Figure 3.3　SARS-CoV-2 Main Variant Prevalence in England from February 2021 to July 2022 (Data source: UKHSA)

In the early stage of the pandemic with infections by the original SARS CoV2 strain, i.e. before July 2020, although the daily number of newly confirmed cases in the UK and the US were steady, the daily number of new deaths was very high. From November 2020 when the alpha variant became dominant, there were small peaks of daily confirmed cases in both countries, but a large peak of the daily death. When the delta variant became dominant in May 2021, the number of daily confirmed new cases and new deaths in both countries rose again, but compared with the previously variant strains, the growth rate of the new death had slowed down significantly. From the period when Omicron variant became dominant from December 2021, the number of daily new cases increased sharply, but the number of daily new deaths did not change much. New subtypes of the Omicron variant soon appeared, but newly confirmed daily cases and new deaths were gradually declined. It was clearly shown that the transmission of the new variant strains has entered a stage of high transmission but caused low death by the omicron variants and its sub-strains. The virulence of omicron strains of SARS-CoV2 has greatly reduced.

Similar to bacteria, viruses continue to mutate during the reproduction process. But unlike bacteria, viruses parasitize in host cells, and the survival and evolution of viruses are closely related to host cell responses. In the early stage of the infection, the exogenous virus could trigger a severe reaction of the host cell, the rates of clinical mortality and severe cases were high. The natural variation of the virus strain either trigger a strong reaction of the  host cell , or mild reaction of the host cell. Due to the concealment of the mild reaction, viruses with weaker virulence have stronger survivability and more concealed transmission ability, which could multiple the transmission speed, but the symptoms are mild.

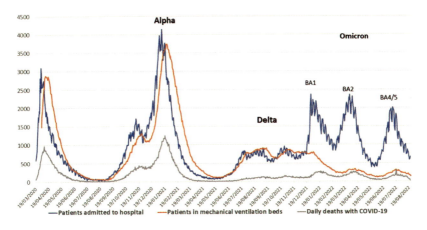

Figure 4.  COVID19 patients in hospital, England.(Data Source: UKHSA)

Data from the UK Health Security Agency (UKHSA) (Figure.4) show that during the period of the Alpha variant infection(September

2020-April 2021), the newly hospitalized patients were severe, and the number of deaths during this period reached more than 1,000 per day. It exceeds the number of severe cases and deaths in the early stage of the original SARS-CoV2 strain in the UK (March 2020-June 2020). When the pandemics enters the delta variant period (July 2021 to December 2021), a smaller peak of hospitalized patients was observed. Although the clinical cases were still severe, compared to the period of alpha variant, the number of severe patients and the death rate had dropped significantly and since then remained at a low level. From December 2021, the Omicron variants strain quickly took the lead, and the number of patients diagnosed with positive virus tests increased sharply, far exceeding previous levels. Although several waves of hospitalization peaks have been set off again, the number of new severe patients and death rate were basically maintained at a low level, which is obviously different from the alpha and delta variants.

## The Protective Effect of the SARS–CoV2 Vaccine

The parasitic nature of the virus makes treatment difficult. So far, there are still lack of effective medicine to treat virus infection in human, vaccine is the best means of defence against viruses. Antibodies produced by vaccination can neutralize the virus to prevent the virus attack or reduce severe illness or death. However, there was no vaccine against SARS-CoV2 produced during the first 12 months of the COVID-19 pandemic, the only preventionwasquarantine or symptomatic treatment. It was predictable that in the early period, the severe disease rate and mortality rate must be relatively high in countries with the LWC policy.

Take England as an example. By August 2021, since the launch of COVID-19 vaccine in early 2021, the two-doses vaccination reached more than 80% of the population; by December 2021, the booster vaccination in England reached more than 60%of the population.

However, it remains to be seen whether the significant decrease in the number of new deaths from the COVID-19 pandemics during the Delta and Omicron variants in England was mainly due to the decreased virulence of the virus itself or the neutralization of the virus after vaccination. More relevant data need to be analysis.

It is no doubt that vaccination has played an important role in the defence against the SARS-CoV2.

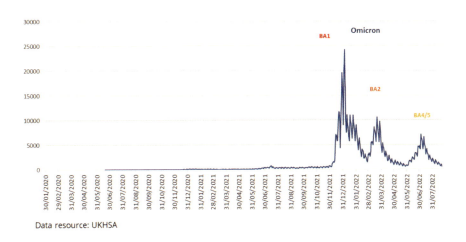

Data resource: UKHSA

Figure 5. New COVID-19 reinfections by specimen data in England (Jan 2020 – Aug 2022) (Data Source: UKHSA)

The data of UKHSA found that a considerable number of patients had second or even multiple re-infection by SARS-CoV2which occurred during the period of the Omicron variant strains. The number of new cases of re-infection were similar among different strains of the Omicron variant (Figure 5). The phenomenon of re-infections was hardly found in the alpha and delta mutant strains. This phenomenon reflects that the Omicron strains were obviously different from the previous strains, or in another words that the vaccines inoculated earlier had lost their defensive effectiveness against the Omicron variants. Genetic analysis shown that there were more than 32 mutation sites in the Omicron strains, it was likely that the immune 'escape' has occurred in the vaccine which was derived from the early virus version. Clearly, a new vaccination against the Omicron variant of the SARS-CoV2 was necessary. In November 2022, England implemented the vaccination against the Omicron variant (called as the fourth dose of COVID virus) for people who over 50 years old.

Table 2. COVID-19 Vaccination Data and Death Rate of Patients Confirmed with COVID-19 Infection in Major Countries

| Country | Vaccinated numbers per 100people | Fully vaccinated per 100 people | Booster doses per 100 people | Mortality rate of COVID19 |
|---|---|---|---|---|
| India | 159.9 | 68.99 | 16.57 | 1.18 |
| Brazil | 239.65 | 80.12 | 51.71 | 1.87 |
| Russia | 127.7 | 54.54 | | 1.74 |
| USA | 171.21 | 65.51 | 31.39 | 1.08 |
| UK | 222.8 | 74.59 | 65.0 | 0.91 |
| France | 234.5 | 78.98 | 60.61 | 0.42 |
| Germany | 232.3 | 76.42 | 62.68 | 0.45 |
| Japan | 302.96 | 81.72 | 68.28 | 0.22 |
| China | 238.97 | 87.3 | 56.67 | 0.12 |

Table (Continued)

| Country | Vaccinated numbers per 100people | Fully vaccinated per 100 people | Booster doses per 100 people | Mortality rate of COVID19 |
|---|---|---|---|---|
| New Zealand | 254.08 | 84.69 | 56.39 | 0.12 |
| South Korea | 251.9 | 82.97 | 75.3 | 0.11 |
| Singapore | 254.75 | 87.5 | 79.1 | 0.07 |

(Data Source: WHO)

Data from World Health Organization (Table 2) show that there were some but not strong  correlation between the vaccination rate of the SARS-CoV2 vaccine and the mortality rate of the COVID-19. Countries with low vaccination rates, especially countries with a lower rate of the booster vaccination, were more likely to have a slightly higher mortality rate. However,  it was remarkably clear that the case fatality rate of COVID-19 in all countries or areas that had implemented the zero-clearing policy were at a low level. It was noticed that , Japan (non-zero-clearing policy countries) and Singapore had relatively lower fatality rates of COVID-19.

## Future Prospective:  Never–ending Challenges

After tens of thousands of years of evolution, survival and development, as part of the food chain in the nature, more  interdependent relationship developed between humans and microorganisms. Genetic mutations exist all the time as natural procedures of evolution during the process of gene replication and species generation.As the  human gene mutations can cause cancer, the microbial genetic mutations can also turn the non-human-related microorganisms into pathogenic agents that can harm human health and even cause epidemics. Therefore, the battles between humans and pathogenic microorganisms will be no doubt to continue.

It is gratifying that although the history of the identification of pathogenic microorganisms by human is less than 150 years, the emergence of vaccines and antibiotics has basically brought under control the infectious diseases caused by most of the human pathogens. However, judging from the outcome of the new coronavirus pandemic and the reality of anti-infection, human beings are still far from managing the law of the occurrence and development of pathogenic microorganisms, and have not yet possessed the ability to protect humans against infection. In many ways, there is still a lot of room for improvement in the fight against pathogen infections.

Looking forward to the future, to improve the ability of humans to fight against pathogenic microorganisms, we need to focus on the following aspects:

1) Accelarate the speed of vaccine development for newly emergent microorganisms and effectively reduce the mortality at early stage of pandemic;

2) Implement the zero-clearing policy at the early stage of the pandemic before the availability of vaccines to block the spread of the viruses;

3) Scientifically apply the clearing and lifting policy and protect the high-risk group to consolidate the achievements from the zero-cleaning policy.

4) Accelerate the development of new antibiotics and scientifically control the use of antibiotics;

5) Innovation in understanding of the genetic evolution of pathogenic microorganisms and the mechanisms of anti-microbial resistance

## About the author

James Q Zhang was qualified in 1985 and worked as an attending physician in the Third Hospital of Peking University for 8 years. In 1997, he completed his PhD study at Clinical Pharmacology Unit, Addenbrooke's Hospital,Gonville & Caius College of the University Cambridge. He is currently a Fellow of Royal Society of Medicine and Scientist of Royal Pharmaceutical Society and a Board member of World Association of Chinese Doctors and Chairman of Overseas Chinese Society for Technology & Business in the UK.

# "对话"大熊猫

文 / 詹姆斯·爱德华·阿亚拉 [美]

译 / 李欢

　　我自小在纽约城里长大,和大自然的距离很遥远。与很多城里长大的孩子们一样,我主要是通过阅读书籍、观看电视纪录片或者到动物园游览的方式,来了解野生动植物。我对各种各样的动物书籍都爱不释手,在纪实类和传说故事类的动物书中体验现实和虚幻的精彩碰撞。值得我们注意的是,纵观人类历史长河,各个地域文化中都有讲述人类与野生动物对话的神话传说。虽然绝大多数都是虚构的故事,但也存在少量的真实元素。例如,在撒哈拉以南的非洲地区,传说人们在一只野鸟的指引下找到了蜂蜜。对于生活在酷热环境中的人们来说,蜂蜜可是珍贵的商品。在一些地区,蜂蜜占当地土著人日常饮食的10%。这是一个非常古老的非洲传说,1588年,一位居住在莫桑比克的葡萄牙传教士乔·多斯桑托斯(Joã dos Santos)首次记录下这个故事,并将其传播到了西方。

　　几百年来,人们一直认为多斯桑托斯记录下的这个故事只是神话传说，但最近人们发现它其实是真实存在的。故事里的主角叫做"蜂蜜鸟"（拉丁名：Indicator indicator），研究表明，这种鸟类确实能够通过独特的叫声和肢体动作与当地人交流，并为他们做向导，寻找蜂巢。两个不同的物种都从这种双赢的关系中获益。蜂巢往往很隐蔽，但人类在鸟儿的引领下，能很快找到它；在人们大力破巢时，鸟儿也能轻松获得其中的蜂蜜、蜂蜡和蜂蛹。据说这种特殊的关系已经延续了数千年。虽然人类通过驯养犬类和马匹等动物，建立了类似的联系，但需要指明的一点是，蜂蜜鸟属于完全野生的物种，人类能与它们交流是非常罕见的。

第一次听说这个故事时，我就对人与动物相互交流的方式产生了浓厚的兴趣，也对人类是否能与动物进行交流非常好奇。由于兴趣使然，我便以此作为自己的职业。现在的我是一名动物行为训练研究员，其中一个主要研究方向是如何通过交流互动的方式，保护大熊猫等珍稀濒危野生动物。目前，我已在位于四川省的成都大熊猫繁育研究基地工作了十余年，研究"国宝"大熊猫的行为，通过正强化训练，和大熊猫"对话"。为了让大家更好地了解我们的工作内容和意义，我们需要先了解一下大熊猫的进化史和它们相互间的交流方式。

大熊猫身上总萦绕着很多谜团，它们踽踽独行，在高山密竹间深居简出。不论是在中国古代传说里，还是在纪实类作品中，都有它们的身影。1869年，法国传教士、博物学家阿尔芒·戴维发现了大熊猫的毛皮，随后猎户们为他带回大熊猫尸体，这是西方世界认识大熊猫的开端，同时开启了大熊猫在分类学上的长久争议。根据最近的DNA分子学研究，科学家最终确定将大熊猫划入熊科。这个研究成果意义重大，让我们能够认识到大熊猫在进化前后的变化、它们与其他熊科动物的区别，以及人类与大熊猫交流的最佳途径。

既然我们确定了大熊猫属熊科，那么它们和其他现存的熊科动物有何不同呢？就大熊猫的进化史来看，我们需要知道大熊猫是现存最古老的熊科动物，这是很重要的一点。大熊猫被誉为"活化石"，它们历经了八百多万年的漫长进化，从食肉动物进化为主要以竹为生的素食者。现在，竹子占到大熊猫日常食物的99%。为了适应食物的变化，大熊猫身体上发生了许多改变，其中最显著的一点在于大熊猫头骨的变化。与其他熊类相比，大熊猫的脑袋很圆，口鼻短而宽，圆圆的脸颊憨态可掬，犹如孩童一般天真可爱。诚然，大熊猫的可爱毋庸置疑，但我们需要明白，它们可爱的外表是为了适应食物而进化来的。为了咬碎坚硬的竹子，熊猫进化出强有力的下颌。它们圆圆的脑袋是因为颅骨上有着发达的矢状嵴（即其颅顶中线脊状的骨头），主要功能是固定其强大的咬肌。大熊猫短粗的下颌骨上附着发达的肌肉群。这种适应性变化大大强化了大熊猫的咬合力，让它们能够轻易地咬碎和咀嚼粗硬的竹竿。所以，如果抛开体重不谈，大熊猫的咬合力远超狼、狮子和老虎，是食肉目动物中最强大的。

大熊猫区别于其他熊类的另一特征：为适应竹类采食需求，进化出了第六根"指头"——伪拇指。伪拇指实际是由腕骨演化而来，方便大熊猫抓握竹子，提高了它们采食竹子的效率，这是其他熊类不具备的特点。但是大熊猫的伪拇指与人类的大拇指不同，它不是真正的对生拇指，因此大熊猫无法做出"ok"的手势。有趣的是，大熊猫转变食性后，头骨和肌肉组织随之进化改变，但是它们的消化系统依然很简单，保留着肉食动物的特点。因此，即便在肠道内特有菌群的帮助下，大熊猫也只能吸收竹子中约17%的营养成分。为了弥补能量相对较低的饮食结构，大熊猫每天用一半左右的时间吃东西，另一半时间睡觉。虽然从科学的角度来讲，这属于适应性的能量储存策略，但一般来讲，你当然也可以说进化后的大熊猫看着慵慵懒懒的。在我们对大熊猫的身体进化机制有更多了解后，可以来关注一下大熊猫彼此之间的交流方式了。

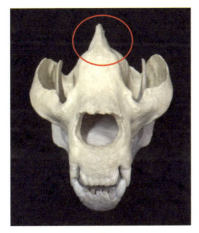 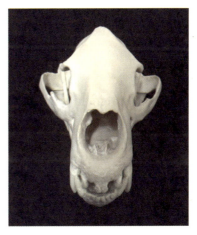

成年大熊猫头骨
红色圈指示的部位就是大熊猫发达的矢状嵴，该骨结构用来固定大熊猫强大的咬肌。

成年黑熊头骨
没有明显的矢状嵴，咬肌也更细长。

图1. 成年大熊猫头骨和成年黑熊头骨

人类高度依赖视觉沟通交流，甚至在自己没有意识到的情况下，都在进行视觉交流。举个例子，当下您在阅读这些文字的时候，我就正在和您进行视觉上的交流！编辑部还希望我提供6张配图，来和您进一步交流。一图能抵千言，不是吗？如果没有红绿灯等视觉交流信号，我们很难在城市里安全驾驶，行人也很难过马路。熊猫当然也能通过视觉进行交流，我们后续就会讲到这个问题，但是通过感官（既简单的嗅觉、气味）交流是它们的主要交流方式。

和其他熊科动物一样，大熊猫通常处于独居状态。即便有时大熊猫的领地会稍有重叠，但大多数情况下，它们都坚守在自己的领地内。它们进化为依靠气味标记来进行交流，不需要真正面对面，跨越空间和时间。大熊猫的气味标记是一种蜡状分泌物，由尾部的肛周腺分泌。这些气味标记中包含着很多的信息，比如大熊猫的个体信息、性别、繁殖情况、年龄甚至亲缘关系等。一年中随着季节变化，气味标记所起的作用也不同。同时，气味标记的功能也会因留标记个体以及接收者的不同而有所差异。

大部分时间里，雌/雄性大熊猫做标记都是为了标记领地，避免和其他大熊猫过多地碰面。但在繁殖期，气味标记发挥的作用则不同。成年雌性大熊猫会留下气味，表示自己已进入发情期，吸引雄性交配。同时，雄性大熊猫也会通过气味标记，留下发情迹象，吸引雌性的注意。此外，发情的成年雄性大熊猫留下的标记，不仅可以吸引雌性，也可以起到威胁或者警示附近成年雄性的作用。未发情或正在带仔的雌性大熊猫，对交配毫无兴趣，会选择避开这类气味标记。同样，亚成年、受伤以及年老的雄性个体，由于无力参与决斗，争取交配权，所以也可能会避开这些标记。总体来说，气味标记属于一种交流方式，可以让住得近的大熊猫，在交配前进行相互了解。不过，在大熊猫"见面"后，就需要采用更加直接的交流方式，实现即时互动。这就和我们人类一样，它们也会通过声音来交流。

熊猫可以发出许多复杂的声音，在不同的环境中，它们通过变换音高、音频或声音长度，来表达各种不同情绪。虽然熊猫宝宝刚出生时还不具备听觉和视觉，但是它们一落地就能发出叫喊声，呼唤母兽的怀抱和安抚。随着宝宝日渐长大，它们的听觉系统逐渐发育，能够回应妈妈的呼唤，如果自己走得较远或者遇到危险时，会跑回妈妈的怀抱。雄/雌性大熊猫达到性成熟后，它们会发出"咩"叫声，表达自己有交配的兴趣；大熊猫在打斗或遇到天敌时，会发出咆哮和吠叫声，以吓退敌人。现有的实验表明，它们能像人类一样，辨别出其他熟识的大熊猫的声音。

与声音交流类似，当大熊猫面对面时，能通过视觉进行交流。总体来看，当前针对大熊猫视觉交流领域的研究尚不深入，仍有待探索。我们知道的是，大熊猫会通过某种身体姿势，传递一些特定的信息。例如雌性大熊猫俯身向前、弓背抬尾是传递自己进入发情期的信号；大熊猫向前扑是向其他大熊猫或者天敌发出警告，不过如果是幼仔间出现这种行为，往往是在嬉戏玩耍。

同样，大熊猫还可以通过触觉进行交流。类似视觉交流，我们目前对于大熊猫触觉交流的了解并不多。我们知道在大熊猫育幼期，母兽和幼仔之间的触觉交流尤为关键。幼仔出生时看不见也听不见，因此在头几周只能通过触觉感知的方式，与母兽建立联系。随着幼仔的逐步长大，它们会和妈妈玩耍，这时的触觉交流对于幼仔的身心健康发展也至关重要。此外，触觉交流也是大熊猫成功交配的重要一环。

了解完大熊猫之间的几种基本交流方式后，我们该如何应用这些知识，实现人与大熊猫的交流呢？首先，我们无法与大熊猫进行气味交流，这明显又尴尬又毫无头绪！但我们可以通过声音、视觉信号和触摸的方式与大熊猫交流。幸运的是，"正强化训练"的方法正好能涵盖到上述几种交流方法。20世纪30年代末，美国心理学家伯尔赫斯·费雷德里克·斯金纳（B.F.Skinner）最早提出正强化训练概念，该概念认为，在人或动物的行为达到预期目标时提供奖励，可以提高其后续再次出现该行为的概率。

其实，正强化训练在我们的日常生活中的应用非常广泛，比如你的学校考试成绩优异，父母可能给你买新衣服或者其他特别的礼物作为奖励。在礼物的鼓励下，你肯定会加倍努力学习。父母持续的奖励，成为你坚持努力学习的动力。这就是一种正强化训练，新衣服激励/强化了你的行为，成为主要的强化刺激物。同理，在大熊猫行为训练中，我们首先要找到主要的强化刺激物，作为激励大熊猫的奖励。

在前文中，我们提到过大熊猫的主食营养较少。因此我们发现像苹果一样高能量的含糖食物，正好可以弥补竹子的低能量，是作为其行为训练主要强化刺激物的不二选择。第一步完成后，在正式开始训练前，我们还需要确定一个第二强化刺激物。这一点非常重要，因为第二强化刺激物有两个作用：首先，它可以帮助大熊猫意识到自己完成了正确的动作；其次，它还是大熊猫即将获得奖励的信号。根据我们对大熊猫声音的了解，音质清脆且独特的响片声是第二强化刺激物的最佳选择。

确定了第一和第二强化刺激物后，我们就可以开始大熊猫的适应性训练了。我们通过吹响片然后即时奖励苹果的方式，让大熊猫适应这两种强化刺激物，训练步骤大致如下：喂食——吹响片，吹响片——喂食，喂食——吹响片，以此类推……均按照俄罗斯心理学家伊万·巴普洛夫（Ivan Pavlov）的研究原则进行，他曾开展过著名的手摇铃铛狗流口水的巴普洛夫实验。我们可以不断地进行重复训练，等到大熊猫一听到口哨声，能立即看向我们，等待苹果奖励，就说明大熊猫已经适应了这两种强化刺激物。这是我们与大熊猫进行交流的突破口和关键一步。从本质上来看，我们就像是教会了大熊猫一个词语——"正确"。虽然这一步骤看似简单无奇，仅仅是一个词而已，但这微不足道的一步对后续的行为训练意义非凡。

准备就绪后，我们终于来到正式训练大熊猫的环节了。首先，训练最基本的一步是如何让大熊猫识别"目标"，其中包括让大熊猫用鼻子触碰训练员手中的短木杆。回顾一下前文，大熊猫主要依赖气味进行交流。因此，任何出现在眼前的新物体，它们都要先闻一闻。当它们向前走来，鼻子触碰到目标竿顶端时，我们需立即吹响片并提供奖励。重复该训练步骤，进行强化，让大熊猫快速识别"目标"，我们还可以增加口头指令或者在竿的顶端做标记，加入听觉和视觉刺激。这项训练也可以辅助大熊猫完成其他复杂的行为训练，因为我们可以采用"目标"法，调整熊猫的位置和身体姿势。例如，只需要把目标竿高举过它们头顶，发出指令，大熊猫就会站立起来；或者用目标竿把它们引到体重秤上，就可以轻松测量大熊猫的体重。通过这些步骤，你与大熊猫建立起基础性联系，后续的行为训练可能会有无限的可能性。

图2. 成都熊猫基地行为训练员引导大熊猫"晶晶"识别目标竿，当它用鼻子触碰到目标竿，就会获得奖励。训练员会立即吹响片，同时从腰间的训练袋中拿出奖励品。

通过应用这些方法，我们在大熊猫饲养管理上取得了长足进

图3. 成都熊猫基地行为训练员引导大熊猫"喜兰"张嘴，接受口腔检查。

步。熊猫基地的大熊猫种群，在幼年时期就接受了行为训练，能够在无麻醉状态下自主配合采血。这一点对于大熊猫保护工作发挥了重要作用，因为在这里，我们开展大熊猫激素水平、营养需求、疾病诊疗和总体福利水平等生物学领域的研究，都离不开大熊猫自主配合采血。

目前，我们已经完成了大熊猫自主接受口腔检查、超声检查、人工采奶、尿液采集以及血压检测等一系列行为训练。和大家看到的一样，通过正强化训练来实现人与大熊猫交流，具有里程碑式的意义。但与想象中不同，训练大熊猫并不是一帆风顺的，常常会受到其他因素影响，甚至还会充满危险。

图4. 有赖于和大熊猫之间建立起的强大互信关系，我们可以采用安全的方式与它们进行密切交流。在检查大熊猫"绩美"的牙齿时，请大家注意看训练员口中的响片和腰间的训练袋。

训练时，大熊猫的食欲会影响到行为训练。正如之前所说，大熊猫的主食竹子营养不高，它们常常渴望得到香甜可口的奖励，这虽是事实，但它们也有不想吃苹果的时候。例如在繁殖期，雌/雄性大熊猫食欲下降，不停地在兽舍里走来走去。同时，我们很难预测它们的后续行为，训练难度增大。在这期间，原先慵懒软萌的大熊猫会性情大变，变得焦躁易怒。怀孕的雌性大熊猫在临产头几天食欲全无，幼仔出生后，母兽攻击性很强。当然，熊猫生病的时候，也没有食欲。在这期间，我们很难进行大熊猫行为训练。此外，大熊猫的咬合力非常强大，不但能轻而易举咬碎竹子，更能轻易地咬伤人。

图5. 通过行为训练方法，开展大熊猫发育情况研究，以确保它们的健康。图中，"绩美"关注着训练员的手，双脚站立。这个姿势可以帮助我们安全地检查大熊猫的发育情况和身体健康状况。

训练大熊猫要注意一些事项。第一条：大熊猫永远是对的。我们的训练工作需要适应大熊猫的节奏。大熊猫是熊类，是电影明星，而我们只是芸芸众生中普通的一员。如果它们想慢下来，那么我们不妨慢一点；如果它们没做好，直接忽略就好，只要它们完成了相应动作，就要立即奖励。要牢牢记住如果和大熊猫产生了什么隔阂，那错肯定在我们，不在大熊猫。第二条：要了解大熊猫个体的差异。因为在训练中，我们需要和每只大熊猫单独相处，以建立强大的互信关系。每一只大熊猫的性格和需求都不尽相同，如果你足够了解每只个体的特点，就能掌握好安全的训练时间。第三条：使用秘密武器——蜂蜜。大熊猫的最爱是蜂蜜，即便最冥顽不灵的大熊猫，也会为了得到蜂蜜而配合训练。第四条，如果大熊猫依旧不配合训练，那请回看第一条。

图6. 由于大熊猫的独特生理特性，我们只能通过超声检查的方式，来确定大熊猫是否怀孕。图中，训练员通过训练和奖励的方式，让大熊猫"雅莉"平躺，配合兽医进行超声检查。基于训练员与大熊猫之间的互信关系，整个超声检查过程没有让大熊猫感到紧张。

我们这里又说到蜂蜜，恰恰契合了文章的开篇，这个非常有意思。蜂蜜主要由蜜蜂采集花蜜酿造而成，它们在人与鸟、人与大熊猫的交流中发挥着关键性作用，令人称奇。跨物种交流的秘密在于发挥美食的吸引力！蜂蜜鸟和人类建立了独特的交流方式，二者获得双赢，那么人类为什么要寻求与大熊猫建立交流联系呢？

大熊猫种群数量曾不幸锐减，甚至一度濒临灭绝，造成这一切的罪魁祸首正是我们人类。但好消息是，中国政府采取了行之有效的措施，保护国宝大熊猫及野外栖息地。中国的野生动物保护工作取得积极成效，野生大熊猫种群数量逐年攀升。最新统计数据显示，现存野生大熊猫数量已达1864只。不过，即便成效显著，大熊猫依然面临着灭绝的风险。为了进一步保护大熊猫，政府主导建立了大熊猫圈养种群。对于大熊猫圈养种群而言，人与大熊猫之间的交流至关重要。通过应用文中提到的大熊猫训练方法，现在国内外大熊猫繁育中心、动物园圈养大熊猫数量已超600只，并保持稳定性增长，达到了自我维持的水平。保护事业是一项双向互惠的工作，通过实现人与大熊猫的交流互动，一方面保障大熊猫种群的繁衍生息，另一方面，试想一下，如果没有大熊猫，人类世界肯定会黯然失色，变得一片寂静荒凉。

## 作者简介

詹姆斯·爱德华·阿亚拉（James Ayala）先生出生于美国纽约市，2005年在安提俄克新英国研究生院获得保护生物学硕士学位，到目前为止已经有超过25年的野生动物工作经验。在过去的10年中，他一直在中国成都大熊猫繁育研究基地从事大熊猫的研究和保护工  作。他的主要研究方向包括应用行为研究、正强化条件反射研究和通过丰富圈养环境来改善濒危物种的繁殖和生存条件研究等。

# Communicating with Giant Pandas

By James Ayala (USA)

Growing up in New York City, I was detached from nature. Like many other city kids, the main way I experienced wildlife was through TV documentaries, trips to the zoo and reading. I loved all sorts of animal books, both the real ones and the storybooks of legends, where fantasy and reality would collide. It's remarkable that throughout human history, across all continents and cultures, there are myths and legends of people communicating with wild animals. The vast majority of these stories are pure make believe but sometimes, though very rare, there is truth in fantasy. For example, in sub-Saharan Africa, there was a legend of a wild bird that led people to find honey. In this hot environment, honey is a precious commodity and, in some communities, makes up around 10% of the diet of the local people. This legend is incredibly old amongst Africans and was first known to the western world in 1588 through the records of a Portuguese missionary living in Mozambique named João dos Santos.

For centuries the report from Dos Santos was believed to be just a myth, however recently it was discovered to be true. The bird is known as the greater honeyguide (*Indicator indicator*) and research has shown these birds do in fact use unique calls and gestures to communicate with the local people and lead them to beehives. This is an example of a mutualism, which is a type of relationship between two different species where both benefit. In this case, the humans benefit by quickly locating the hard-to-find beehives and the birds benefit by humans breaking into the hives and giving the birds easy access to the honey, wax and young bees inside. It's believed this special relationship developed over thousands of years. It is important to point out though, that while humans have developed similar relationships with animals that have been domesticated, like dogs and horses, this is a rare case of communication between humans and a completely wild free-living species.

When I first learned about this, I became fascinated about the different ways and possibilities that humans could communicate with animals, so fascinated that I chose this as a career. Now, as a researcher of animal behavior, one of my main areas of study is to see how we can use communication to conserve rare and endangered wildlife, like the giant panda. I have spent the last ten years working at the Chengdu Research Base of Giant Panda Breeding in Sichuan Province, studying the behavior of this iconic species and how we can use positive reinforcement training to communicate with our pandas. In order to understand how we do this and why, we first need to learn a little bit more about how giant pandas evolved and how they communicate with each other.

There has always been a mystery surrounding giant pandas. Because of their solitary, reclusive nature and the fact that they live in high elevation, remote bamboo forests, they existed on the border of legend and reality amongst the ancient Chinese. Pandas were first known to the western world in 1869, when a French missionary and naturalist named Armand David was given the fur of a giant panda. Later hunters brought him the body of a giant panda, which started the long debate as to how to classify the panda taxonomically. With the recent advance of molecular studies, using DNA, scientists have definitively classed giant pandas as a species of bear in the Family Ursidae. This clarification is very important because it allows us to understand the changes pandas have undergone during their evolution, what makes them unique compared to the other bear species and, in this specific instance, what are the best ways to communicate with them.

Now that it is clear that giant pandas are bears, how are they different from the other living bears? Considering their evolution, it is important to point out that pandas are the oldest existing member of the bear family. Pandas are known as "living fossils" and have been evolving over the course of eight million years. During this long period, pandas evolved from an omnivore that ate meat to an herbivore that survives by exclusively eating bamboo. Ninety-nine percent of the panda's diet is bamboo, adapting to this diet has changed pandas in many, many ways. Probably the most noticeable change is in the panda's skull. A panda's head is quite round, compared to the other bears, with a short broad muzzle, giving them a chubby, cute almost childlike appearance. While there is no point arguing how cute pandas are (they are), it is worth noting these features evolved as a result of pandas needing incredibly powerful jaws to crush bamboo. The roundness of the panda skull is mostly due to their large sagittal crest, a bony structure on the top of their skull, which serves as an anchor point for their powerful jaw muscles, which attach to their reduced broad mandible (lower jaw). This adaptation optimizes the panda's bite pressure, allowing them to break and chew even very hard bamboo stems. As a result, if you control for body mass, pandas have one of the most powerful bites in their taxonomic Order Carnivora, and can even bite harder than wolves, lions and tigers.

Another way that giant pandas have changed, compared with other bears, as a result of their bamboo diet, is that they evolved to have a sixth "finger" known as a pseudo thumb. This "finger" is actually a fused wrist bone and allows pandas to grasp and hold bamboo, which is not physically possible for other bears. This bone doesn't function like a true opposable thumb, like yours and mine, pandas could never make the "ok" symbol with their fingers, however this small bone again optimizes how efficiently pandas can eat bamboo. Interestingly, while the skeleton and musculature of pandas have evolved around their bamboo diet, they still retain the simple digestive system of a meat-eating animal. Because of this, even with the help of specialized bacteria that live in their intestines, pandas only digest around 17% of the available nutrients from bamboo. Pandas compensate for this relatively low-nutrient diet by spending around half the day eating and the rest of the day inactive. While scientifically speaking, this is an adaption to conserve energy, in everyday terms, yes, you can say pandas have evolved to be lazy. Now that we know a bit more about the physical evolution of pandas, we can focus on the different ways pandas communicate.

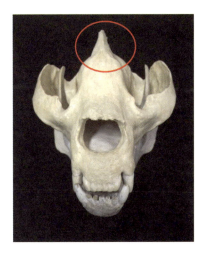 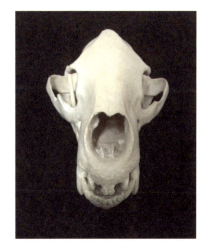

**The skull of an adult giant panda.** Notice the large sagittal crest circled in red. This bone structure is an anchor point for the giant pandas strong chewing muscles.

**The skull of an adult black bear.** Notice the absence of a pronounced sagittal crest and the longer thinner muzzle.

Figure 1. The skull of an adult giant panda vs. the skull of an adult black bear

As a human, we rely so much on visual communication, so much so that you don't even realize when you are doing it. For example, right now I am communicating with you visually as you read these words! The editors even requested I provide six pictures for this story to communicate with you further. A picture is worth a thousand words, right? We can't drive safely in the city or cross the street without using visual communication in the form of traffic lights. Pandas certainly communicate visually, and we will discuss that a little later, but using chemosensory communication, or simply scents and smells, is a pandas primary means of communicating.

Pandas, like other bears, are generally solitary. There is some overlap in the territories between pandas but, for the most part, they keep to themselves. As a result, they have evolved to communicate across space and time, without physically meeting, by leaving scent marks. A panda scent mark is a waxy secretion that is produced by the anogenital gland located under the base of the panda's tail. These markings convey a number of things including a unique identifier for each panda, their sex, reproductive status, age and even possibly kinship information. These marks serve different functions depending on the time of year, and serve multiple functions depending on the age and sex of the sender and also on the receiver of the mark.

In both male and female pandas, for most of the year, these marks delineate their territory and aid in preventing any unwanted interactions with other pandas. However, during the breeding season, these signals serve a different function. During the breeding season, an adult female will scent mark to announce her estrous and attract males, while an adult male will signal his interest in mating and hope to get a female's attention with his marks. These marks also serve another function, in the case of adult males, during the mating season, the same mark he will leave to attract female pandas can be interpreted as a challenge or a warning to nearby adult males. Female pandas that are not in estrous or have young cubs will also be affected differently and likely avoid these marks, because they are not interested in mating. Lastly, sub-adult, injured or older males, during the mating season, will also likely avoid these marks as well because they are not able to fight during mating competitions. Regardless of the context, scent markings serve as a method of communication so that pandas may learn about neighboring pandas prior to them actually meeting, however when they do meet, pandas need to switch to a more direct means of communication that works in real time. For this, just like you and I, they use vocalizations.

Pandas make numerous vocalizations that vary by pitch, frequency and duration to express a range of emotions depending on the context. All giant panda cubs are born deaf and blind however, they vocalize immediately after birth stimulating their mother to hold and nurse them. When cubs are older, their hearing develops and they respond to their mother's calls and will return to her if they wander too far or if there is danger. When pandas are sexually mature, both males and females will use a "bleat" call to show interest in mating and when pandas fight or are faced by a predator, they will roar and bark to frighten and intimidate the threat. Previous experiments have also shown, again like you and I, that pandas can recognize the vocalizations of other familiar pandas.

Like vocalizations, pandas will communicate visually when they are closer together. In general, visual communication is poorly understood in giant pandas and an area that deserves future research. We do know that certain postures and gestures serve specific meanings for pandas. One of these postures is called lordosis and communicates that a female panda is interested in mating by raising her tail and arching her back. Another posture or gesture used by pandas is a lunging behavior, this serves as a warning and a threat of violence between pandas or to a predator, however this same gesture is used playfully by cubs and can be an invitation to wrestle.

Lastly, pandas also communicate through touch. Again, like visual communication, tactile communication is poorly understood with giant pandas. We do know that tactile communication is essential during the cub-rearing period between mothers and their infant. As cubs are born deaf and blind, touch is the only way cubs can experience the first weeks of life and bond with their mother. As cubs grow older, playing with their mother, which involves tactile communication, is critical for the healthy physical and mental development of the cub. Lastly, communicating through touch is important during the mating period for successful copulation.

Now that we understand the basic ways that pandas communicate with each other, how can we as humans apply this to communicating with pandas? For obvious reasons we cannot communicate using odors with pandas, that would get messy and awkward! That leaves us vocalizations, visual cues and touch to communicate with giant pandas, luckily there is a technique called positive reinforcement training that incorporates these methods. Positive reinforcement was first developed by the American psychologist B.F. Skinner in the late 1930's. This technique involves rewarding an animal each time a desired action occurs with the goal to increase the chances of the action occurring again in the future.

Positive reinforcement is often used in our daily lives, without us knowing. For example, if you score high on a school exam, your parents may buy you something special, like new clothes. This will increase the chance that you will study harder for each future test because you really like the rewards they gave you. As long as your parents continue to reward you, you will continue to work hard in school. This is positive reinforcement and your new clothes are what we call a primary reinforcer because they motivate or reinforce your actions. We use the same exact principle with giant pandas. The first part of training giant pandas is finding out what sort of reward would motivate a panda and serve as a primary reinforcer.

Remember, earlier we spoke about the panda's nutrient poor diet? We have found that because giant pandas are specialized to feed on low calorie bamboo, high calorie sugary things like apples, are excellent rewards for giant pandas, and are very useful as a primary reinforcer. Once we have chosen a primary reinforcer, we need one more step before we can train pandas and that is to add a secondary reinforcer. This is really important and it serves two functions: first, it lets the panda know that they did something correctly and second, it is a promise that the pandas will be rewarded. Using our knowledge of how pandas communicate vocally, we chose a whistle as our secondary reinforcer because it is easily heard and distinguishable from other sounds.

Now that we have both a primary and secondary reinforcer, it's time to begin conditioning our giant pandas. We first establish our primary and secondary reinforcer with the pandas by blowing our whistle and then immediately feeding the panda. It goes something like this, whistle – food, whistle – food, whistle – food, etc, etc. This is called conditioning and is based on the principles that were first studied by the Russian Phycologist Ivan Pavlov, who famously conditioned dogs to salivate at the sound of a bell. We will continue this step, over and over again, until we know that the pandas are conditioned. We can tell the panda is conditioned when we blow the whistle and the panda immediately looks at us expecting food. This is the breakthrough moment and the main step in communicating with pandas. Essentially, you can think of it as though we have taught the panda one single word, the word is "correct". While this seems simple and insignificant, it's only one word after all, this small little step is worth 100 miles when it comes to training.

Now, with all of that out of the way, we are finally ready to start training pandas. The first and most basic thing we train is how to "target". "Targeting" involves teaching pandas to touch their nose to a pole. This behavior draws back to our knowledge of panda communication, as pandas communicate mainly with smell, any new object you show them, they will first try to smell it. When a panda moves forward to sniff the tip of our target pole, we whistle and reward them. Repeating and reinforcing this behavior quickly trains the panda to "target". We will also say the word "target" to add a vocal cue, and clearly mark the tip of the pole so it serves as a visual cue. Training this behavior makes other much more

Figure 2. A trainer at the Panda Base teaches a panda named Jing Jing to "target". Once the panda touches her nose to the pole she will be rewarded. The trainer has a whistle in his mouth to signal the panda and rewards in the metal bucket at his hip.

complicated behaviors that much easier, as "targeting" lets us control the position and posture of the panda. As an example, to teach a panda to stand, you simply need to hold the target pole above their head and ask them to "target". If you want to weigh a panda, hold the target over a scale. The possibilities for training are nearly limitless once you have established these basic steps with the animal.

Using these methods, we have made tremendous progress in how we care for our pandas. At an early age, all of our pandas are trained to participate in voluntary blood draws so that we may collect their blood without anesthesia. This one single action has had a massive impact on the conservation of giant pandas. Just about every aspect of our understanding of panda biology, from their hormonal levels to nutrition requirements, from disease treatments to their overall well-being, have been based off of research conducted on the blood collected

Figure 3. A trainer at the Panda Base teaches a panda named Xi Lan to open his mouth for a dental exam.

voluntarily through training at the Panda Base.

To date, we have taught our pandas to volunteer for dental checks, ultrasound exams, milk collection, urine collection, blood pressure checks and many, many other behaviors. As you can see,

Figure 4. Because of the strong bond that we build with our pandas, we can work closely with them in a safe way. In this case, Ji Mei is having his teeth checked. Notice again the whistle and the bucket of food at the trainer's waist.

communicating with giant pandas, using positive reinforcement, has been a huge accomplishment, but are there limitations and risks involved in training pandas, it can't be as wonderful as it sounds, right? Unfortunately, there are limitations to training and yes there are risks involved.

When training pandas, we are limited by the pandas' desire for food. Again, I said earlier that pandas have a low nutrient bamboo diet, and are almost always ready for a sweet treat, this is true, except when they aren't. Both adult male and female pandas lose their appetites and become restless,

Figure 5. We use training to study how our giant pandas develop and to ensure they are healthy. Here Ji Mei "targets" to his trainer's hand and stands on his hind legs. This position allows us to safety check his body condition and monitor his growth.

unpredictable and difficult to train during the mating season. During this period, the usually super lazy, cuddly pandas, can even get aggressive. Pregnant females will also lose interest in food a few days before giving birth, and can also become aggressive after their cub is born. And of course, if a panda is sick, they may lose their appetite. These are the most difficult and dangerous times for us to train pandas. Remember, pandas evolved to have an extremely powerful bite and can easily crush bamboo, well they can also easily crush human bones too. Luckily, there are four rules that we follow to safely train them, even during these challenging periods.

Rule number one, *the panda is always right*. We need to let the panda pick the pace that we work at. The pandas are the movie stars, we're just people after all and they are bears! If they want to work slowly, go slowly. If they misbehave, ignore it, and then reward them as soon as they do what you asked. It's important to remember, if there is any misunderstanding, the fault is always ours, not the panda. Rule number two, *know your panda*. Because we have to work closely with each individual panda during training, we build a strong, mutual bond that is based on trust. Each panda has a unique personality and needs, if you know your panda then you will know whether it is safe or not to work with them. Rule number three, *use our secret weapon honey*! Pandas love honey, just about more than anything, even the most stubborn panda will usually cooperate for honey. Rule number four, *if the panda still does not cooperate go back to rule number one*!

It's a funny that with honey, we are back full circle. It's amazing that honey, which is basically flower nectar that is partially digested

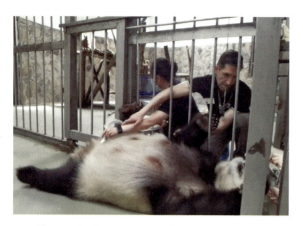

Figure 6. Due to the giant panda's unique biology, determining for certain if a panda is pregnant can only be done by ultrasound examination. Here, Ya Li is being examined with ultrasound by the Panda Base veterinarian. Ya Li is trained and rewarded for laying completely still during the exam. Again, because of the bond she has with her trainer, these exams can be done safely and with very little stress.

and regurgitated by bees, would play a key role in driving the communication between a species of bird and humans, as well as between humans and pandas. The secret, it seems, between cross-species communication is using something delicious to eat! As the greater honeyguide and humans developed this unique method of communicating as a mutualism, in which both species benefit, why did humans seek to develop this method of communicating with giant pandas?

Sadly, humans are responsible for the decline of the giant panda population and we nearly drove them to extinction. Luckily, the Chinese government has made tremendous efforts to conserve this national treasure and its habitat. As a testament of the government's dedication to conserving wildlife, the wild population of giant pandas is slowly recovering, with currently 1864 individuals living in the wild. While this is a great accomplishment, giant pandas are still vulnerable to extinction. To further safeguard the species, the government established a captive population and it's with these captive pandas where our efforts at communication have proven essential. Using the methods I described to train pandas, the captive population has now grown to a self-sustaining level, with over 600 individuals housed in breeding centers and zoos both in China and abroad. It is here, communicating and working together with pandas, that we can ensure the survival of this precious species, to our mutual benefit, because a world without pandas would be a very bleak and desolate place for all of humanity.

### About the author

Born in New York City, USA, Mr. James Ayala completed a master's degree in conservation biology from Antioch New England Graduate School in 2005 and has over 25 years of experience working with wild animals. For the past 10 years, he has engaged in the research and conservation of giant pandas in China at the Chengdu Research Base of Giant Panda Breeding. Mr. Ayala's main research interests include applying behavioral research, positive reinforcement conditioning and environmental enrichment to improve the management, breeding and welfare of captive endangered species.

# 白天还是夜晚：
# 探索猫头鹰饮食和习惯的演变

文／托马斯·斯坦哈姆［美］
译／张晓

## ▌ 对大自然的热爱

我在3岁的时候拥有了第一本关于恐龙的书。翻看着书，我学会了很多令人着迷但已灭绝的生物的名字，比如暴龙和古巨龟。这激发了我对科学和自然的兴趣，最终引领我成了一名科学家。我的童年生活充满了寻找化石、捕捉昆虫、收集岩石和矿物的经历。这些广泛涉猎的兴趣之外，始终最让我着迷的是鸟类。世界各地有1万多种鸟类。我们不可能避开鸟类。不管是最高的山，还是最远的海洋或者沙漠，不管是冰封的地球两极，还是我北京公寓的窗外，鸟类无处不在。鸟类是恐龙唯一的后裔，它们的飞行能力激发了很多人的想象力。

科学家们提出关于我们周围世界的问题，然后努力探索问题的答案。科学研究者提出了许多有关鸟类的有趣的问题，比如他们羽

毛的颜色的起源、它们是如何飞行的、气候变化对鸟类的影响，以
及鸟类为什么迁徙等。作为一名科学家，我通过研究鸟类的进化来
揭示鸟类生物学的各个方面。鸟类的化石研究需要利用科学、数
学甚至非科学学科等不同领域的知识和技术。尽管我是鸟类专家，
在六大洲见到过数千种鸟类，我总能提出新的有趣的问题来进行研
究，然而有一组鸟类对我来说仍然有点神秘，因为它们大多隐藏在
夜里，这就是猫头鹰。

想想大多数猫头鹰每天生活的世界，那就是黑暗。假如你是一
只猫头鹰，那你生存的首要问题是什么？怎么找到食物？吃什么？
什么时候去找吃的？接下来，作为一名科学家，你如何回答这些问
题？你需要什么样的科学证据？长期以来，生物学家一直在收集数
据（来自野外观察、唾余、骨骼、遗传学和其他领域），进行假设
并验证。如今的科学家们在研究问题时不会拘泥于一个学科领域，
而是整合不同领域的证据来解答自己所在专业的问题。正如下文所
说，我们在各个科学领域进行探索，不仅是为了提问，也为了探索
问题的答案。在对猫头鹰和综合鸟类的研究中，我运用了行为学、
地质学、生物学、古生物学、统计学和几何学等学科的数据和方
法，还有满满的好奇心，来探索有趣的科学之路。

## 猫头鹰的多样性

猫头鹰以其主要在夜间（或夜行性的）捕食和活动而与众不
同。由于这种差异，世界各地的文化都将猫头鹰与智慧、神秘、死

亡、幸运，甚至哈利·波特的魔法世界联系在一起。

猫头鹰是鸮形目鸟类的俗称。现存的猫头鹰种类在鸮形目中分为两个科，谷仓猫头鹰科（Tytonidae仓鸮科）和真猫头鹰科（Strigidae 鸱鸮科），许多已灭绝的物种被归为各自的类群。如今，在各大陆（南极洲除外）和许多岛屿上共发现了200多种猫头鹰。作为顶级捕食者，猫头鹰是世界各地陆地生态系统的重要组成部分，帮助构建所在地的生态群落。猫头鹰的饮食、体型、声音甚至习性都各不相同。这种多样性是它们在大约5500万至6000万年的漫长的进化历史中逐渐形成的，已知最古老的猫头鹰化石来自欧洲和北美的古新世晚期。

猫头鹰的体型范围之广令人难以置信，最大的猫头鹰雕鸮（包括所谓的鹰鸮）翼展接近2米，最小的猫头鹰姬鸮翼展只有26厘米，体重约40克。5500多万年前的最早的猫头鹰化石也表明，猫头鹰的体型迅速进化，一些早期灭绝的物种几乎与现存最大的物种一样大。虽然大多数种类的猫头鹰绝大部分是夜间活动的，但并不是所有种类都在夜间活动。有些物种更喜欢在白天保持清醒和狩猎。然而，关于白天活动的这段进化史，在很大程度上我们并不了解，没有深入研究。

## ▌ 猫头鹰的食物

作为一个群体，猫头鹰的食物多种多样，包括脊椎动物和无脊椎动物。也许猫头鹰最常见的猎物是那些在夜间也很活跃的动物，如小型哺乳动物（如啮齿动物和食虫动物）和无脊椎动物（包括昆虫和蜘蛛）。最大的猫头鹰，如雕鸮，可以捕获像狐狸或兔子一样大的哺乳动物。然而，包括体型最大的猫头鹰在内的大多数猫头鹰也会吃大量不同种类的昆虫和其他无脊椎动物，而不仅仅是哺乳动物。当然，即使是体型最大的猫头鹰也无法直接吞下狐狸那么大的动物，而对于体型较大的猎物，它们必须用锋利的钩状喙和强壮的双脚将猎物撕成碎片然后吞下。

我曾发现一个因吞食较大的猎物而导致猫头鹰死亡的例子。我和一名学生解剖了一只美洲雕鸮，这只猫头鹰被发现死在美国加利福尼亚州的一个植物园里，它的胃里满满当当，有一整只加利福尼亚蝾螈和几只耶路撒冷蟋蟀的消化残余。这种蝾螈的皮肤和身体被一种叫做河豚毒素的天然毒物所覆盖，这是一种非常强大的神经毒素，对大多数食肉动物具有天然的威慑力。显然，毒素并没有阻挡住这只猫头鹰，它快速吞下整个蝾螈，这很可能导致它在一分钟内麻痹并死亡。

尽管猫头鹰主要在夜间活动，在黑暗中搜寻和捕获猎物，但我们实际上已对猫头鹰的饮食有相当多的了解。生物学家是怎么知道这些的呢？猫头鹰捕食各种各样的动物，但无法消化许多猎物的坚硬部分，如牙齿、骨头、羽毛，还有毛发。哺乳动物可以吞下骨头，经过整个消化系统（从胃到肠）并最终形成粪便。与此不同，猫头鹰会将难以消化的东西堆积在胃中并反刍，将它们化作

图1. 猫头鹰吐出的唾余，发现于中国西部，长8厘米，包含许多小啮齿动物骨骼和毛发。

丸状颗粒从嘴里吐出（图1）。猫头鹰吃的几乎所有东西都会记录在这些唾余中，包括猎物的骨头、牙齿、毛发、羽毛和其它难以消化的部位。在一晚的狩猎和进食后，白天猫头鹰会在树上、悬崖上或洞穴中栖息和睡觉，这时它们通常会咳出这些唾余。由于经年累月地生活在一个栖息地，栖息地下面的地面上就会堆积起大量的唾余。生物学家们在世界各地收集这些唾余，以研究和记录猫头鹰的饮食。他们仔细地破开这些唾余，并辨认出骨头、牙齿和昆虫，以了解不同种类的猫头鹰在不同的生态环境中和不同的历史时期内都吃什么。这些唾余不仅告诉科学家猫头鹰吃什么，还告诉了生物学家猫头鹰栖息的地方生活着哪些动物（在猫头鹰一晚的飞行范围内）。

猫头鹰是优秀的捕食者。猫头鹰通常会捕食一个区域内常见的任何小型哺乳动物，而较少捕获稀有的哺乳动物。它们栖息处的唾余反映了不同物种骨头和牙齿的数量，揭示了这种差异。我在北京检查过一只雕鸮的唾余，唾余里含有一只长耳猫头鹰的骨头，这非常罕见，令人惊讶。猫头鹰不断地采集周边环境中各种动物的样本，这一点有点像生物学家。通过对大量唾余的长期检查，科学家可以追踪小型哺乳动物和物种，在多年长时间段内的变化情况。尽管大多数猫头鹰通常是捕食一个地区中较常见的脊椎动物和无脊椎动物，但一些猫头鹰也会表现出对某类食物的偏好，就像我们也会偏爱某种食物一样。例如，我曾在非洲了解到一种猫头鹰几乎只吃青蛙，我在中国西部发现了一个唾余，它的成分几乎完全是甲虫。猫头鹰的食谱菜单也会随一年四季而变化。长耳鸮在冬天来到北京，在寒冷的月份里享受这里特定的食物。在天坛和北京的其他公园，这些猫头鹰吃了许多冬眠中的蝙蝠。虽然我们不知道猫头鹰如何在夜间找到蝙蝠，并捕捉和吃掉它们，但很明显，长耳鸮在这方面相当成功，而且不在北京的时候，也就是一年中的其他时间，它们似乎不会吃很多蝙蝠。

## ▌ 猫头鹰的特殊技能

为了成为一名成功的夜间猎手，猫头鹰进化出了许多特殊的特征。它们有强有力的喙和锋利的爪子，可以抓住并杀死猎物。为了帮助抓取猎物，猫头鹰脚趾上的所有骨头（趾骨）表现出差异性，即脚趾上相连的每节骨头（趾骨）在朝着趾尖的方向次第变长。此外，它们的第四个脚趾可以朝前或者朝后，以帮助抓紧挣扎中的猎物。猫头鹰很早就进化出了这样的脚和喙，这些特征甚至出现在最早的化石中。猫头鹰的羽毛有分叉的或毛刷般的边缘，这种羽毛使它们的飞行几乎无声无息，让它们在夜间尽可能静悄悄地接近猎物。猫头鹰的头骨在鸟类中也是独特的。它们耳朵的位置不对称，左右两侧不平齐。这种不对称性使他们不仅可以精确定位声音在水平轴上的位置（就像我们一样），而且可以确定声音在垂直方向上的位置。对一只栖息在树上的猫头鹰来说，这有助于它在黑暗中倾听树下某个地方的哺乳动物的动静。

也许猫头鹰最大的差异性进化表现在眼睛。由于夜间光线暗，猫头鹰进化出了大大的前置眼睛。它们有很好的双眼视觉（与我们相似），而且有几乎可以转动一周的长长的脖子，可以很好地观察周围的三维空间。此外，白天时，它们硕大的眼睛能够使它们比其他白天强光下活动的物种接收更多的光线，并且能让它们在黑暗中看见东西。像其他爬行动物和鸟类一样，猫头鹰的眼睛中有围绕瞳孔和虹膜的重叠的圆环状骨头（称为巩膜骨），形成类似于管状望远镜的结构，这有助于猫头鹰获得更好的夜视能力（图2）。尽管听力和视力有所提高，猫头鹰的味觉和嗅觉能力却有所下降甚至丧失。对夜行猫头鹰的基因分析表明，它们失去了一些其他鸟类常有的与味觉和嗅觉有关的基因。科学家们认为这是因为嗅觉和味觉对于在晚上觅食时没那么有用。

## 回到白天

请记住，并非所有猫头鹰都在夜间活动。有些通常在黎明或黄昏时分出来，很少一些则几乎全在白天活动，更喜欢白天。这些白天活动的"少数派"猫头鹰包括猛鸮（Surnia ulula）、雪鸮（Bubo scaniacus）、北方鸺鹠（Glaucidium gnoma）和穴小鸮（Athene cunicularia）。它们在猫头鹰家族树（系统发育学）上不是彼此的近亲，这表明，一些猫头鹰的这种回归白天的特征发生在其进化史的不同时期。一些大约5500万年前的最早的猫头鹰化石表明，这些早期灭绝的猫头鹰的身体类似于现存猫头鹰，但眼睛却更小。较小的眼睛表明，最初的猫头鹰不是夜行性的，它们可能像其他鸟类一样是在白天活动的。在数百万年的进化过程中，猫头鹰才转变出了我们所熟知的夜间生活的习惯。科学家们还不知道猫头鹰这种倾向于夜间活动的习惯是何时进化来的，这是一个非常值得未来深入研究的问题。

然而，最近的一个发现有助于揭示猫头鹰何时从夜间改为白天活动。在中国青藏高原的边缘发现了一只近650万年前已灭绝猫头鹰的化石骨架（图2）。这个几乎完整的骨骼包括头骨、四肢和身体的大部分三维结构，甚至还有一些很少能保存下来的身体部分，如舌头的骨头、气管的骨环、翅膀和腿的骨腱、胃里一些被消化的猎物骨头，令人惊讶的是还有眼骨（巩膜骨）。这个迷人的化石骨架，让我们研究了许多不同的问题，如这只已灭绝的猫头鹰与哪些动物有关，

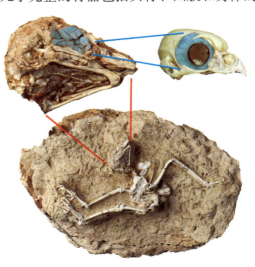

图2．来自中国的已灭绝的猫头鹰（Miosurnia diurna）的骨骼（下部）及其头骨（左上）与鸺鹠属猫头鹰（Glaucidium）的头骨（右上）的对比。为了便于比较，眼睛的巩膜骨处理为蓝色。

它吃了什么，它在夜间还是白天活动。如果没有保存了这么多的解剖特征的化石，那么开展这种详细研究几乎是不可能的。对胃部区域的骨骼碎片的检查表明，它们来自一种小型哺乳动物（可能是啮齿动物），它们被胃酸深深腐蚀，这表明猫头鹰的最后一餐是在死亡前几个小时。通过测量其眼窝中的梯形巩膜骨（图2中以蓝色突出显示），我们能够利用几何学将其与活猫头鹰骨骼比较来重建其眼睛的大小和形状。通过统计程序，我们将其与500多种在白天或晚上活动的其他鸟类、爬行动物的眼睛（巩膜骨环）进行了比较。结果表明，这种灭绝已久的猫头鹰的眼睛更像白天的动物（尤其是昼行猫头鹰），而不像夜间猫头鹰。通过将该化石骨骼与世界各地猫头鹰的进行比较，这种被我们命名为Miosurnia diurna的已灭绝猫头鹰与昼行性的北方鹰鸮和鸺鹠属的侏儒猫头鹰（在夜间不出没）最为接近，北美鸺鹠也属于这种侏儒猫头鹰。这种已灭绝很久的昼行猫头鹰与现存的昼行猫头鹰关系密切，这就提出了一些进化方面的新问题。使用一种被称为祖先状态重建的统计技术（结合了物种谱系与大小、形状、行为数据等），我们发现，这群猫头鹰的近亲在600多万年前由Miosurnia、北方鹰鸮和侏儒猫头鹰进化而成，它们逐渐改变了夜间活动的习惯。因此，与其说现在的北方鹰鸮是一种孤立的、奇怪的昼夜物种，倒不如说它是数百万年来改变了夜行习惯的猫头鹰群体的一部分，它们的亲戚如今在世界各地都能找到。我们可以看到这种进化对这群猫头鹰的影响，较小的眼睛适应了白天，较小的眼睛也影响了头骨的整体形状。Miosurnia的行为有点像它的近亲——鹰，在树上搜寻小型哺乳动物，然后迅速飞近并用脚抓住它。

六百多万年前，Miosurnia在中国生活的地区有已灭绝的马、大象、犀牛、鬣狗、秃鹫和鸵鸟等动物。总体而言，该地区看起来与现在的非洲大草原非常相似，有大片的草原和零星的树木。而今，许多昼行猫头鹰正是在这样开放式的栖息地生活，这种类型的栖息地可能会影响它们的进化。还有很多问题有待我们去探索，比如了解猫头鹰何时、为什么以及如何恢复白天活动的习惯。是因为饮食改变（以白天活动的哺乳动物为食）吗？还是因为环境的变化（森林栖息地的丧失）？未来的科学家将通过新发现的化石、现代统计工具、科学和自然各领域的数据等来解答这些问题。

## 总结

猫头鹰的多样性提供了许多有趣的生物信息，这使得好奇的科学头脑提出了有趣的问题。虽然科学家们已经对猫头鹰和其他鸟类有了相当的了解，但还有很多地方需要进一步研究。一般来说，回答一个科学问题会引出另一个问题。你对猫头鹰有什么问题吗？科学是因问题和好奇心而向前发展的。科学家的工作其实大都是一点一点加深我们对某一问题的认识，每个新的答案都是向前迈进的一小步，但一个新发现或一个独特的提问，可能会对我们对某一问题的认识以及如何思考这个问题产生巨大影响，并彻底改变未来研究的方向。例如上文的例子中，这个来自中国的猫头鹰新化石彻底改变了我们对数百万年来世界各地猫头鹰昼夜生活习性演变的看法，研究人员将在未来几年里研究这一发现的影响。这就是科学的魅力，一项研究可以改变未来许多问题的方向。科学家明天会提出什么问题？你接下来会研究什么问题？它将来又会产生什么影响？

（王颖协助审核了本文专业内容的翻译，特此感谢。）

## 作者简介

托马斯·斯坦哈姆（Thomas Stidham）博士是北京中国科学院古脊椎动物与古人类研究所脊椎动物进化与系统学重点实验室的教授。他是现代鸟类化石研究和进化方面的专家。作为科学家，斯坦哈姆博士利用稳定同位素分析、CT扫描、化石、解剖等技术和数据，研究鸟

类演变以及数百万年来气候和环境变化如何影响鸟类等问题。他发表了从北极到南极的鸟类研究报告，其中包括第一个来自青藏高原的鸟类化石的报告。作为中国科学院大学兼职教授，托马斯还教授和培养研究生，并在北京积极开展科普活动，包括在中国古动物馆、周口店北京人遗址及其博物馆、北京周边的山区以及学校。他努力激发学生对科学的好奇心，鼓励所有年龄段的人热爱并投身科学和自然。

# Tracking the Evolution of Owl Diet and Habits Night (and Day)

By Thomas Stidham (USA)

## ▌ Passion for Nature

I received my first book on dinosaurs when I was three years old. Constantly flipping the pages to learn all of the names of the fascinating extinct creatures pictured in that book, like *Tyrannosaurus and Archelon*, helped to spark a life-long interest in science and nature that led eventually to my career as a global scientist. My childhood was filled with searching for fossils, catching insects, and collecting rocks and minerals everywhere I went. Despite those wide interests, it is birds, with their more than 10,000 species around the world, that constantly capture my interest. You cannot escape birds. From the highest mountain, to the most remote ocean or desert, and the ice-covered poles of the Earth or outside my apartment window in Beijing, there are birds. Birds are special as the only living descendants of dinosaurs, and their ability to fly captures many imaginations.

Scientists ask questions about the world around us, and work hard to answer them. Scientific studies of the great diversity of birds bring up so many interesting questions from the origin of their fantastic feather colors and how they fly to how climate change impacts birds over time and why birds migrate. As a scientist, I investigate different aspects of the biology of birds through studying their evolution and fossil record using information and techniques from across different fields of science, math, and even non-science subjects. Even though I am an expert on birds having seen thousands of species on six continents, I always can come up with new fascinating questions to research, but one group of birds in particular continues to be a bit mysterious for me since they are largely hidden in the night, owls.

Think of the world that most owls live in everyday. It is dark. Imagine that you are an owl. What would be your first questions about their lives? How would you find food, what would you eat, and when would you look for it if you were an owl? Next as a scientist, how would you go about answering those questions, and what scientific evidence would you need? Biologists have been collecting data (from field observations, pellets, skeletons, genetics, and other fields) and testing hypotheses about those questions for a long time. In the modern era, scientists do not stick to one subject area when looking for answers and they integrate evidence from different fields to answer questions in their areas of expertise. As you will see in the text below, we search across the sciences not only to ask, but also to answer research questions. In my studies of owls and birds in general, I have used data and methods from subjects like behavior, geology, biology, paleontology, statistics, and geometry, as well a great deal of curiosity, to pursue interesting scientific pathways.

## ▌ Owl Diversity

Owls stand out from most other birds with their largely nighttime (or nocturnal) and predatory activities, and because of this difference, cultures around the world have associated owls with wisdom, mystery, death, luck, and even the magical world of Harry Potter.

Owls, as a whole, are classified in the group named Strigiformes. The living species of owls are divided into two large groups within Strigiformes, the barn owls (Tytonidae) and the typical owls (Strigidae), with many extinct species placed into their own groupings. Today, there are more than 200 species of owls found on all continents (except Antarctica) and many islands. As skilled top predators, owls are important parts of terrestrial ecosystems around the world where they help to structure the ecological communities where they live. Owls are diverse in their diets, sizes, sounds, and even their habits. That diversity has grown over their very long evolutionary history from about 55 to 60 million years ago to today with the oldest known fossils of owls from the late Paleocene in Europe and North America.

Owls have an incredible range in body sizes with the largest owls being species in the genus Bubo(which includes the so-called eagle owls) with wings span near two meters, and the smallest species is the Elf Owl (*Microthene whitneyi*) with a wingspan of only 26 centimeters and a body mass of about 40 grams. Even the earliest fossils of owls from more than 55 million years ago show that owls quickly evolved a wide range in their body sizes with some early extinct species being nearly as big as the biggest living species. While most species of owls are largely nocturnal, not all choose the night. There are some species that prefer instead to be awake and hunt during daylight hours (diurnal activity).However, this daytime evolutionary history largely has been hidden and not studied in depth.

## Owl Diet

Owls as a group eat a wide variety of prey items from across vertebrate and invertebrate animals. Perhaps the most common prey animals of owls are ones also largely active at night like small mammals (such as rodents and insectivores) and invertebrates (including insects and spiders). The largest living owls such as the Eurasian Eagle Owl (*Bubo bubo*)can capture mammals as large as a fox or hare. However, most kinds of owls, including the biggest owls,also will consume a large number of different types of insects and other invertebrates, not just mammals. Of course even the biggest owls cannot swallow an animal as large as a fox, and for larger prey, they have to tear the body apart into pieces small enough to swallow using their sharp hooked beak and strong feet. However, owls will swallow the entire bodies of smaller animals when they can.

I discovered one such case of swallowing whole that led to the death of the owl. My dissection with a student of a Great-Horned Owl (*Bubo virginianus*) that was found dead in a botanical garden in California (USA) revealed a full stomach, and when we opened it, the stomach contained partially digested parts from a couple of Jerusalem crickets and the entire body of a California Newt (*Taricha torosa*). The skin and body of this species of newt is covered in a kind of natural poison called tetrodotoxin, which is a highly potent neurotoxin and a natural deterrent to most predators. However in this case, the fast acting toxin did not deter the owl, and because of the strength of the toxin, swallowing the whole newt quickly likely resulted in the paralysis and death of the owl within one minute.

Even though owls are largely active at night, and search and capture their prey in darkness, we actually know quite a lot about the diet of owls. How do biologists know so much about what owls eat?As bird predators, owls kill and eat a wide variety of animals. Owls cannot digest hard parts from many of their prey species like teeth, bones, feathers, and hair. Unlike mammalian predators who will swallow bones that pass through their entire digestive system (from stomach to intestines) and end up in their feces, owls accumulate these hard to digest items in their stomachs and regurgitate them out their mouths as a series of compact pill-shaped pellets (Figure 1). Nearly everything an owl eats can be recorded in these regurgitated pellet-shaped masses of bones, teeth, hair, feathers, and other indigestible body parts of their prey. Owls typically cough up these pellets after a night of

Figure 1. An 8 cm long regurgitated pellet from an owl in western China with many small rodent bones and hair exposed on the surface.

hunting and eating when they rest and sleep on their daytime roost located in a tree, on a cliff, or in a cave. As a result of the continued use of a single roost over days, months, or even years, thousands of bones, teeth, and other prey items can accumulate on the ground beneath the roost. Biologists collect these pellets around the world to study and document the diet of owls. They take apart these pellets carefully and identify the bones, teeth, and insect parts to see what owls eat across different species of owls, across the landscape, and over time. Not only do these lists of animals in the pellets tell scientists what owls eat, they also tell biologists what animals live around the owl's roost (within one night's flight).

Owls are excellent hunters. Typically owls eat whatever small mammals are the most common in an area, and capture more rare mammals less frequently.These differences are reflected in the number of bones and teeth of different species that accumulate under their roosts. Some pellets reveal surprise meals, as when I examined a pellet from a Eurasian Eagle Owl (*Bubo bubo*) in Beijing that contained the bones of a Long-Eared Owl (*Asio otus*), a rare predatory event.Owls are a bit like biologists in that they constantly sample the diversity of animals in their environment. By examining the contents of many pellets over a long period of time, scientists can track long-term changes in small mammal populations and species over many years. Even though most owls will consume the more common vertebrates and invertebrates in an area, some individual owls can show preferences for certain types of foods just like us with our favorite foods. For example, I have seen some pellets from a roost in Africa where the owl ate almost exclusively frogs, and I found a pellet in western China composed of only beetle parts. An owl's menu also can change through the year. Long-Eared Owls (*Asio otus*) come to Beijing in the winter and enjoy a special diet during those cold months. At the Temple of Heaven and other parks across Beijing, those owls eat many hibernating bats. Although we do not know how the owls locate the hibernating bats at night in order to catch and eat them, it is clear that Long-Eared Owls are quite successful at this endeavor, and they do not appear to eat many bats at other times of year when they are not in Beijing.

## ▮ Owl Specializations

In order to be a successful nocturnal hunter, owls have evolved many specialized features. They have powerful grasping feet with sharp claws to hold and kill their prey. The individual bones of their toes (phalanges) show a modification for helping to grab prey in that each successive bone (phalanx) in the toe is longer than the previous one towards the tip of the toe. In addition, the fourth toe of their foot can face forwards or backwards to help with holding items or struggling prey firmly. These features of their feet and beak evolved early among owls and are present even in the fossils of the earliest species of this group. Owls also have feathers with frayed or brushy edges. These kinds of feathers make their flight nearly silent, allowing them to approach prey as quietly as possible at night. The skulls of owls are unique among birds too. Their ears are asymmetrically positioned, not level with one another on the left and right sides. That asymmetry allows them to not only pinpoint where a sound lies on a left to right axis (like we can do), but also on a vertical up-down axis. That is very helpful when you are an owl perched in a tree listening in the darkness for a mammal somewhere on the ground below you.

Perhaps the greatest evolutionary change in owls is their eyes. With the low light of their nighttime activities, owls have evolved large front-facing eyes. They have good binocular vision (similar to us), and along with their very long neck, they can turn their heads nearly all the way around to survey the three-dimensional space around them in detail quite well. In addition, their very large eyes let in far more light than species active during the day with the bright sun, and their big eyes allow them to see in the dark. Like other reptiles and birds, owls have a ring of overlapping bones in their eyes surrounding the pupil and iris (called scleral ossicles) forming something similar to a telescope tube,which helps to give owls superior night vision (Figure 2). Despite increases in hearing and vision, owls have decreased or even lost some of their abilities in taste and smell. Genetic analysis of nocturnal owls has shown that they have lost some genes related to taste and smell that other types of birds usually

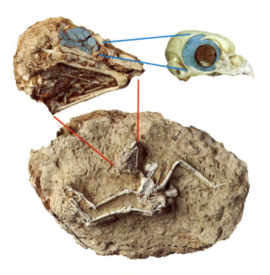

Figure 2. The skeleton of the extinct owl *Miosurnia diurna* from China (bottom) with its skull (top left) in comparison to the skull of the pygmy owl *Glaucidium* (top right). The scleral ossicles of the eye are false colored blue for comparison.

have. Scientists think they lost some of those smell and taste abilities because they are not as useful for finding food at night.

## ▌ Owls Return to the Daylight

Remember, not all owls are active during the night. Some come out mostly at dawn or dusk in the twilight hours, and even a few are nearly completely diurnal and prefer the day. Those few daylight or diurnal owls include the Northern Hawk Owl (*Surnia ulula*), the Snowy Owl (*Bubo scandiacus*), the Northern Pygmy Owl (*Glaucidium gnoma*), and the Burrowing Owl (*Athene cunicularia*). They are not each other's closest relatives on the owl family tree (phylogeny), and show that this return to the day for some owls occurred at different times during their evolutionary history. Some of earliest fossils of owls from about 55 million years ago indicate that while they had bodies similar to living owls, these early extinct owls instead had smaller eyes. Those smaller eyes suggest that the first owls were not nocturnal and that they were probably active during the day like nearly all other kinds of birds. It was only millions of years later in owl evolution that they switched to the nocturnal habits that we associate with living owls. Scientists currently do not know when owls entered the night as their preferred habit, and that is a good research question to pursue in the future.

However, a recent fossil discovery is helping to uncover when some owls switched from nocturnal to back to diurnal habits. The beautiful fossil skeleton of a nearly 6.5 million year old extinct species of owl was found in rocks on the edge of the Tibetan Plateau in China (Figure 2). This nearly complete skeleton includes the skull, limbs, and most parts of the body in three dimensions, and even has some rarely preserved body parts like the bones of the tongue, the bony rings of the trachea, bony tendons in the wing and leg, some partially digested bones in the stomach area, and amazingly, the bones of the eye (scleral ossicles) as well. This spectacular fossil skeleton allowed us to research many different questions about who this extinct owl is related to, what did it eat, and was it active during the night or day. This type of detailed study has not been possible with other fossil owls that do not preserve so many anatomical features. Close examination of the bony fragments in the stomach area of the skeleton showed that they were from a small mammal (likely a rodent)and they had been etched deeply by stomach acid suggesting that the owl's last meal was hours before its death. By measuring the individual trapezoidal-shaped scleral ossicles in the eye sockets of the fossil (highlighted in a blue color in Figure 2), we were able to use geometry and comparisons to living owl skeletons to reconstruct the size and shape of the eye. Using statistical programs, we compared that eye reconstruction to the eyes (rings of scleral ossicles) of over 500 species of other birds and reptiles that are active during the day or at night. That statistical comparison showed us that the eyes of this long extinct owl were most like those of daytime animals (particularly diurnal owls) and not like nocturnal owls. Using details of the anatomy of the skeleton of the fossil and comparison across of the living groups of owls around the world, we were able to determine that this extinct owl that we named Miosurnia diurna is most closely related to the diurnal Northern Hawk Owl and the pygmy owls of the genus Glaucidium(whose species do not come out at night)which includes another diurnal owl, the Northern Pygmy Owl (*Glaucidium gnoma*). The discovery of a long extinct diurnal owl closely related to living diurnal owls suggested some new questions about their evolution. Using another statistical technique called an Ancestral State Reconstruction (which combines size, shape, or behavioral data with the family tree), we found that this evolutionary group of owl relatives formed by *Miosurnia*, the Northern Hawk Owl, and the pygmy owls evolutionarily changed their preference away from nocturnal habits more than six million years ago. So rather than the living Northern Hawk Owl being an isolated strange diurnal owl, we discovered that it is actually part of a larger group of owls that rejected the night overmany millions of years, and their living relatives are found around the world today. We can see the impact of that evolutionary change on this group with their overall smaller eyes adapted to the daytime, and those smaller eyes influence the overall shape of the skull in these owls. *Miosurnia* likely behaved as its close diurnal relatives do by acting a bit like a hawk, watching for small mammal prey from a tree perch and flying quickly towards the animal to catch it with its feet.

The area in China where *Miosurnia* lived more than six million years ago was filled with extinct horses, elephants, rhinos, hyenas, vultures, and ostriches, and overall,the area would have looked quite similar to the modern savannas of Africa with their predominant grasslands and a few scattered trees. That open type of habitat is where many of the diurnal owl species live today around the world, and that habitat may influence their evolution. There are many more questions for us to answer relating to understanding how, why, and when owls returned to diurnal habits. Was it a change in diet (eating diurnal mammals)? Was it a change in environment (loss of forest habitats)? Scientists of the future will tackle those questions with new fossil discoveries, modern statistical methods, and gathering data from different areas of science and nature.

## ▌ Summary

The diversity of owls presents a lot of interesting biological information that leads a curious scientific mind to ask intriguing questions. While scientists have discovered much about owls and other birds, there is so much more to investigate and understand. In general, answering one scientific question will lead to another one. What questions do you have about owls? Science advances through questions and curiosity. While much of the work of scientists progresses slowly with each uncovered answer to a question as a step forward, a single new discovery or unique question can have an oversized impact on what we know, how we think about a problem, and completely change the direction of future research. For example in the case above, a single new fossil of an owl from China completely changed what we thought about the evolution of diurnal habits among owls around the world over millions of years, and researchers will be tackling the implications of that discovery for many years to come. The almost revolutionary results of this kind of research are one of the amazing aspects of science where one study can change the direction of so many future questions across subject areas. What questions will scientists have tomorrow or the next day? What question will you investigate next, and what impact will it have?

## About the Author

Dr. Thomas Stidham is a professor of the Key Laboratory of Vertebrate Evolution and Systematics in the Institute of Vertebrate Paleontology and Paleoanthropology of the Chinese Academy of Sciences in Beijing. He is a leading expert on the fossil record and evolution of the modern groups of birds from around the world. As an  active research scientist, Dr. Stidham integrates data from a wide variety of techniques and data sources like stable isotope analysis, CT-scanning, fossils, anatomical dissection, and more to tackle big questions about how birds evolved over time and how changes in climate and environment impacted birds over millions of years. He has published research on birds from the Arctic to the Antarctic, including the first fossil bird from the Tibetan Plateau. Thomas also teaches and trains graduate students as an adjunct professor of the University of Chinese Academy of Sciences, and conducts public science outreach in Beijing with talks and activities for children and families at the Paleozoology Museum of China, the Zhoukoudian Peking Man site and museum, nature sites in the Beijing mountains, and school classrooms across the city. He endeavors to encourage scientific curiosity in students and engagement with science and nature by people of all ages.

# CHAPTER 2 第二章

## 生活中的科技

### Science and Technology in Life

# 慢粒，由令人"谈之色变"的血癌转换成慢性病

文／王义汉 [美]

译／林汉英

## 慢性粒细胞白血病

慢性粒细胞白血病（Chronic Myelocytic Leukemia，CML），简称"慢粒"，是一种起源于骨髓多能造血干细胞的恶性克隆增殖性疾病。常见的诱因可能为环境污染、辐射、化学药物或致癌物质接触（例如油漆）等。

骨髓是承担我们人体中造血功能的组织，（红）骨髓中包含有一种多能造血干细胞（Haematopoietic Stem Cells，HSCs），这种细胞通过源源不断的分化和增殖，生成各种更加成熟的血细胞，如红细胞、白细胞和血小板等，再经由血流进入外周血液循环，到达各个"岗位"发挥其生理作用。这其中，红细胞主要负责运送氧气、血小板，起到止血功能，白细胞则担任防御感染（细菌、真菌、病毒等）的作用，所以骨髓还具有重要的免疫功能。而当肿瘤细胞的

恶性增殖侵占骨髓中正常的造血空间，抑制了正常造血干细胞的增长时，将会影响人体骨髓的造血能力。

慢性粒细胞白血病患病早期的表现不明显，不利于疾病早期的发现和治疗，例如疲劳、发热、贫血、出血和脾脏肿大等症状，视患者个体情况而定（定期体检很重要哦！）。慢粒患者的血象结果通常会出现白细胞数显著升高、红细胞及血小板异常等情况。

## ▍ "魔术子弹"格列卫的诞生

为什么我们说靶向药物格列卫的出现是"革命性的突破"？靶向药物是什么？与其他药物又有什么区别呢？

靶向药物，是指被赋予了靶向（Targeting）能力的药物，就像竞技比赛中运动员需要瞄准预先设定的靶标进行射击一样，格列卫等靶向药物可以专攻特定的突变基因或蛋白（称之为"靶点"），能选择性杀伤肿瘤细胞，对正常细胞损害较小，因而不良反应少而轻微。而传统化疗药物普遍缺乏靶向性，对患者正常细胞和组织进行无差别杀伤，带来严重的毒副作用。

公元2000年以前，白血病是人人"谈之色变"的恶性疾病，慢粒患者的五年存活率仅为30%左右，意味着每100名患者在确诊慢粒后仅有30名存活时间超过5年。"1995年1月，我拿着检验为何背痛的结果走进密歇根州的医生办公室，医生告诉我，我确诊了慢粒，只有3年时间了。"Mel Mann回忆道，"而在一次加入格列卫临床试验后的回诊时，我看到一位曾经虚弱到需要长期依靠轮椅出行的老年女士，从医生办公室出来后，从我身边健步走过。"（故事来源：MD Anderson Center官网，作者：Mel Mann）。

2001年5月，瑞士诺华公司（Novartis）宣布，其用于治疗慢性粒细胞白血病的小分子靶向药物格列卫（Gleevec），获得美国食品药品监督管理局（Food and Drug Administration，FDA）批准上市。同年，格列卫登上了美国著名《时代周刊》（Time）杂志的封面（如图1）。

图1.《时代周刊》杂志封面

格列卫的上市，使慢粒的10年总体生存率提高到了84%！它的诞生，体现了各领域一代又一代的科学家不屈不挠、勇于攻坚的勇气和韧性：

### ①费城染色体（Philadelphia Chromosome）的发现

1960年，宾夕法尼亚大学肿瘤研究所的彼得·纽维尔（Peter Nowell）和大卫·亨格福德（David Hungerford），首次发现CML患者的46条染色体中，有一条异常的短，这引起了他们的兴趣。经过多次观察后，他们确定，CML肿瘤的形成与染色体的变异直接相关。为了纪念他们所在的城市费城（位于美国宾夕法尼亚州东南部），便把这条染色体命名为费城染色体。但此时造成染色体异常的原因却还未被解答。

图2．费城染色体的发现者之—Peter Nowell教授（图片来源：宾夕法尼亚大学纪念网站）

②首次发现染色体易位现象

1973年，基于DNA研究技术的发展，芝加哥大学的珍妮特·罗列（Janet Rowley）解决了彼得·纽维尔和大卫·亨格福德遗留下来的问题。她发现，CML患者的46条染色体中，22号染色体缺失的长度刚好等于9号染色体多出来的长度（如图4），据此她推断费城染色体（BCR-ABL）是22号染色体与9号染色体一部分发生易位的结果。而Janet在其他白血病和淋巴瘤细胞中，也发现了十多个类

图3．奥巴马给珍妮特·罗列颁发"总统自由勋章"（图片来源：芝加哥大学医学中心）

似的易位。她的发现为后来针对特定基因异常癌症的药物开发奠定了基础。

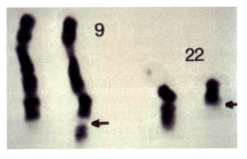

正常22号染色体（图片来源：公开资料）

一些白血病患者的第22号染色体要明显更短（图片来源：《自然》）

图4. 正常的第22号染色体与一些白血病患者的第22号染色体对比图

### ③针对费城染色体设计靶向药物（STI571）

在靶向药物出现以前，癌症治疗的常规手段是人们较为熟知的放疗和化疗，这些疗法在杀死癌细胞的同时，也会损伤人体内其他正常运作的健康细胞，可以说是"杀敌一千，自损八百"。为了研制出更精准的治疗手段，1993年，布莱恩·德鲁克（Brian J.Druker）博士、生物化学家尼克·莱登（Nick Lydon）及一众研发人员在诺华早期先导化合物的基础上，进行思考及反复结构修改，使之能够特异针对CML细胞，最终开发出STI571（俗称格列卫），这就是电影《我不是药神》里大名鼎鼎的神药"格列宁"。

### ④格列卫破茧而出，慢粒白血病治疗取得突破性进展

在STI571的研发过程中，由于药物在剂型、生产上的困难，且加之药物针对的病人数量较少，担心开发新药的巨额投资无法收回

等问题，诺华一度想放弃这个项目的研发。

数千慢粒患者得知此事后，联名请愿，请求诺华增加STI571的生产规模以满足扩大的临床试验需求。时任诺华公司首席执行官丹尼尔·魏思乐（Daniel Vasella）表示"这封信简直让人无法回避"。他说服了公司里的其他反对者，加大了STI571的产能。1998年6月，格列卫启动了Ⅰ期临床试验。

2001年，在万众期待下，格列卫终于获批上市了！此时距Nowell首次发现慢粒致癌基因费城染色体已近40年！

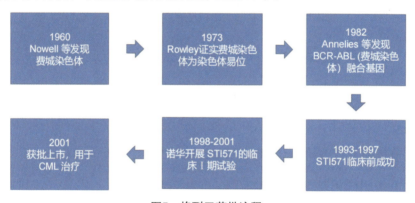

图5. 格列卫获批流程

临床研究结果表明：服用格列卫一段时间后，约95%的病人其白细胞恢复到正常水平，有60%病人的费城染色体未检出。格列卫大幅提高了慢粒患者的生存期，那些对放、化疗有严重副作用的患者、苦于等待适配骨髓捐赠的患者和在有限的生命时限里积极求生的患者，自此可以像患糖尿病、高血压一样，只要日常遵医嘱服药、定期接受检查，便能如健康人一般工作、运动、生活，能够重新融入社会。

从此，慢性粒细胞白血病成为慢性病，变得不再让人恐惧。

▍ **靶向药物的迭代——科学家们应对"耐药"的作战！**

那么，仅靠格列卫就能从此彻底将慢粒白血病变得可控吗？答案是否定的。

我们先简单了解格列卫治疗的作用原理：格列卫是一种酪氨酸激酶抑制剂，也称为正构抑制剂。激酶，在我们人体中具有调节、控制细胞生长、分化及凋亡的功能，它从三磷酸腺苷（Adenosine-Triphos phate，缩写为ATP），一种控制生物体内能量转换和传递的物质）处获得能量，并把一个磷酸基团转移到某些氨基酸上（例如酪氨酸）。在肿瘤细胞中由于基因变异，导致激酶功能失控，进而触发（肿瘤）细胞不可控的增殖和生长。格列卫直接和激酶在三磷酸腺苷（ATP）位点结合，导致ATP无法进入，癌细胞失去能量来源，直接被"饿死"。这就是激酶抑制剂的作用原理。

一部分慢粒白血病患者（约15%—20%）在服用格列卫后不久，会产生药物耐药性，使之失效。激酶非常聪明，就像战场上作战的士兵，和药物"搏斗"一段时间后，吸取了"作战经验"，改变了"作战策略"，即它改变了自身的形状（基因位点的突变），使得格列卫无法完美地和靶点结合，"道高一尺，魔高一丈"，新的挑战出现了。

这一次，基于前期科学发展和技术研究的积累，更多药企投入这场与"万病之王"的抗争之中，针对格列卫耐药问题的新药研发激烈展开。查尔斯·索耶斯（Charles Sawyers），2009年美国拉斯克医学研究奖（Lasker Medical Research Award）临床医学研究奖获得者，和百时美施贵宝制药公司（Bristol-Myers Squibb Company，BMS）合作研发出能有效对抗格列卫耐药的二代药物达沙替尼（Dasatinib），同样的二代药物还有格列卫原研厂家诺华于2007年上市的尼洛替尼（Nilotinib）。

这些药物已经可以解决由格列卫引发的大部分耐药问题，使慢粒患者多了一层保障，但一旦慢粒患者发生某种基因突变时，就面临着无药可医的困境，那就是守门残基T315I突变！它就像足球守门员一样死死守住"球门"，阻止药物和靶蛋白的结合，使其难以发挥药效。在T315I守门残基耐药突变面前，所有一代、二代药物均败下阵来。

科学家们又一次面临严峻的挑战！

## ▌ 十年磨一剑——创新小药企 ARIAD 的突围

阿瑞雅德（Ariad）是一家以结构辅助药物设计为特色的新锐生物制药企业，由一群来自哈佛、MIT的教授和工业界的人士共同创立经营。它位于马萨诸塞州剑桥市，离MIT校园很近。可别看Ariad规模小，它所在的地方，汇聚了众多来自世界各地的跨国大药企，同时也孕育出很多小而精的初创企业，新药研发的竞争在这一带如火如荼地进行着。而在其中的Ariad，正是慢性粒细胞白血病第三代药物帕纳替尼（Ponatinib）的诞生地！

图6. 阿瑞雅德制药公司

"醉翁之意不在酒"，帕纳替尼（AP24534）最初并不是特别针对慢性粒细胞白血病研发的，其设计思路源于研究骨质疏松药物，后转向由于激酶突变引发的伊马替尼耐药问题。在其研究期间，公司遭遇了大批研发人员离职、资金困难、研究技术瓶颈等困境，帕纳替尼的研发一度一筹莫展。但就是靠着Ariad科学家们的一股拼劲儿，在距格列卫上市10多年之后，这款能够针对一代药物格列卫、二代药物尼洛替尼、达沙替尼耐药，特别是针对守门残基T315I突变有效的第三代慢粒药物——"帕纳替尼"被批准上市了！

但是，针对靶向药物耐药的研发从未停止！帕纳替尼上市的一年后，被发现引起一部分病人较严重的心血管副作用，被FDA从市场短暂召回，贴上黑框警示后重新上市。2021年10月，慢粒四代药物阿恩尼布（Asciminib）在美国获批上市。与此同时，国内也有一款全新机制的最新一代变构抑制剂TGRX-678，由深圳市塔吉瑞生物医药有限公司成功开发出来，目前正在北京大学人民医院进行人体临床Ⅰ期试验。这两款药物另辟蹊径，运用了不同于以往的全新的结构和作用机制，可以同时针对第一、二、三代慢粒药物的耐药和不耐受问题。

阿恩尼布和TGRX-678作用于BCR-ABL靶点的一个全新部位，肉豆蔻酰口袋。这完全有别于第一、二、三代药物——它们都作用于ATP结合位点（正构位点抑制剂）。癌细胞需要结合ATP取得能量，抑制正构位点相当于卡住了癌细胞的"咽喉"。而变构位点抑制剂相当于以"下三路"进攻，突然袭击，对一代、二代、三代耐药的癌细胞打了个措手不及，全线崩溃，能取得意想不到的效果。

## 我国与全球药物研发的差距

从慢粒一代、二代药物的时间线上看，我国的新药研发速度一直大幅落后于全球。在2021年以前，慢粒白血病领域国内没有一款进口或国产的第三代药物获批。甚至第一代药物格列卫进入中国都很晚，且价格昂贵，造成中国慢粒病人"望药兴叹"。

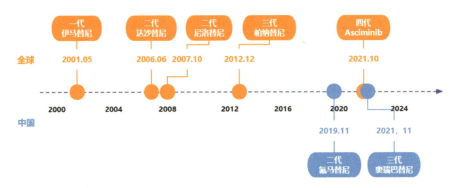

图7. 中国与全球药物研发的差距

一款新药的诞生，从药物发现到获批上市，包含了药物设计、化学合成、化学分析、生物（体内外细胞）检测、毒理、药理、药代动力学、工艺、制剂研究等多个技术环节（如图8），进入临床试验后，还重点需要临床医学的支持，是一个整合化学、生物、药学、医学、统计学等多个综合学科相关理论及实践的系统化"大工程"。

图8. 新药研发流程

我国的生物医药行业仍与世界水平存在较大差距。近年来，从国家到各地方，陆续推行了许多产业监管及扶持政策，涉及药物研发、临床试验、药品审批、医保集采、医药平台等，意在加快推动我国生物医药产业发展。除了政策、资金等外部支持外，拥有具备优秀科学素养和掌握高端科研技术的医药行业的从业人员，才是真正能够支撑药物研发、行业发展的重要基础。

**推荐阅读**

1. 《神奇的抗癌药丸》（Magic Cancer Bullet）

作者：[瑞士]Daniel Vasella（魏思乐）著

本书是第一次对于Gleevec药物的整个研制过程的权威报道。

2.《十亿美元分子》

(The Billion-Dollar Molecule: The Quest for the Perfect Drug)

作者：[美] 巴里·沃思 著

讲述制药界现象级黑马 Vertex Pharmaceuticals（福泰制药）的创业故事，谱写从实验室到华尔街的传奇。

## ●参考文献

1. Goldman, J. M.（2010）. Chronic Myeloid Leukemia: A Historical Perspective. Seminars in Hematology, 47（4）, 302–311. doi:10.1053/j.seminhematol.2010.07.001

2. 来自National Institutes of Health和MD Anderson Center 的公开资料

## 作者简介

王义汉，湖北荆州人。本科毕业于中国科学技术大学。1992年赴海外深造，取得美国纽约大学（NYU）化学博士学位。毕业后加入美国创新药企阿瑞雅德制药公司（Ariad Pharmaceuticals）担任首席科学家，扎根于靶向新药研发和对抗癌症药物耐药的研究。

作为核心成员，王义汉博士在Ariad与团队一起开发出多个国际Ⅰ类新药，包括已获批上市的抗慢粒药物IClusigTM（Ponatinib）、抗非小细胞肺癌药物AlunbrigTM以及RidaforolimusTM等。他还是美中生物医药协会（CABA）、全美华人生物医药联盟（All-CABPA）以及新英格兰美中医药开发协会（SAPA-NE）的主要发起人之一。

看到国内一些癌症患者面临用药难、用药贵的问题，王义汉博士一心想回归故土，运用自己在国外积攒的学识和经验，研制出中国自己的创新良药。他的想法获得了家人及朋友们的鼎力支持。2014年，王义汉博士回国，在深圳市南山科技园区创立了塔吉瑞（TargetRx），致力于研发克服耐药的最新一代小分子靶向药。成立至今已累计申报国内外发明专利200余项。其中，国际领先的抗慢粒（BCR-ABL）变构抑制剂TGRX-678和抗肺癌ALK抑制剂TGRX-326已于2021年启动Ⅰ期临床试验。

2017年，王义汉博士及其团队入选"第五批国务院侨办重点华侨华人创业团队"；2020年，他获得"2020年深圳创新领袖人物20强"荣誉；2021年，他获得"新时代深圳百名创新奋斗者"荣誉。

# CML, from the Dreaded Blood Cancer to the Chronic Disease

By Wang Yihan (USA)

## ▍ Chronic Myelogenous Leukemia

Chronic Myelocytic Leukemia (CML), short for "CML", is a malignant clonal proliferative disease originating from bone marrow pluripotent hematopoietic stem cells. Common triggers may be environmental pollution, radiation, exposure to chemicals or carcinogens (such as paint) etc.

Bone marrow is the tissue responsible for hematopoietic function in our body. (Red) bone marrow contains Haematopoietic stem cells (HSCs), which differentiate and multiply continuously to give rise to various more mature blood cells such as red blood cells, white blood cells and platelets, reaching each "post" to play its physiological role through the blood flow into the peripheral blood circulation. Among them, red blood cells are mainly responsible for transporting oxygen, platelets for hemostasis, and white blood cells for defense against infection (bacteria, fungi, viruses, etc.), so bone marrow also has an important immune

function. And when the malignant proliferation of tumor cells occupy the normal hematopoietic space in bone marrow, inhibit the growth of normal hematopoietic stem cells, will the hematopoietic ability of human bone marrow will be affected.

The early symptom of chronic granulocytic leukaemia is different from person to person, like feeling fatigue, calorific, having anaemia, haemorrhage and splenomegalia, is not apparent, which doesn't help the detection and treatment of certain disease, therefor regular check-up is very important! The hemogram results of CML patients usually show significantly increased white blood cells, as well as abnormal RBC and platelet.

## The Birth of Gleevec, Magic Bullet

Why do we call the emergence of the targeted drug Gleevec a "revolutionary breakthrough"? What are targeted drugs? How is it different from other drugs?

Targeted drugs refer to drugs that have been given the ability of Targeting. Just like athletes need to target a predetermined target in an athletic competition, targeted drugs such as Gleevec can target specific mutated genes or proteins (called "targets") and selectively kill tumor cells with less damage to normal cells. Therefore, adverse reactions were few and mild. Instead, traditional chemotherapy drugs are generally lack of targeting, which can indiscriminately kill normal cells and tissues of patients, bringing serious toxic and side effects.

Before 2000, leukaemia was a malignant disease, and the five-year survival rate of CML patients was only about 30%, meaning that only 30 out of 100 patients survived more than five years after being diagnosed with CML. "In January 1995, when I walked into a doctor's office in Michigan with the results of tests to see why I had back pain, I was told I had CML and had three years to live." "On a return visit after joining the Gleevec trial, I saw an elderly woman, who had been so frail that she had to rely on a wheelchair for a long time, walking past me at a good bat from the doctor's office." (MD Anderson Center official website by Mel Mann).

In May 2001, Novartis announced that Gleevec, a small molecule targeted Drug for the treatment of chronic myelogenous leukemia, got approved by the Food and Drug Administration for marketing. In the same year, Gleevec appeared on the cover of Time magazine.

Figure 1. Cover of Time magazine

The advent of Gleevec increased the overall 10-year survival rate of CML to 84%! Its birth brings together the rich knowledge, perseverance, courage and tenacity of generations of scientists in various fields:

### ① The Discovery of the Philadelphia Chromosome

In 1960, Peter Nowell and David Hungerford from the University of Pennsylvania cancer Institute, first discovered that one of the 46 chromosomes in CML patients was abnormally short, which caught their attention. After several observations, they confirmed that the CML

Figure 2. Peter Nowell, one of the discoverers of the Philadelphia chromosome (photo credit: University of Pennsylvania Memorial website)

tumor formation was directly related to chromosomal mutations. The chromosome was named the Philadelphia Chromosome in honor of their city. But the cause of the chromosomal abnormality is still unknown.

## ② Chromosome Translocation Found for the First Time

In 1973, Janet Rowley from the University of Chicago solved the problems left by Peter Nowell and David Hungerford, based on the development of DNA research techniques. She found that in 46 chromosomes in CML patients, the length of the deletion on chromosome 22 was exactly the same as the extra length on chromosome 9 (see figure), from which she deduced that the Philadelphia chromosome (BCR-ABL) was the result of a translocation between chromosome 22 and a portion

Figure 3. Obama awarded Janet Rowley the Presidential Medal of Freedom (source: Uchicagomedicine)

of chromosome 9. Janet found more than a dozen similar translocations in other leukemia and lymphoma cells. Her discovery laid the foundation for the later development of drugs that target cancers with specific genetic abnormalities.

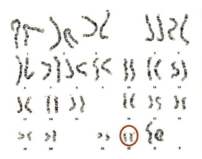

Normal chromosome 22 (Source: Public information)

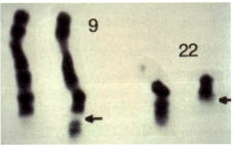

Chromosome 22 is significantly shorter in some leukemia patients (Source:Nature)

Figure 4. Comparison between the normal chromosome 22 and those of leukemia patients

### ③ To Design Targeted Drugs for Philadelphia Chromosome (STI571)

Before the advent of targeted drugs, the conventional approach to cancer treatment was known as radiation and chemotherapy, which not only killed cancer cells but also damaged other healthy cells in the body, so to speak "kill one thousand and self-damage eight hundred". To develop a more precise treatment, in 1993, based on the leading compounds of early novartis and repeated structure modification, Dr. BrianJ.Druker, the biochemist Nick Lydon, and a team of researchers finally developed STI571 (commonly known as Gleevec), which could directly target CML cells. It turned out to be the famous elixir of Dying to Survive.

④ Gleevec Emerged from Chrysalis, Making "Breakthrough" in the Treatment of Chronic Leukemia.

During the development of STI571, Novartis wanted to give up the development of STI571 several times concerning that the huge investment in the development of new drugs would not be recouped, due to the drug dosage form and production difficulties, and the small number of patients targeted by the drug.

Thousands of CML patients signed a petition asking Novartis to scale up the production of STI571 to meet expanding clinical trials. Daniel Vasella, the chief executive of Novartis at the time, said the letter was "inescapable". He persuaded other naysayers in the company to increase production capacity of STI571. In June 1998, Gleevec initiated the Phase I clinical trial.

In 2001, with much anticipation, Gleevec was finally approved for going on sale! It had been nearly 40 years since Nowell first discovered the CML oncogene, Philadelphia chromosome.

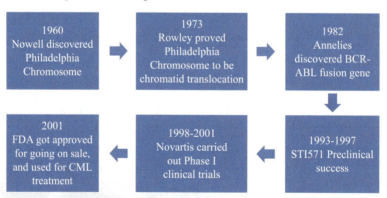

Figure 5. The approval process of Gleevec.

Clinical studies showed that after a period of taking Gleevec, white blood cells returned to normal in about 95 percent of patients and the Philadelphia chromosome was not detected in 60 percent of patients. Gleevec significantly improved the lifetime of patients with CML, and those who suffered severe side effects of radiotherapy and chemotherapy, who were waiting for the suitable bone marrow donations, or positively seeking to survive in the limited lifetime, could be able to reintegrate into the society like healthy people, working, doing sports and living normal life as long as they took daily prescribed medication and regular examination, like diabetics and people with hypertension.

Since then, CML has become a chronic disease, no longer to be feared.

## Iteration of Targeted Drugs—Scientists Battle 'Drug Resistance'!

Well, will Gleevec alone make CML completely controllable from then on? The answer is No.

Let's start with a brief overview of how gleevec works: Gleevec is a tyrosine kinase inhibitor, also known as an orthosteric inhibitor. Kinase, which regulates cell growth, differentiation, and apoptosis in our body, obtains energy from ATP (Adenosine triphosphate, a substance that controls the conversion and transfer of energy in living organisms) and transfers a phosphate group to certain amino acids (e.g. Tyrosine). In tumor cells, mutations in genes cause kinase function to go out of control, triggering uncontrolled proliferation and growth. Gleevec binds directly to the kinase at THE ATP site, preventing ATP from entering, deprives the which meant it changed its shape (gene locus mutation),

preventing Gleevec from reaching the targets. As the Chinese idiom goes,

"Virtue is one foot tall, the devil ten foot.", a new challenge came out.

This time, based on the accumulation of early scientific development

and technical research, more pharmaceutical companies went into the

fight against the "King of all diseases", and the researches of new drugs

dealing with the drug-fastness of Gleevec were carried out fiercely. Charles

Sawyers, Winner of the 2009 Lasker Award for Clinical Medicine Research,

collaborated with Bristol-Myers Squibb Company(BMS), bringing in

Dasatinib, a second-generation drug that works against gleevec resistance,

as well as Novartis' Nilotinib, which was produced by Gleevec's original

maker and was introduced to the market in 2007.

These drugs were able to solve most of the drug resistance problems

caused by Gleevec, so that CML patients had a layer of security. But

once a certain gene mutation occurred in the GML patients, they had to

face the dilemma of no cure. That was, the gatekeeping residue T315I

mutation! It was like a soccer goalkeeper to defend the "goal," preventing

the combination of drugs and target proteins, and making it difficult to

play its efficacy. All first - and second-generation drugs failed in the face of the T315I gate-keeping residue resistance mutation.

The scientists were facing another tough challenge.

## ▮ Decade of Grinding a Sword—A Breakthrough of ARIAD, an Innovative Small Pharmaceutical Company

Ariad is a vigorous new biopharmaceutical company specialized in structurally assisted drug design. It was founded by a group of harvard and MIT professors and industry professionals, and located in Cambridge, Massachusetts, near the MIT campus. Despite Ariad's small size, the region is home to many of the world's biggest multinational drug companies, as well as to many small but sophisticated start-ups. The competition for new drugs was fierce in the region, where Ariad became the birthplace of Ponatinib, a third-generation drug for chronic myeloid leukemia.

"The drinkers mind is not in the cup." Ponatinib (AP24534) was not developed specifically for chronic myelogenous leukemia, but was originally designed for working on osteoporosis drugs,

Figure 6. ARIAD Pharmaceuticals

and later turned to imatinib resistance caused by kinase mutations. During the research, the company went through a number of problems including staff departures, financial difficulties and technical bottlenecks. But thanks to the concerted effort made by Ariad scientists, more than a decade after Gleevec was launched, Ponatinib, a third-generation CML drug was approved to go on sale. It could effectively deal with the drug resistance to the first and second generation targeted drugs, Gleevec, Nilotinib and Dasatinib, and in particular, the gate-keeping residue T315I mutation.

However, the research on targeted drug resistance never stops! A year after it got the licence, Ponatinib was briefly pulled from the market by the FDA for it was found to be causing serious cardiovascular side effects in some patients, and then re-marketed with a black box warning. In October 2021, the fourth generation CML drug, asciminib, was approved for marketing in the United States. At the same time, a new and the latest generation of allosteric inhibitor TGRX-678, was successfully developed by Shenzhen Tagirui Biomedical Co., LTD. It is currently undergoing phase I clinical trials in Peking University People's Hospital. These two drugs break a new path, using a new structure and mechanism of action that is different from the past, and can simultaneously deal with the drug resistance and intolerance of the first, second and third generation CML drugs.

Asciminib and TGRX-678 act on a novel part of the BCR-ABL target, the myrisyl pocket. This is entirely different from the first, second and third generation of drugs, which all act on ATP-binding sites (inhibitors of the constitutive site). Cancer cells need to bind to ATP for energy, and inhibiting the positive construction sites is like blocking the "throat" of cancer cells. Allosteric site inhibitors are equivalent to "the next three ways" of attack, sudden attack, the first, second and third generation of drug resistant cancer cells were taken by surprise, the whole line collapse, can achieve unexpected effects.

## The Gap Between China and the World in Drug R&D

From the time line of the first and second generation of CML drugs, the speed of new drug research and development in China has been significantly behind the world. Before 2021, no single imported drug or domestic third-generation drug had been approved in the field of CML. Even Gleevec, the first-generation drug, was introduced to China late and it was expensive, causing Chinese CML patients to "feel hopeless" and have to take huge risks to buy drugs abroad. This predicament is deeply reflected in the film Dying to Survive, which triggered great shock.

The birth of a new drug, from drug discovery to approved listing, contains drug design, chemical synthesis, chemical analysis, biological (cells in vivo and in vitro) test, toxicology, pharmacology, pharmacokinetics, process, preparation research, and other techniques (as shown in figure). After entering clinical trials, the support of clinical medicine is in need. It is a systematic "huge project" integrating the theory and practice of chemistry, biology, pharmacy, medicine, numerical system and other comprehensive disciplines.

Figure 7. New drug development process

There is still a big gap between China's biomedical industry and the world level. In recent years, many industrial supervision and support policies have been implemented from the national to local levels, involving drug research and development, clinical trials, drug approval, medical insurance procurement, pharmaceutical platforms, etc., which aims at accelerating the development of China's biomedical industry. In addition to external support such as policies and funds, what makes the significant foundation to support the medical research and industry development is to have employees with excellent scientific literacy and high-end scientific research skills. I believe that with the joint efforts of all of you, the experience of CML patients in Dying to Survive will become history forever in the near future.

## Recommended reading

1. *Magic Cancer Bullet*

By Daniel Vasella (Switzerland)

This book is the first authoritative report of the entire development of Gleevec.

2. *"The Billion-Dollar Molecule: The Quest for The Perfect Drug"*

By Barry Worth

It tells the story of Vertex Pharmaceuticals, a dark horse phenomenon in the pharmaceutical industry, from the lab to Wall Street.

## ●References

1.Goldman, J. M. (2010). Chronic Myeloid Leukemia: A Historical Perspective. Seminars in Hematology, 47(4), 302–311. doi:10.1053/j.seminhematol.2010.07.001

2.Open Sources

3.National Institutes of Health

4.MD Anderson Center

### About the author

Wang Yihan was born in Jingzhou, Hubei province. He graduated from University of Science and Technology of China. In 1992, he went abroad for further study and got his doctorate in chemistry from New York University. After graduation, he joined Ariad Pharmaceuticals, an American innovative pharmaceutical company,  as the chief scientist, and devoted himself to the development of targeted new drugs and anti-cancer drug resistance.

As a core member, Dr. Wang worked with the team at Ariad to develop several international class I drugs, including IClusigTM (Ponatinib), AlunbrigTM, and RidaforolimusTM, which have already been approved for marketing. He is also one of the initiators of Chinese- American BioMedical Association (CABA),

Alliance of Chinese-Amrican Biotechnology and Pharmaceutical Associations (ALL-CABPA), and Sino-American Pharmaceutical Professionals Association-New England (SAPA-NE).

Seeing that a number of cancer patients in China were facing the problem of lacking drugs and high prices, Dr. Wang Yihan made up his mind to return to his hometown and develop China's own innovative medicine with his knowledge and experience accumulated abroad. His idea won great support from his family and friends. In 2014, Dr. Yihan Wang returned to China and founded TargetRx in Shenzhen Nanshan Science and Technology Park, which is committed to developing the latest generation of small molecule targeted drugs to overcome drug resistance. Since its establishment, it has applied more than 200 domestic and foreign patents for invention. Among them, TGRX-678, a world leading allosteric inhibitor against CML BCR-ABL, and TGRX-326, an anti-lung cancer ALK inhibitor, started phase I clinical trials in 2021.

In 2017, Dr. Wang Yihan and his team were selected as "The Fifth Batch of Key Overseas Chinese Entrepreneurial Team of Overseas Chinese Affairs Office of the State Council". In 2020, he was selected as one of the top 20 Shenzhen Innovation Leaders of 2020. In 2021, he was awarded the 100 Innovation Strivers of Shenzhen in the New Era.

# "成像"的科学基础

文／储扎克［美］

译／林汉英

　　我今天想和大家讨论一下"成像"的科学基础。大家都知道什么是拍照吧？简单地举个例子，你手里如果有手机或者相机，想拍一张照片或者自拍一下，拍照片这个过程就叫成像。手机、相机以某种方式进行某些操作，将其所看到的复制下来，并保存至手机、相机，但是这是怎么做到的呢？今天我们就一起来看看什么是成像，成像的科学原理又是什么。

## ▌我的研究方向

　　我的研究方向是光学，英文就是optics。那么什么是光学呢？

　　光学可以简单地理解为就是研究光的科学，例如太阳光。我们可以用光学解决生物、医学方向的一些问题。比如，你去看病的时候，医生需要了解你得了什么病，可能就需要去化验你的血液，血液的化验通常需要用到光学，比如通过显微镜看到血液，或者看到化学测试的颜色。

今天,我们来深入讨论与成像相关的科学,利用光学研究细胞这个尺寸的成像。细胞是身体微小的部分,它非常小以至于肉眼都无法看到,而我们的身体里有上万亿个细胞,我们怎么才能把这么小的细胞拍下来呢?举个例子,我要给我的小猫拍一下它的毛发,很难清楚地拍出其中一根毛发,而细胞比头发丝还要细小十倍到百倍,那我要怎么办才能看清楚细胞呢?这里就要使用一种有特殊的成像技术的设备——显微镜,这就是我研究方向的一部分——开发性能更先进的显微技术来帮助人类提升医疗水平。

## ▍什么是成像

医疗领域中使用的现代显微镜和其他设备确实很先进且高科技,但这样的技术并不是突然发生的。为了更好地研究微观世界,人们就成像进行了上百年的研究,逐渐完成了从零到一的突破,才有了今天先进的显微技术。虽然被称为高科技,但其依托的基本原理实际上是一位古代中国人——墨子发现的。大约在两千多年前,墨子发现了光与影的关系,了解到光以近乎直线的轨迹运动,并用这个发现进行了"小孔成像"的实验,这个最初的相机也成为现代成像技术的基础。

我们看到一颗非常漂亮的大树就会想用相机把它拍下来变成照片,这在今天看起来很容易,几乎每个人口袋里都有个相机。那么相机内部是如何成像的呢？这里光的作用就体现出来了。如果光直射到树叶上就会发生散射现象，那么光会向着相机散射，但是散射本身是不能成像的。就好像我们拿一张纸在树叶的后面，纸上是不能形成清晰的图像的，这是因为从树叶上某一点反射的光是散射在纸上的，即便它来自树叶上的某一点，也不会返回到纸上一个相应的点。

那怎么办呢？中国两千多年前的墨子就用小孔成像的原理解决了这个问题，针孔的作用就是只让来自物体上某一点的一束光通过小孔，投射到纸上的某一点，物体上的每个点在纸上都有一个姊妹点，这样就形成了像。这个系统被称为"针孔相机"。

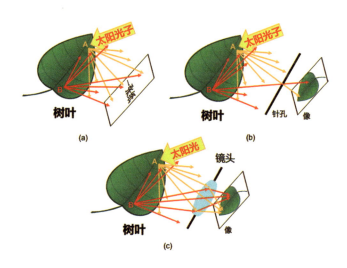

图1.（a）树叶上不同点（A,B）的光会到达纸上的同一个点，无法区分这两个点，所以纸上不能成像；（b）针孔成像；（c）镜头成像

## ▌ 如何成像

人类的眼睛就是一个天然的相机，一个很自然的相机，因为我们已经看到了外界的景物，实际上就是成了一个像。现代的相机原理很大程度上就是模拟了我们眼睛的成像功能。

生命科学中最简单的眼是一种古生物——鹦鹉螺的眼睛。鹦鹉螺的眼睛也相当特别——它缺少人类眼睛那样的晶状体，它的眼睛就是个单个的针孔，就像针孔相机一样。经过亿万年的进化，人类的眼睛已经不是简单的针孔眼了。这是因为针孔相机（或者说针孔眼）存在一个缺陷，只有很少量的光线能穿过针孔，其余的光都浪费了。所以透过针孔形成的像非常暗，光线暗的时候就更看不清了。就好比有老虎在暗处，针孔眼会害得人被老虎吃掉。感知危险的需求就需要我们人类的眼睛要看得清楚，要不断进化。现在我们人类利用晶状体，得以让眼睛收集到更多的光，形成更清晰的图像。因为成像要求物体上的一个点投射到图像上的一个点（这被称为"点对点条件"），晶状体需要"弯曲"来自物体上每个点的光，这样它们只会转向图像中的一点。这是怎么做到的呢？这就涉及了折射这一现象。

就好比我们在一个装着水的杯子里，放上一根吸管，大家可以看到吸管本身是直的，但是从杯子外面看起来就像弯折了一样。这就是光的折射——光由一种介质进入另一种介质时，传播方向就改变了。

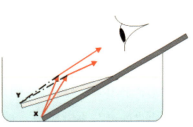

图2. 在液体中的吸管是直的，但看起来是弯折的，因为光由一种介质进入另一种介质时，传播速度改变，产生一定的偏离角度。

大家现在可以观察一下相机或者智能手机的镜头，你会发现它们都不是完全平面的，这是因为，光线通过平面的玻璃时，并不会改变光的传播方向，只是传播路线发生了改变。要改变光的方向就必须使光通过曲面玻璃，这样就改变了穿过玻璃的光的方向，不同方向的光就可以汇聚到一个点，我们称之为聚焦，这个光线聚集的点就叫聚焦点，从镜头到聚焦点的距离叫焦距，标记为"f"。

## ▎"Camera"是什么意思

相机的英文是Camera，它是什么意思呢？Camera其实是拉丁语camera obscura的缩写，其中，camera = room（房间），obscura = dark（黑暗的），所以按字面解释就是"暗室"的意思，因为最早的相机就是一个"房间"。文艺复兴时期很多艺术家就在一个房间打一个孔，利用小孔成像原理将外面的风景在墙面上成像，使得他们的绘画更加逼真。18世纪初期，基于镜头的光学照相机问世后，人们将其称为针孔照相机。后来，随着它的流行，人们将其简称为照相机。

手机自带的相机和显微镜有什么区别呢？

现在我们对成像的科学基础有了一些了解：当光线从物体的一点"聚焦"到图像中的一点时，图像就形成了。在现代成像系统中，这是通过"透镜"来完成的。那么，如果所有的图像都是这样形成的，为什么我们的手机不能给一个细胞拍照呢？原因在于图像系统是如何设计的。

一方面，手机相机只有一个镜头，这限制了它的放大倍数，也限制了它能看到的最小物体。另一方面，显微镜使用两个透镜（一个称为"物镜"，另一个称为"管透镜"），这种透镜的组合使显微镜具有非常高的放大倍率（这意味着它可以使小的东西看起来非常大），并且不仅能够看到一个细胞，甚至可以看到一个细胞的一

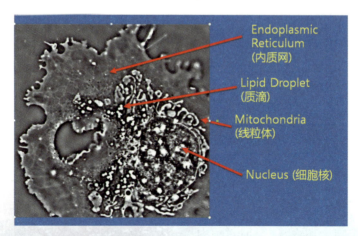

图3. 通过超斜照明高分辨率相衬显微镜技术，科技家可以清晰地看到细胞内部的大部分结构

部分（如细胞核）。

事实上，我们的手机摄像头真的可以"变成"显微镜，只要我们在它上面再加一个镜头，作为"物镜"，就能增加手机的放大率。如今，你甚至可以在流行网站上以很低的价格买到这样的镜头，所以好奇的同学都可以在自己家里制作一台显微镜。

## ▌ "成像"科学基础总结

俗话说"眼见为实"，从古到今"成像"可以说一直是人类科学进步的关键部分。几千年前，人类发现了成像现象，证实了光在直线上从一点传播到另一点，并利用这一知识创造了"针孔相机"。文艺复兴时期的艺术家们利用这个原理绘制和临摹细腻的风景画。随着现代技术的发展，人们已经可以利用光学镜头实现将物体一个点发射的多条光线通过镜头再重新合成一个点，从而形成与针孔成像系统相比，更明亮且具有更多功能的现代的成像系统。今天我们看到的高清彩色照片和影片，都是"成像"技术不断发展的结果。成像系统涵盖了手机、相机、摄像机，以及其他与日常用途及艺术相关的系统，还涉及太空探索、医疗保健和许多其他应用的高度复杂的科学系统。年轻的学生可以用他们的手机相机来探索成像的知识和原理，或许在未来，下一个先进成像技术的发明者就是你！

## 作者简介

储扎克在罗切斯特大学获得了光学专业学士和博士学位。随后，他在加州大学戴维斯分校生物光子学中心继续从事博士后研究。2015年，储扎克离开美国来到中国科学技术大学，成为精密机械与精密仪器系的教授和博士生导师。现在，在妻子和两只爱猫的陪伴下，储扎克渴望运用他的光学知识，为人类和动物同伴们作出贡献，让世界变得更加美好。

# The Scientific Basis of "Imaging"

By Zachary J. Smith (USA)

Today I want to talk about the scientific basis of imaging. We all "know" what it means to take an image, right? For a simple example, if you take a photo or a selfie with your smart phone or camera, the process of taking photos is imaging. Somehow the camera is doing *something* to make a copy of what it's looking at, and saving it on my phone. But how does it do that? Today, let's figure out what imaging really means, and its scientific principle.

## My Research Direction

My research field is called "optics" , but what is "optics"?

It can be simply explained as a science focused on light, such as sunlight. Optics can be applied to solve biological and medical problems. For example, when you go to see a doctor, he/she needs to know what your disease is, and you may need to take a blood test, which often uses optical science, like looking at your blood through a microscope, or looking at the color of a chemical test.

Today, let's probe deeper into the science of imaging, using optics to study the imaging of tiny things like cells. A cell is a tiny part of our body. It's so small that we can't see it with our naked eyes, and our bodies contain trillions of cells. How can we take a photo of such a tiny object? For example, if I want to take a picture of my kitten's hair, it's hard to clearly photograph one single hair. But cell's are 10 or even 100 times smaller than a single hair. So how can I see the cells clearly? I have to use a special imaging technology device, the microscope, which is part of my specific research direction, ——developing more advanced microscopy technology to help advance human healthcare.

## What is Imaging

Modern microscopes and other optical devices used in healthcare are really advanced and high-technology. But this technology didn't come about suddenly. To better look into the micro world, humans have been studying imaging for hundreds of years. Through the slow progress across many generations, we finally lead up to today's highly advanced microscopy technology. Even though they are "high tech", their basis is still very fundamental science that was actually discovered by an ancient Chinese named Mozi. About two thousand years ago, he discovered the relationship between light and shadow, learning that light moves in nearly-straight lines and used this to conducted the "pinhole imaging" experiment, forming the first "camera" that is the basis of modern imaging technology.

When we see a very beautiful big tree, we want to use our camera to take photos of it, which seems easy in today's world, where everyone carries a camera in their pocket. So how does the image form inside the camera? That's where the light plays its role. If light hits directly on the leaves, the light scatters towards the camera, but this scattering can't produce an image on its own. If we put a piece of paper behind the leaf, we won't get a clear picture. That's because the light reflected from a single point on the leaf is scattered on the paper, and even though it came from a single point on the leaf, it doesn't "come back" to one single point on the paper.

So what can we do? More than two thousand years ago, Mozi solved this problem with the pinhole imaging principle. The function of the pinhole is to only let only a single light ray from a single point on the object through it to reach a single point on the paper. Each point on the object has its sister point on the paper, and this forms the image! This system is called the "Pinhole Camera."

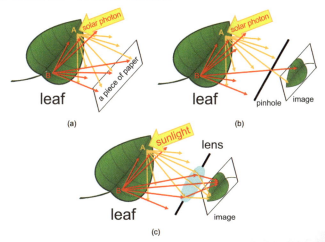

Figure 1. (a) The light from different points(A,B) on the leaf will reach the same point on the paper. Since the two points can not be distinguished, there is no image on the paper. (b) Pinhole imaging. (c) Lens imaging

# How Imaging Works

Human eyes are a natural camera. When we actually see something, it is the result of imaging. Modern camera largely imitates the imaging function of our eyes.

The simplest eye in life science is that of an ancient creatures called the nautilus. It's so special——it lacks the lens of the human eye and its eye is just a single pinhole, just like a pinhole camera. After billions of years' evolution, our human's eyes are no longer simple pinhole eyes. This is because pinhole cameras (or pinhole eyes!) have a flaw: only a tiny amount of light gets through the pinhole, the rest of the light is wasted. So pinhole images are very dark, and don't work well in dim light. If there is a tiger in the dark, our pinhole eyes will get us killed. The need to perceive the danger demands our human eyes to see clearly, and to evolve. Now our eyes use something called a "lens", which allows us to collect more light, but still make a clear image. Because imaging requires one point on the object to reach only one point on the image (this is called the "point-to-point condition"), the lens needs to "bend" light from each point on the object, so they turn back towards only one point in the image. How is that done? This involves the phenomenon of refraction.

When we put a straw in a cup with water, we know that the straw itself is straight, but it looks like it is bent from the outside of the cup. This is the refraction of light —— if light travels from one medium into another, its direction changes. You can now look at the lens in your camera or smartphone, and you will find out that none of them are completely flat, because when the light travels through the flat glass, its direction doesn't change. To change the direction of the light, we must make it go through curved glass. This changes the direction of the light travelling through it, and those light rays from a single point in the object finally converge to a point. We call this process "focusing," and this point where the rays converge is called the "focal point." The distance from the lens to the focus point is called the focal length, marked as "f".

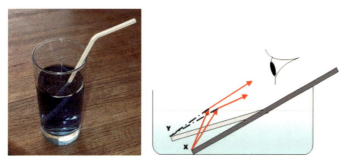

Figure 2. The straw is straight, but appears bent because the speed of light traveling from one medium to another changes, creating certain deviation.

## What is a Camera Called a Camera?

What does camera mean? Camera is actually the short form of Latin words *camera obscura. camera* means room, *obscura* means dark, so a "camera" is literally a "dark room". This is because the earliest cameras were really a "room". Many Renaissance artists made a hole in one room wall, and then applied the pinhole imaging principle to form an image of the landscape outside on the wall, making their paintings more real. After the optical, lens-based camera was invented in the early 18th century, it was also called a *camera obscura*. Later, when it became popular, they were simply called a camera.

What is the difference between a cell phone camera and a microscope?

Now we have some understanding of the scientific basis of imaging: an image is formed when light from one point on an object is brought back to "focus" on one point in the image. In modern imaging systems, this is done through a "lens." So if all images are formed in this way, why can't our cell phone take a picture of a cell? The reason is because of how the image system is designed.

A cell phone camera has only one lens, which limits its magnification, and limits the smallest object it can see. A microscope, on the other hand, utilizes two lenses (one is called the "objective" and the other is called the "tube lens"). This combination of lenses allows the microscope to have a very high magnification (meaning that it can make small things look very big), and has the ability to see not only one cell, but even one part of one cell (like the cell nucleus).

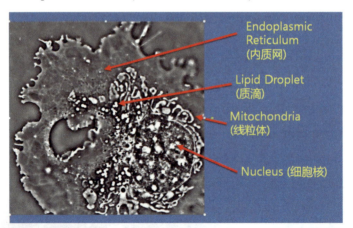

Figure 3. Scientists can see most of the structures inside cells clearly by using ultra oblique high-resolution phase contrast microscope.

In fact, our cell phone camera can actually be "turned into" a microscope, if only we add a second lens to it, to act as the "objective" lens and increase the cell phone's magnification. These days you can even buy such a lens on popular websites for a low cost, so that almost any curious student can build a microscope in their own home.

## Summary of the Scientific Basis of Imaging

The old adage says "seeing is believing," and imaging has been a key component of scientific progress from the ancient world until today. Humans discovered the phenomenon of imaging thousands of years ago, verifying that the light travels from point to point in a straight line, and using this knowledge to create the "pinhole camera". Renaissance artists used this principle to paint and copy detailed landscapes. With the development of modern technology, people can use optical lenses to focus multiple rays emitted from one point of an object through the lens and then re-synthesize a point, thus forming a modern imaging system with brighter images and more functions compared to a pinhole imaging system. The high-definition color photos and films we see today are the result of the continuous development of imaging technology. Imaging systems span the range of cell phone cameras, video cameras, and other systems used for art and "every day" purposes, as well as highly complex scientific systems used for space exploration, healthcare, and many other applications. Young students can use their cell phone's camera to probe into the knowledge and principles of imaging and maybe invent the next advanced imaging technology in the future!

外国专家科学讲堂
Foreign Expert Science Classes

## About the Author

Zachary J. Smith got his educational start in Rochester. It is at the University of Rochester that Zach has finished his bachelor and doctoral degrees in optics. Then, he pursued his postdoctoral research at Center for Biophotonics at the University of California, Davis. In 2015, Zach left the U.S. for the University of Science and Technology  of China to become a professor and doctoral supervisor at the Department of Precision Machinery and Precision Instrumentation. Together with his wife and two cats, Zach has been desiring to turn his knowledge in optics into contributions to both human races and fellow animals.

146

# 照　明

文 / 吴晖锽 [ 马来西亚 ]

本文将介绍照明，大体分为以下几个部分：照明的简介、与照明相关的一些重要定义、灯具的种类及其特点、电气照明设计和照明的方法。

## 照明的简介

首先简要介绍光。光是一种电磁波，有各种频率和波长，能够穿透空间。光随不同光的本源和穿越物质的不同而变化出多种色彩，而且阳光本身的色彩也随大气条件和一天时辰的变化而变化。我们日常看到的阳光是太阳大气层粒子受激励跃迁辐射所产生的，阳光的实质是电磁波在高空中同地球上方的粒子及云层等发生碰撞后，大部分反射到太空中，少部分通过折射进入大气层到达地球。

光由红、橙、黄、绿、青、蓝、紫等单色光组成，紫外线波长100nm（纳米）～400nm<可见光380nm～770nm（紫蓝青绿黄橙红）<红外线770nm~1mm（毫米）。其中，红外线是频率介于微波

与可见光之间的电磁波，它的波长更长；紫外线则不能引起人们的视觉反应，它是频率比蓝紫光高的不可见光；可见光是人们所能感光的极狭窄的一个波段，它的波长范围很窄。X射线、r射线是常见的紫外区部分，占太阳辐射总能量的7%；紫、蓝、青、绿、黄、橙、红光是常见的可见光区部分，占总能量的50%；红外区部分则占总能量的43%。

| 颜色 | 波长(纳米) |
|------|-----------|
| 紫 | 380—450 nm |
| 蓝 | 450—495 nm |
| 绿 | 495—570 nm |
| 黄 | 570—590 nm |
| 橙 | 590—620 nm |
| 红 | 620—770 nm |

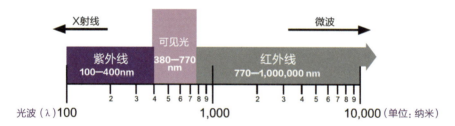

图1. 不同颜色的单色光及其波长

常见的发光类型有白炽灯、电致发光、气体放电和光激发。对于白炽灯形式，固体和液体在加热到1000摄氏度左右的温度时会发出可见辐射，白炽灯利用灯丝电阻电流的热效应使灯丝温度上升至白炽程度而发光。电发光是将电能直接转换为光能的发光现象，它是一种物理现象，当电流通过某些固体，如半导体或荧光粉材料时，就会产生光。对于气体放电形式，当气体原子受到具有一定能量的电子碰撞时会被激发和电离而发光，其光谱与存在的元素的特征相同。光激发光形式是物体依赖外界光源进行照射从而获得能量产生激发从而发光的现象，即一种波长的辐射通常被固体吸收然后以另一种波长重新发射。

2015年全球照明用电量估计为3910太瓦时，占全球总用电量的19%。照明可以分为公共照明与商业照明、厂矿（工业）照明、社区家居照明和室外照明。其中公共照明与商业照明占全球光产生量的41%，而室外照明占约12%。可以看到，照明是日常生活的重要组成部分，我们应对它有更清晰的认知。

## 照明的一些重要定义

为了更好地描述照明，我们常用流明来描述光源发出的总可见光功率。流明是描述光通量的单位，表示一个单位时间内光源发出的可见光总量。"1流明"就是1坎德拉（cd）的点光源在单位立体角（1球面度）内所发出的光通量。

光的亮度是在给定方向上的光的强度和密度的量度，它描述的是穿过某一特定区域或从某一特定区域发出并落在给定的立体角内的光的数量。它是反映发光体（反光体）表面发光（反光）强弱的物理量。亮度的单位是坎德拉/平方米（cd/m²），也就是每平方米的烛光分数。亮度是一个主观的量，与发光面的方向也有关系，同一发光面在不同的方向上其亮度值也是不同的，通常是按垂直于视线的方向进行计量的。值得注意的是，亮度和流明有本质上的区别，流明是描述光通量的单位，亮度指的是物体发光强度，也是指发光体光强与光源面积之比。

照度指单位面积上所接受可见光的光通量，单位为勒克斯（Lux或 lx），是用于指示光照的强弱和物体表面积被照明程度的量。总体来说，1勒克斯=1流明的光通量均匀分布在1平方米面积上的照度；1流明=发光强度为1坎德拉的点光源在单位立体角内发射的光通量；1勒克斯=发光强度为1坎德拉的点光源在半径为1米的球面上产生的光照度。

照度的均匀性是指光在一个区域上的均匀分布，视场中特定区域与邻近区域之间（如工作面与工作面邻近区域）照明分布的差异程度。不均匀的照度会产生亮斑和暗斑，这可能会分散人的注意力，让他们感到不适。在照度均匀性较差的条件下工作，眼睛容易疲劳，易产生眩光效应，影响视觉操作，降低视觉作业绩效。

眩光是视野内相对明亮的物体给灯光使用者带来的一种感觉。它是指视野中由于不适宜亮度分布，或在空间或时间上存在极端的亮度对比，以致引起视觉不舒适和降低物体可见度的视觉条件。明亮的物体位于黑暗环境中时，眩光最有可能出现。

光源的显色性是其逼真地再现物体颜色能力的一个指标，指光源在与标准参照光源相比时对物体颜色产生的颜色效果。显色性是0到100之间的一个指数，较低的值表示显色性差，较高的值表示显色性好。其他使用的指数是1A（极好），1B（好），2（中等），

3（低）和4（很少或几乎没有）。

色温是表示光线中包含颜色成分的一个计量单位，它的单位是开尔文（K）。在3300K以下，光源被认为是"暖光"，5300K以上的光源被认为是"冷光源"。高色温光源照射下，如亮度不高则给人们一种阴冷的气氛；低色温光源照射下，亮度过高则会给人们一种闷热的感觉。色温低的光偏黄，比如白炽灯为2800K左右，色温高的光偏蓝，比如紫光灯为9000K以上。一般认为，标准白色光色温为6500K，阴极射线管（CRT）所发出的白光约为5500K。当温度升高到一定程度时，颜色开始由深红、浅红、橙、黄、白、蓝，逐渐改变。

**表1. 色温对照表**

| 烛光 | 超暖白 | 暖白 | 冷白（月光） | 日光 | 阴天蓝 | 晴天蓝 |
|---|---|---|---|---|---|---|
| 1800K | 2800K | 3000K | 4000K | 5000K | 6500K - 7500K | 8000K - 12000K |

## 灯具的种类及其特点

高强度放电的照明可以分为白炽灯、卤钨灯、荧光灯、高压钠灯、低压钠灯、汞蒸气灯、金属卤化物灯、混合灯、LED灯等。

图2. 自左至右分别为：紧凑型荧光灯，高压钠灯，低压钠灯，金属卤化物灯

白炽灯是一种热辐射光源，它是将灯丝通电加热到白炽状态，利用热辐射发出可见光的电光源。白炽灯可实现70%—90%的能量转化为热能，显色指数为1A，色温为2500k—2700k。白炽灯具有显色性好、光谱连续、使用方便等优点，寿命为2000小时，因而被广泛应用。

卤钨灯是填充气体内含有部分卤族元素或卤化物的充气白炽灯，其原理是在灯泡内注入碘或溴等卤素气体，高温下升华的钨丝与卤素进行化学作用，冷却后的钨会重新凝固在钨丝上，形成平衡的循环，避免钨丝过早断裂。卤钨灯的显色指数为1A，属于温暖色温，寿命约为4000小时。

荧光灯属于气体放电光源，接下来介绍荧光灯的发光原理。首先，荧光灯的一端电极发射的电子以高速通过电子管，直到与汞原子的一个电子发生碰撞。其次，撞击使汞原子的电子偏离轨道，当它突然恢复原位时，就会产生紫外线辐射。最后，当紫外线辐射到达磷光晶体时，脉冲传播到晶体中的一个活性中心，这里发生了与上一步骤中描述的类似的行为。然而，这一次产生了可见光。不同型号的紧凑型荧光灯直径和效率不同，在20℃—30℃的环境温度下紧凑型荧光灯最有效，它相比于其他类型灯具要小得多。荧光灯适用于天然采光的房间照明或要求环境舒适的照明场所，在开关频繁的场所不宜采用，环境温度过高或过低的室内外场所也不适于采用。

钠灯是利用蒸汽放电产生可见光的电光源。高压钠灯是一种高强度气体放电灯泡，用于户外和工业应用，主要由镇流器、高压电子起动器、陶瓷电弧管、氙气填充（钠、汞）等组成，使用时发出金白色光，具有发光效率高、耗电少、寿命长、透雾能力强和不诱虫等优点，高压钠灯的寿命不超过2.4万小时。虽然高压钠灯使用有许多优点，但是显色性差。而低压钠灯最高功效为100—200流明/瓦，它的光质量最差，颜色呈现黑色、白色或灰色阴影，因此仅限于户外应用。低压钠灯的显色指数为3，色温呈现黄色，其寿命小于1.6万小时。

图3. 高压钠灯用于户外和工业应用

图4. 低压钠灯仅限于户外应用

汞蒸汽灯是利用汞放电时产生汞蒸气获得可见光的电光源，由带汞和氩气的电弧管和石英管、第三电极（外涂荧光粉的灯泡、外玻璃管）组成，具有使用寿命长，初始成本低的特点，其寿命为1.6万—2.4万小时。然而汞蒸汽灯的功效只有30—65流明/瓦，显色指数为3，色温呈现中级。自镇流高压汞灯相比于其他类别的灯具省去了镇流器，以自镇流灯丝来替代，无须其他任何附件，旋入灯座即可点燃，具有发光效率高的优点。

金属卤化物灯的工作原理与钨卤灯类似，但它的颜色、尺寸和等级选择余地更大，金卤灯具有发光效率高、显色性能好、寿命长（6000—2万小时）等特点。此外，金属卤化物灯的效率也比其他类型的照明更高，可达80流明/瓦。

混合灯是"二合一"类型的照明灯，一个充气灯泡中含有两个光源，因此适用于防火区域。混合灯具有较高的功率因数，可达到0.95，其典型额定功率可达160瓦。它的效率可为20—30流明/瓦，寿命不超过8000小时。

LED灯是最新款节能灯，它能以极窄的光谱发射可见光，并能产生"白光"。白光LED的能耗仅为白炽灯的1/10、节能灯的1/4，具有显著节能的特点。此外，其寿命可达10万小时以上，对普通家庭照明可谓"一劳永逸"，现已应用于交通信号灯、显示屏、汽车信号灯等领域。

对不同类型的灯进行对比可以发现，白炽灯色光接近于太阳色，荧光灯的照明效果较差；卤钨灯和白炽灯则具有极佳的显色指数，高压钠灯和低压钠灯的寿命较长，但低压钠灯的显色指数较差。

## 电气照明设计

照明的设计有两个目标，分别为提供合适数量的光和提供合适质量的光，二者相辅相成，缺一不可。

较好的照明是可以提高生产力的，因此设计师面临的两个主要问题：选择正确的照明水平和选择光线质量（显色）。不同应用条件下所推荐的光水平具有较大差异。用于不经常使用和/或偶尔执行简单视觉任务的房间和区域的一般照明（最低要求为室外流通区域、户外商店、畜栏的最低照度）、室内一般照明（最低要求为满足照明任务的最低服务照度）和视觉上严格要求的额外局部照明是常见的照明设计场景（精细的工作，如仪器的小零件、制表、雕刻等）。对应这三种设计场景，照度水平（勒克斯）要求范围从20到3000勒克斯不等。

反射镜是一种利用反射定律工作的光学元件，它可以影响光线到达面积和分布模式。反射镜可以被分为扩散反射和镜面反射。扩散反射在具有油漆或粉末涂层的白色表面，可达到70%—80%的反射率，但反射率随时间下降；镜面反射则是抛光面或镜面反射，可达到85%—96%的反射率，反射率随时间衰减。

镇流器和点火器是照明常见的组成装备，镇流器是日光灯上起限流作用和产生瞬间高压的设备，作为限流装置有助于荧光灯的电压积聚；点火器则是金属卤素灯和钠蒸汽灯中的重要装备。

## ▍照明的方法

照明的方法有许多种，本文介绍三种：瓦特密度法、流明法或光通量法和点对点法。瓦特密度法是一种粗略计算的方式，按照照明装机功率/平方米计算，一般仅供检查使用；流明法或光通量法是照明方案设计中最常用的方法；点对点法适用于由于需要一个或多个光源而照亮的点，通常用于泛光照明计算。流明法需要考虑灯的数量、每盏灯的瓦数、每盏灯的效率、利用系数、折旧系数和维修系数等变量的取值。

## 作者简介

　　吴晖锽（Hui-Hwang GOH）是电气工程领域的专家，是一名电气咨询顾问、国家能源委员认证电能管理师，现任广西大学电气工程学院电气工程系主任，曾任马来西亚敦胡先翁大学（UTHM）副教授。2019年获得"东盟杰出青年科学家"称号。

　　吴晖锽目前的研究领域包括：电力系统，可再生能源，能源效率，多标准决策（MCDM），电能质量等。由于具有较高的学术水平和工程经验，他经常受邀担任期刊评审员、主席以及各种国内外会议的顾问。同时，他是英国工程委员会（ECUK）和马来西亚工程师局（BEM）注册特许工程师和专业工程师，他被选为中国电机工程学会会士（FCSEE, Chinese Society for Electrical Engineering），英国工程技术学会会士（FIET, The Institution of Engineering and Technology，其前身是The Institution of Electrical Engineers（IEE）），东盟工程院院士（FAAET），马来西亚工程师学会会员（FIEM, The Institution of Engineers, Malaysia），也是国际电气和电子工程师协会（IEEE）的高级会员（Senior Member）。作为2019年度第一批来桂杰出青年科学家，他一直致力于支持中国"一带一路"和RECP战略，致力于中国东盟能源中心的建立，代表广西大学参加各类东盟国际相关会议、联系东盟各个国家。

# Illumination

By Hui-Hwang GOH [Malaysia]

In this science lecture, you will learn about illumination. The lecture is generally divided into the following sections: a brief introduction to lighting, some essential definitions in lighting, different types of illumination and their characteristics, electrical lighting design and methods of illumination.

## ▌ I An Introduction to Lighting

Let's start with the light. Light is a kind of electromagnetic waves of various frequencies and lengths that penetrate space. Light varies in color with different light sources and materials it passes through, and the color of sunlight itself varies with atmospheric conditions and the time of day. The sunlight we see on the daily basis is produced by the excited transition of particles in the solar atmosphere. The essence of sunlight is that high-speed moving particles collide with particles and clouds above the Earth in the high sky, and most of them are reflected into space, while a small part of them enter the atmosphere and reach the Earth through refraction.

Light consists of red, orange, yellow, green, blue, and purple, with the ultraviolet wavelength of 100nm ~ 400nm<Visible light 380 ~ 770nm <Infrared 770nm (nano) ~1mm (mm). Infrared is an electromagnetic wave with a frequency between microwaves and visible light. It has a longer wavelength. Ultraviolet light can not cause people's visual response, it is a frequency higher than blue violet invisible light; Visible light is the very narrow band of light that people can sense. It has a very narrow range of wavelengths. X-rays and r rays are the common ultraviolet region, accounting for 7% of the total solar radiation energy. Purple, blue, cyan, green, yellow, orange and red light are common visible light regions, accounting for 50% of the total energy. The infrared region accounts for 43% of the total energy.

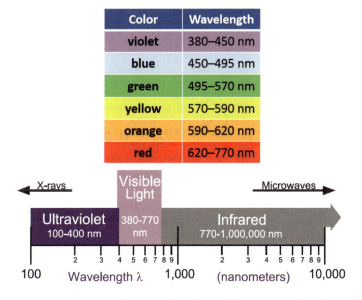

| Color | Wavelength |
|---|---|
| violet | 380–450 nm |
| blue | 450–495 nm |
| green | 495–570 nm |
| yellow | 570–590 nm |
| orange | 590–620 nm |
| red | 620–770 nm |

Figure 1. Different light color and its wavelength

The most popular types of luminescence include the incandescent lamp, electroluminescence, gas discharge, and light excitation. Solids and liquids emit visible radiation in the form of incandescent lamps when heated to around 1,000 degrees Celsius. Incandescent lamps produce light by utilizing the thermal effect of the filament's resistor current to raise the temperature of the filament to an incandescent level and cause it to emit light. Electroluminescence is the direct conversion of electrical energy into light energy. It is a physical phenomenon that produces light when an electric current is passed through certain solids, such as semiconductors or phosphor materials.For the gas discharge form, when the gas atoms are collided by electrons with a certain energy, they will be excited and ionized to emit light, and the spectrum is the same as that of the existing elements. Light excitation is a phenomenon in which an object is irradiated by an external light source to obtain energy and generate excitation leading to luminescence, that is, radiation of one wavelength is usually absorbed by a solid and then re-emitted at another wavelength.

With global lighting consumption estimated at 3,910 terawatt hours in 2015, accounting for 19% of the world's total electricity consumption. There are many different types of lighting categories, including public and commercial lighting, factory and mine (industrial) lighting, community household lighting, and outdoor lighting. Public and commercial lighting account for 41% of total global light generation, with outdoor lighting accounting for around 12%. As can be seen, lighting is an important part of our daily life, and we should be clearly aware of that.

## II Essential Definitions of Lighting

To better describe illumination, lumens are commonly used to show the total visible power emitted by a light source. Lumen is a unit of luminous flux, representing the amount of visible light emitted by a light source per unit time. "1 lumen" is the luminous flux emitted by a point source of 1 candela (cd) at a unit solid Angle (1 sphericity).

The brightness of light is a measure of the intensity and density of light in a given direction, and it describes the amount of light that passes through or emanates from a particular region and falls within a given solid Angle. It refers to the physical quantity of luminescence (reflection) on the surface of the luminescent body (reflector). Brightness is measured in candelas per square meter ($cd/m^2$), or candlelight fractions per square meter. Brightness is a subjective quantity, and the direction of the luminous surface is also related. The brightness values of the same luminous surface in different directions are different, and usually it is measured in the direction perpendicular to the line of sight. It is worth noting that there is an essential difference between luminance and lumen. Lumen is a unit that describes the luminous flux. Luminance refers to the luminous intensity of an object, and also refers to the ratio of the luminous body's luminous intensity to the area of the light source.

Illuminance refers to the flux of visible light received per unit area and is measured in Lux or lx. A quantity used to indicate the intensity of light and the extent to which an object's surface area is illuminated. In general, the luminous flux of 1 lux =1 lumen is evenly distributed over an area of 1 square meter.1 lumen = luminous flux emitted by point light source with luminous intensity of 1 candela in unit solid Angle; 1 lux = illuminance produced by a point source with luminous intensity of 1 candela on a sphere with radius of 1 m.

The uniformity of illuminance refers to how uniformly light is distributed across a certain area. Because of the uneven illumination, bright and dark regions are created, which can be distracting and upsetting for some people. Workers who work in a setting with insufficient illumination uniformity experience eyestrain and glare, which affects their visual operations and the performance of their visual tasks.

Glare is the feeling that a relatively bright object in the field of vision gives to the light user. It refers to the visual conditions that cause visual discomfort and reduce the visibility of objects due to inappropriate brightness distribution or extreme brightness contrast in space or time in the visual field. Glare is most likely to occur when a bright object is contrasted against a dark background.

The ability of a light source to represent the color of an item realistically is indicated by the color rendering of the light source. In the color rendering index scale, numbers ranging from 0 to 100 are given, with lower values indicating poor color rendering and higher values indicating acceptable color rendering. There are also more indexes: 1A (excellent), 1B (very good), 2 (moderate), 3 (poor), and 4 (low) (Little or almost none).

Color temperature is a measure of how much color a light contains, measured in Kelvin (K). Below 3300K, light sources are considered "warm" and above 5300K "cool". Under the irradiation of high color temperature light source, if the brightness is not high, it gives people a bleak atmosphere, while of low color temperature light source, too high brightness will give people a stuffy feeling. Light with low color temperature tends to be yellow, such as about 2800K for incandescent lamps, while light with high color temperature tends to be blue, such as over 9000K for purple lamps. It is generally believed that the color temperature of a standard white light is 6500K and the white light emitted by a CRT (Cathode Ray Tube) is about 5500K. The Kelvin color temperature unit is expressed by the absolute temperature K. When the temperature rises to a certain degree, the color starts to change from dark red, light red, orange, yellow, white and blue.

Table 1. Color Temperature Chart

## ▌ III Types and Characteristics of Lighting

HID lights include incandescent lamps, halogen tungsten lamps, fluorescent lamps, high-pressure sodium lamps and low-pressure sodium lamps, mercury vapour and metal halide lamps, mixed-light lamps, and LED lamps.

Figure 2. From left to right: Compact Fluorescent Lamps, High Pressure Sodium (HPS) Lamps, Low Pressure Sodium (LPS) Lamps, Metal Halide Lamps

The incandescent lamp is a form of thermal radiation light source. It heats the filament to the incandescent state through electrical heating and then emits visible light as a result of heat radiation. When it comes to color rendering index, incandescent lights can convert between 70% and 90% of their energy into heat. Their color temperature ranges from 2,500 to 2,700K, and they have a color rendering index of 1A. The advantages of incandescent lighting include superb color rendering, a continuous spectrum, usability, a long lifespan of 2000 hours and etc. Therefore, it is widely used.

The halogen tungsten lamp is an inflatable incandescent lamp filled with halogen elements or halides. Its principle is to inject halogen gas such as iodine or bromine into the bulb. At high temperature, sublimated tungsten wire and halogen react chemically, and the cooled tungsten will re-solidified on the tungsten wire, forming a balanced cycle to avoid premature rupture of tungsten wire. Halogen tungsten lamps have a color rendering index of 1A and a lifespan of approximately 4,000 hours.

Fluorescent lamps are gas discharge light sources, and the luminous principle of a fluorescent lamp is discussed in further detail. First, electrons emitted from an electrode at one end of the fluorescent lamp travel at high speed through the tube until they collide with an electron from a mercury atom. Second, as the mercury atom snaps back into position, the collision deflects the electrons of the mercury atom, resulting in the emission of UV radiation. Finally, the ultraviolet light reaches the phosphorescent crystal, where the pulse propagates to an active center in the crystal, where activity similar to that described in the preceding step occurs. This time, though, visible light was produced as a result.Compact fluorescent lamps are available in a variety of diameters and efficiencies. Compact fluorescent lamps operate at their most efficient levels between 20 and 30 degrees Celsius and are substantially smaller in size than other types of lighting. Fluorescent lamps are suitable for room lighting with natural lighting or lighting places requiring a comfortable environment. They should not be used in places with frequent switching and indoor or outdoor places where the ambient temperature is too high or too low.

The sodium lamp is an electric light source which produces visible light by vapor discharge. High voltage sodium lamp is a high intensity gas discharge bulb for outdoor and industrial applications. It is mainly composed of ballast, high voltage electronic starter, ceramic arc tube, xenon filling (sodium, mercury), etc., which emits a golden white light when used. It has the advantages of high luminous efficiency, less power consumption,  a service life of 24,000 hours at most, strong fog penetration ability and no insect trapping. However, it has poor color rendering. Low pressure sodium lamps, which have a maximum

Figure 3. High pressure sodium lamps are used in outdoor and industrial applications

Figure 4. Low pressure sodium lamps are restricted to outdoor use

efficiency of 100-200 lumens per watt, have the lowest light quality and appear in shades of black, white, or gray, so are restricted to outdoor applications. The low pressure sodium lamp has a color rendering index of 3, a yellow color temperature and a life of less than 16,000 hours.

The mercury vapor lamp is an electric light source which can obtain visible light by using mercury vapor generated during mercury discharge. It is composed of arc tube and quartz tube with mercury and argon, and the third electrode (light bulb coated with phosphor and glass tube). It has the characteristics of long service life and low initial cost, and its lifespan is 16000-24000 hours. Mercury vapor lamps, however, have an efficiency of only 30-65 lumens/w, a color rendering index of 3, and an intermediate color temperature. Compared with other types of lamps, self-ballast high-pressure mercury lamp eliminates the ballast and replaces it with self-ballast filament. Without any other accessories, it can be lit by simply screwing into the lamp holder, and has the advantages of high luminous efficiency.

Metal halide lamps work similarly to tungsten halide lamps, although they are available in a wider range of colors, sizes, and grades than tungsten halide lamps. In addition to a high luminous efficiency and good color rendering capabilities, metal halide lamps have a long-life expectancy of 6,000 to 20,000 hours. Apart from that, the efficiency of metal halide lamps can be up to 80 lumens per watt higher than that of other sources of illumination.

Mixed-light lamps are a "two-in-one" type of lighting, in which a single gas-filled bulb contains two light sources and is therefore suitable for fire-resistant areas. The mixed-light lamp has a high power factor up to 0.95, and its typical power rating is up to 160w. Its efficiency can be 20-30 lumens/watt, life does not exceed 8000 hours.

LEDs, the most recent generation of energy-saving lamps, generate visible light in a relatively narrow spectrum and so produce 'white light.' The energy consumption of a white LED light bulb is one-tenth that of an incandescent light bulb and one-quarter that of an energy-saving light bulb. It has the characteristics of significant energy saving. Furthermore, because of its long lifespan (up to 100,000 hours), it can be called "permanent" for regular home illumination. It has been used in a variety of applications, including traffic signal lights, display screens, and automotive signal lights, among others.

When comparing different types of lamps, it can be found that the color of incandescent lamp is close to the sun color, while the lighting effect of fluorescent lamp is poor. Halogen tungsten lamps and incandescent lamps have excellent color rendering index, high pressure sodium and low pressure sodium lamps have long life, but low pressure sodium lamps have poor color rendering index.

## ▮ IV Electrical Lighting Design

Lighting is designed with two goals: to provide the right amount of light and to provide the right quality of light.

Better lighting has been shown to increase productivity, therefore designers are faced with two major challenges: determining the appropriate lighting level and determining the quality of light (color rendering). The appropriate light levels can fluctuate significantly depending on the application conditions. The general light of rooms and and regions in which lighting is used infrequently and/or rarely, and simple visual tasks are conducted (minimum requirements for outdoor circulation areas, outdoor stores, corral the minimum illumination), general indoor lighting (minimum requirements for the minimum service with the task of illuminance), and strict requirements on the vision of additional local lighting (fine delicate work, small parts of instruments, tabulation, engraving, and so on) are common lighting design scenarios . The illumination levels (luxes) necessary for these three design situations range from 20 to 3,000 luxes depending on the situation.

A mirror is an optical element that uses the law of reflection to influence the area and distribution pattern of light rays. Mirrors can be divided into diffuse reflection and specular reflection. Diffuse reflection with paint or powder coated white surface, can reach 70%-80% reflectivity, but the reflectivity decreases with time. Specular reflection is polished or specular, of which the reflectance can achieve 85%-96% , and the reflectivity decreases with time.

Ballast and igniter are common components of lighting equipment. Ballast is a device that limits current and generates instant high voltage in fluorescent lamps. As a current limiting device, it contributes to the voltage accumulation of fluorescent lamp. Igniter is an important equipment in metal halogen lamp and sodium vapor lamp.

# ▌ V Methods of Illumination

There are various methods of illumination, three of which are mentioned in this article: watt density method, lumen or luminous flux method, and point-to-point method. Watts density method is a rough calculation of the installed power of lighting per square meter, usually for inspections only; Lumen method or luminous flux method is the most commonly used method in lighting scheme design. Point-to-point method applies to points that require one or more light sources,  and is commonly used in floodlighting calculations. Lumen method takes into account the value of variables such as the number of lamps, wattage per lamp, efficiency per lamp, utilization factor, depreciation factor and maintenance factor.

**About the author**

Hui-Hwang GOH received the B.Eng (Hons.) degree in Electrical Engineering, the M.Eng. degree in Electrical Engineering, and the Ph.D. degree from the UniversitiTeknologi Malaysia (UTM), Johor, Malaysia, in 1998, 2002, and 2007, respectively.

Dr. Goh is a fellow of the Institution

of Engineering and Technology (IET), U.K. He is also a fellow of the ASEAN Academy of Engineering and Technology (AAET) and the Chinese Society for Electrical Engineering (CSEE), a Chartered Engineer under the Engineering Council United Kingdom (ECUK), and a Professional Engineer under the Board of Engineers, Malaysia (BEM). His research interests include embedded power generation modeling and simulation, power quality studies, wavelet analysis, multi-criteria decision-making, renewable energies, and dynamic equivalent.

Currently, he is a professor, head of Electrical Engineering department, and Junwu Scholar at the School of Electrical Engineering, Guangxi University. As the first batch of outstanding young scientists to come to Guangxi in 2019, he has been committed to supporting China's Belt and Road Initiative and RECP strategy, and is committed to the establishment of the China-ASEAN Energy Center. Guangxi University participates in various ASEAN international conferences and contacts with ASEAN countries.

# 轻生活：生态村与适宜的技术

文 / 罗杰威 [意大利]

译 / 林汉英

　　生态村模式是一种非常有趣的生活方式，与我们每天在城市和城镇所经历的非常不同。生态村不遵循城市或乡村大多数社区的一般规则，并与它们有一些根本性的差异，呈现出人类与自然环境之间一种新的关系形式。生活在生态村的人们相信，他们追求的是"另外一种"生活方式，不是现代化，更不是消费主义，而是一种不同的存在过程。这并不意味着要回到过去几代人那种不舒适的生活，生态村可以非常舒适，重点在于生活方式的不同，人与人、人与自然间关系的不同。

## 生态村的定义

　　一个简单的定义：生态村是一种特意创建的社区，人们自由联系，不受约束，目标是创造一个自给自足、对生态影响小、以可持续发展为基础的居住地。罗伯特·吉尔曼[①]和黛安·吉尔曼于1991年提出生态村的构想，主要基于四点：人口规模，功能全面的居住地，人类的活动无害地融入自然界中，以及能够支持人类健康成长、成功地延续到无限期的未来。

"人口规模"指的是生态村的大小需要被限制在一定的范围内，以使得每个居民都能够认识社区中的其他人，也被其他人所认识。小规模还能够使社区里每个成员觉得他/她是有能力影响整个社区的决策的。这样的一个社区的人数上限是500人。而在非常稳定的、孤立的环境中，这个数字可能达到1000人。在典型的工业化社会中，一个生态村包含的人数通常会较少，甚至少于100人。

"功能全面的居住地"指的是生态村具备所有生活必需的功能，并且各项功能间是均衡的。这些功能包括居住、食物的供给、制造业、休闲、社交生活、商业等。

"人类的活动无害地融入自然界中"指的是坚持人与其他生命平等的理念，人类不是试图主宰自然，而是在自然中找到自己的位置。另一个重要原则是物质的循环利用，而非工业社会典型的线性利用。这就要求生态村使用可再生能源而不是化石燃料；把有机废物做成堆肥返回土壤而不是将它们填埋进垃圾场，放入焚烧炉或排到下水道里；尽可能地回收废弃物，并且避免使用有毒有害物质。

---

① 罗伯特·吉尔曼：《生态村挑战》："发展一个和谐的社区——与自身和自然和谐共存——是一项艰巨的挑战，但却是可以实现的。"《语境》杂志，1991年夏季版，第10页。

"能够支持人类健康成长"这个原则确立了生态村在根本上是一个人类社区，如果不以真正意义的人类健康为核心，那么这些社区不可能成功。什么是"健康的人类成长"呢？简而言之这是一种身体、情感、精神和灵性等所有人类生活方面平衡且整体的成长。这种健康成长不仅仅通过单独的个体来表现，更应该通过社区的整体表现出来。

"能够成功地延续到无限期的未来"，最后这个原则，即可持续性的原则，需要生态村村民们长期坚持，包含了对有关公平和非剥削的深刻承诺——对当今世界的其他地方、人类和非人类以及所有未来的生命的承诺。①

生态村是一个系统。每个生态村的关键都是"可持续社区"的理念，是一群人组织起来创建一个人类可以成功地发展直到无限未来的生命系统。②

依据全球生态村网络（GEN）③，生态村是一个城市或农村社区，人们致力于建设一个在资源使用方面对地球影响较小的支持性的社会环境。为了实现这一目标，生态村整合了不同的生态生活方式和流程，如下：永续种植、生态建筑、可持续生产、可替代能源、闭环概念、废料管理、社区建设实践。

生态村这个概念不仅与节约能源和使用可再生资源有关，也与

---

① 罗伯特·吉尔曼：《生态村挑战》："发展一个和谐的社区——与自身和自然和谐共存——是一项艰巨的挑战，但却是可以实现的。"《语境》杂志，1991年夏季版，第10页。
② 出处同上。
③ Global Ecovillage Network（GEN）全球生态村网络。网站https://ecovillage.org

社会可持续发展有关。

## ▋ 生态村的关键因素

现在重要的是讨论生态村的关键因素有哪些。生态村是非常现实的东西。在乔纳森·道森的一篇报道中，生态村按照一个可持续发展的社区来设计，这样一个全面运转的社会由以下几部分组成。[①]

道森在他的书中将生态村的一些最重要的元素总结如下：[②]

1. 社区成员自力更生；

2. 精神性；

3. 社群主义；

4. 共居；[③]

5. 小型平等主义社区，遵循生态原则、性别和种族之间的平等权利；

6. 中间技术的使用；[④]

7. 开创了强烈反对消费主义的教育运动；

① 乔纳森·道森：《生态村庄：可持续发展的新前沿》，绿皮书出版社2006年版，第14页。
② 这些观点是乔纳森·道森在《生态村庄：可持续发展的新前沿》中讨论的一些概念的综合，第14—18页。
③ 最初在丹麦创建，之后在国际上传播，可以定义为一种低能耗的人类社区，房屋围绕一个公共点建造。
④ 在我们的讨论中，我们称这个问题为多尺度方法和适当技术。

8. 生态可持续性；

9. 社区生活、决策和治理只能基于自下而上的方法。对于生态村来说，还有一些来源于其他出处的要素也非常重要；

10. 永续栽培<sup>①</sup>设计；

11. 由当地天然材料建造的建筑；

12. 依靠自己的（离网）电力供应；

13. 利用可再生能源/替代技术；

14. 利用可持续农业实现粮食供应自给自足；

15. 服务于有需要的特定人群；

16. 家庭手工业；

17. 参与公共决策；

18. 解决冲突的既定程序；

19. 建立与生态村社区联系的流程和沟通技巧。

在生态村中，本地化的理念非常重要。这个想法可以应用于任何形式的生产，无论工业还是农业。它可能涉及当地资源的管理、回收，甚至是当地范围内的决策。

---

① 简而言之，它可以被定义为"对人类有用的多年生或自我延续的植物和动物物种的整合、进化系统"（比尔·莫里森、大卫·霍姆格伦，D. *Permaculture One*, Tagari Publications, 1978年），它由单词"永久农业"组成。其他出版物有：大卫·霍姆格伦，《永续栽培:超越可持续性的原则和途径》，Holmgren Design Services, 2002年；彼得·贝恩和大卫·霍姆格伦，《永久耕作手册：城镇和乡村花园耕作》，新社会出版社，2012年。

生态学界有一句名言，后来成为生态学领域最有意义的思想之一：全球化思考，本地化行动。

这是生态学的核心哲学之一。它也成为生态村理念中的一个关键思想。这句话出自帕特里克·格迪斯（Patrick Geddes），他是生物学家，同时也是地理学家和社会学家，还是早期绿色城市规划的重要人物。这个重要概念的含义是什么呢？要理解和解决局部问题，就必须了解全球范围内的动态。最后，解决方案虽然是局部的，但一定要与更大的世界联系起来。

"全球化思考，本地化行动"可以有多种解释，但我们至少需要考虑三个主要视角。首先必须考虑到的是生态学的逻辑。其次是决策问题。最后一点尤为重要，可以定义为多尺度方法（MSA）。

## ▍理念、决策与方法

第一点强调生态理念。"生态村"这个词包含"生态"，这是非常重要的。生态村拒绝任何形式的大型定居点（城市、特大城市和类似的）。生态村的基础是生态和可持续性，尤其是生态保护意识，因而主张以限定人数的小型社区形式存在。根据经验，生态村从来不会是大规模的。有的社区只有两个人，有的社区有50到150人。500人似乎是一个真正可持续发展的社区的最大规模。[①]有可能找到更大的，多达1000人甚至2000人的社区，但随后可能会出现

---

① 乔纳森·道森：《生态村庄：可持续发展的新前沿》，绿皮书出版社2006年版，第15页。

其他问题，特别是与自然资源的使用有关的问题。我们必须记住，生态村的关键之一是要形成与自然资源保持平衡、废物得到回收利用，以及所有生活环节形成闭环的可持续发展的社区。

这意味着生态村总体上是非常小的。这没有什么不好。一位著名的经济学家曾断言：小就是美。[①]小的即为精致的，不消耗太多能量的。它就像一个小男孩或一个小女孩，恰恰因为小，才会美。

关于第二点，即决策，生态村社区做决策前的讨论过程非常有趣。在生态村中，决策大多是地方性的，但尊重东道国的规定。事实上，一些规定比国家的法律要严格得多。它必须至少尊重三个实体：国家、当地社区，最重要的是自然。在许多生态村的案例中，做决定之前整个社区可以各抒己见直至达成一个大家都满意的且独到的解决方案。社区的每一个成员都有表达自己意愿的自由。这些各自的立场不会造成混乱，相反会促成社会的充分和谐，因为每个人的意见都必须被倾听。

在生态村，做决策的策略是随着经验逐渐积累出来的。社区合作行动，不同的部分和专业知识技能得以统筹协调，最终形成决定。这种方法的优点之一是决策和行动直接来自现场经验。另一个积极的方面是，在生态村中最终的决策将直接惠及当地社区，这个结果源自成员之间直接和更好的交流，造就了负责人讲道德的行为。这种情况之所以发生是因为每个人都参与了这个过程，个

---

① 恩斯特·弗里德里希·舒马赫，《小即是美：一项经济学研究，仿佛人是重要的》，哈珀·柯林斯出版集团，2010年。

人的建议被倾听，并可能会影响其他人的生活，从而产生了更多负责任的行为。其缺点也是众所周知的：该方法需要大量的时间来推进。

我们要提及的第三点与一个非常复杂的问题有关：多尺度方法（MSA）。现在，集中管理和私有化往往代表进步，每件事都有版权，包括那些应该属于公共领域的东西，而我们主张知识的自由共享。这种趋势的主要逻辑是，如果我分享我的知识，你会变得富有，而我不会变得贫穷。知识的传播无异于"思想的碰撞"，艺术家们就是遵循这一概念进行创作的。正是由于分享知识的理念，他们才得以使不同文化和谐统一，创造出美。历史上，共享知识是人类文明的根本基础之一。历史是由信息（和基因）的扩散交织传播而形成的。如果一个人或一个团体拥有一个想法或专利的所有权，最后这个部分也许就不可能发展了，因为它的扩散（和进化）受到严格的限制。

有一种与之相反的哲学，那就是开源伦理。

开源是一个术语，最初指的是开源软件（OSS）。开源软件是源代码被设计为公开访问的代码——任何人都可以看到、修改并以他们认为合适的方式发布。开源软件是以一种分散和协作的方式开发的，依赖于同行评审和社群生产。开源软件通常比专有软件更便宜、更灵活、寿命更长，因为它是由群体而非单个作者或公司开发的。开源已经超越软件生产本身，成为一种风气和工作方式。开源运动利用开源软件的价值和去中心化生产模式来寻找解决社区和行业问题的新方法。[①]

在开源软件运动的案例中，一切都是免费的，没有自上而下的决策，没有管制，没有商业意图，没有任何形式的控制。这在生态村战略中是非常重要的。它必须是全球性的、非营利性的、绝对自由的、反对任何形式的控制或强制。这是开源知识的本质，在直接应用于制造领域时需结合适宜的技术。

开源意味着对世界的慷慨。一个人把知道的东西在互联网上分享，不指望任何回报。让我们甘愿贡献自己的技能、知识和时间给需要的人，仅有的理由是为了帮助他人、相互支持以及期待好的结果。我们不知道他们是谁，也不知道他们为什么需要这些信息，但我们会给予，仅仅是因为人之本性。

有一个术语很好地总结了这个概念，它是上述全部讨论的关键："ubuntu"（乌班图）。这是来自科萨/祖鲁文化的语言。它由词根"–ntu"组成，意思是人类，是最高意义上的人类。科萨语、祖鲁语或恩德贝莱语的完整短语是：Umuntu ngumuntu ngabantu.[②]其深层含义是：我存在，因为你存在。[③]或者说，我们之所以为

---

① 来源：Red Hat网站，《什么是开源？》一文的"概述"，访问2022-01-17。网址https://www.redhat.com/en/topics/open-source/what-is-open-source.

② 引用自克莱尔·E.奥本海姆，《纳尔逊·曼德拉和Ubuntu的力量》，《宗教》2012年第3期，第369—388页。网址：doi: 10.3390 / rel3020369.

③ 我们感谢我们的一位学生，他在2007年向我们解释了这个话题。我们故意没有提到他的名字，因为ubuntu的概念是众所周知的，我们把自己的生命奉献给别人，而不考虑自己。他从别人那里学到这个概念，并贡献给我们。这是开源。

人，是因为他人的存在。①

与所有其他立场相比，开源哲学有一个很大的优势：不存任何个人专有的知识，只有共享知识。大家有义务分享自己获得的东西。没有任何发现属于个人。每一种形式的知识都是基于他人的知识，而单个人的贡献存在于一个更大的知识系统中。科学亦是如此。每一个发现都是基于所谓的研究背景，这些不是一个人的成果，而是整个群体的工作成果。个人工作中的每一项小小的创新之所以成为可能，都要感谢他或她从社群里获得的教育。

## ▍适宜的技术——开源网站 Appropedia.org

在这方面，一个非常重要的话题是适当和可持续的技术。关于使用适宜技术建设生态村的讨论涉及一个颇为困难的话题，即管理上的成本效益和适度投资。换句话说如何使用好资源在不浪费金钱和材料的前提下实现某个目标。在生态村领域有一个非常著名的开源网站，致力于解决建筑和日常生活中的技术问题。下面我们来聊聊"Appropedia"。

Appropedia.org类似维基百科，致力于适宜技术的分享。我们认为近年来多尺度方法（MSA）的主要贡献之一就是开放源码知识（OSK），即共享信息。这个网站帮助人们找到适合当地经济和条件的解决方案。每个人都可以使用非常简单的命令编辑和修改该网

---

① 引用自克莱尔·E.奥本海姆，《纳尔逊·曼德拉和Ubuntu的力量》，《宗教》2012年第3期，第369—388页。网址doi: 10.3390 / rel3020369.

站的信息。Appropedia的宗旨在网站本身就有明确的声明：致力于通过使用合理原则和适宜技术、原始研究和项目信息来开发并分享在可持续发展、减少贫困和国际发展方面的协作解决方案。①

这个网站的理念在于分享信息，主要针对发展中地区和扶贫。基于这个原因，其提供的大多数解决方案都是极其简单、能够自建以及低成本的。在这方面，这个项目的理念与生态村的非常相似，低成本和低技术。实际上，Appropedia是更大的项目，它帮助人们过上有尊严的生活。

这个网站有趣的地方（也是我们非常欣赏的地方）是，他们不仅发布有效的解决方案，也发布失败案例。在大多数情况下，网站发表的文章涉及解决扶贫可持续性、低规模方法、参与性方法等实际问题的技术、应用和解决办法。与中高技术相反，这里没有大企业参与。因为解决方案大多涉及低技术，它们非常简单，实施效果也比较普通。这似乎是一个弱点，但在生态村的逻辑中，这反而是很大的优势，正因为如此建设变得容易且低成本。

Appropedia以及所有的维基项目都在不断的发展中。它在开源软件中被称为"滚动发布"，即没有新旧版本的更替，但社区每天都会执行更新。

总而言之，通常复制（抄袭）是非常糟糕的，往往被教授和科学家批评。倒序制造（通过拆解分析某产品获取其制造原理，进而

---

① 来源：Appropedia.org。访问2022-01-22。https://www.appropedia.org/Appropedia: About # What_Appropedia_is

仿制）也是一种犯罪行为。但在某些情况下，复制（仿制）是好的，而Appropedia的理念正是如此。Appropedia打算公开一些开源知识，并推动人们复制。这是开源的固有逻辑。但这里还有一个更重要的经验：复制对方法和工具的改进很有用。每一次复制都不是被动的行为。复制意味着获得一些知识，并最终根据我们的需要而改变。复制也意味着改变一些想法使之顺应我们自己的需求，最终的产品和原来的已经不一样了。复制意味着寻求实施方案。各种想法，无论是正确的还是错误的，都会被大家公开讨论，再由社区复制、评估，最后加以改进。

## 作者简介

罗杰威，建筑师、博士、教授，毕业于米兰理工大学。自2021年任浙江大学建筑工程学院特聘教授、博士生导师，天津大学建筑学院客座教授；2004—2021年，任天津大学建筑学院全职教授、国际交流办公室副主任、仿生建筑与规划研究中心创始人和主任，研究团队由来自世界超过34个不同国家的学生组成。目前，已出版10本专著、13本合作书籍和1部小说，发表400多篇文章；已在中国和国外辅导60多篇硕博士论文。在中国高校和世界各国院系间建立20多份合作协议；天津大学建筑学院和萨里大学建筑系硕士双学位、天津大学建筑学院和米兰理工大学硕士及博士双学位三个双学位项目的起草者和负责人；担任教育部中阿旱区特色资源与环境治理国际合作联合实验室咨询专家、QS世界大学排名亚欧排名审校专家、SCI和SSCI期刊审稿专家。

主要研究方向涉及建筑设计、建筑规划中的仿生方法、城市规划、传统建筑和村庄的修复、现代建筑史、传统建筑之形而上学、可持续建筑、生态村、人工智能在建筑中的应用等。自2005年以来，完成两项国家自然科学基金项目"中外生态村的比较研究与实践"与"中国生态村落中零排放建筑的MSA方法研究——关于适用指南的综合策略"，和一项天津市社会科学基金项目"中国新型绿色居住区新标准研究"。积极参与中国贫困村的扶贫规划、中国"厕所革命"规划。2017—2018年，参与贵州省台江县、河北省石家庄市和黑龙江省林甸县的贫困村扶贫发展项目。

作为意大利注册建筑师，他一直在中国和国际公司担任首席建筑师和顾问建筑师，从事各种项目的建筑和城市设计工作。2004年，在中国负责意大利环境和领土保护部、米兰理工大学和清华大学合作的"中意环保节能建筑–SIEEB"项目的技术和实施。2005—2006年，作为天津大学建筑学院、天津市和米兰理工大学合作项目的负责人，负责静园（末代皇帝溥仪天津故居）的修复技术、调研和教学计划。2010年，获得天津市政府颁发的"海河友谊奖"，以表彰其对中国的文化贡献。他还是意大利阿斯彭研究所成员。

他在中国和其他国家多次组织关于物质和非物质遗产调查以及自建建筑的研讨会。

他是一名专业摄影师。他是自由软件GNU/Linux的倡导者。

# The Lightness of Living: Eco-Villages and Appropriate Technologies

By Paolo Vincenzo Genovese (Italy)

A very interesting form of living, very different from what we experience every day in our cities and town, is the Eco-Village model. Eco-Villages does not follow the common rules of most of settlements, urban or rural. They have some radical differences which propose a new form of relationship between people and natural environment. People who live in an Eco-Village are convinced in pursuing an "alternative" way of living compared to modernity and especially consumerism. It is a different *process of existence*. This does not mean to come back to the uncomfortable life of the past generations. An Eco-Village could be extremely comfortable. The key point is being *different in the living approach*, in the relationship between people and people and people and nature.

## ▊ Definition of an Eco-Village

A simple definition: an Eco-Village is an intentional community of people in free association, without constriction, with the goal to create a settlement based on self-sufficiency, limited ecological impact, and on sustainability largely intended. Robert and Diane Gilman, in 1991, proposed the idea of Eco-Village based on four points: human-scale, full-featured settlement in which human activities are harmlessly integrated into the natural world in a way that is supportive of healthy human development and can be successfully continued into the indefinite future.[①] And this means:

**"A human-scale…"** * Human-scale refers to a size in which people are able to know and be known by the others in the community, and where each member of the community feels he or she is able to influence the community's direction. […]. The upper limit for such a group is roughly 500 people. In very stable and isolated situations it can be higher, perhaps as high as 1,000, while in situations typical of modern industrial societies it is often lower, even less than 100.

**"…full-featured settlement…"** * A "full-featured settlement" is one in which all the major functions of normal living — residence, food provision, manufacture, leisure, social life, and commerce — are plainly present and in balanced proportions.

[…]

**"… in which human activities are harmlessly integrated into the natural world…"** * […]. [There] is the ideal of equality between humans and other forms of life, so that humans do not attempt to dominate over

---

① Robert Gilman, *The Eco-village Challenge. The challenge of developing a community living in balanced harmony - with itself as well as nature - is tough, but attainable,* In Context magazine, Summer 1991, p. 10. In:
https://web.archive.org/web/20041213201638/http://www.context.org/ICLIB/IC29/Gilman1.htm

nature but rather find their place within it. Another important principle is the cyclic use of material resources, rather than the linear approach [...] that has characterized industrial society. This leads eco-villages to the use of renewable energy sources [...] rather than fossil fuels; to the composting of organic wastes which are then returned to the land rather than sending these to a landfill, incinerator, or sewage treatment plant; to the recycling of as much of the waste stream as possible; and to the avoidance of toxic and harmful substances.

**"... in a way that is supportive of healthy human development..."** * This fourth principle recognizes that eco-villages are, after all, human communities, and without genuine human health at the core, these communities are unlikely to be successful. What is "healthy human development"? [...] Suffice it to say here that I see this as involving a balanced and integrated development of all aspects of human life — physical, emotional, mental, and spiritual. This healthy development needs to be expressed not just in the lives of individuals, but in the life of the community as a whole.

**"... and that can be successfully continued into the indefinite future."** * This last principle - the sustainability principle - forces a kind of honesty on eco-villagers. [...] The sustainability principle brings with it a profound commitment to fairness and non-exploitation — toward other parts of today's world, human and non-human, and toward all future life.[1]

An Eco-Village is a system. The key issue of every Eco-Village

---

① *Ibid.*

外国专家科学讲堂
Foreign Expert Science Classes

is the idea of "sustainable community", a group of people organized to create a system of life where the human development can be successfully continued into the indefinite future.[1]

According with Global Ecovillage Network (GEN)[2], Eco-Villages is an urban or rural community of people who strive to integrate a supportive social environment with a low-impact on Planet Earth in terms of use of resources. In order to achieve this goal, the Eco-Village integrates different methods and processes of ecological life such as:perma-culture, ecological building, sustainable production, alternative energy, close-cycle concept, waste management, community building practices.

This concept is not only in terms of energy saving and use of renewable resources, but also in terms of social sustainability.

## Key Factors of an Eco-Village

It is important now to discuss about what are the key factors of an Eco-Village. An Eco-Village is something extremely realistic. According to a report by Jonathan Dawson an Eco-Village is designed to be a sustainable community, so that a fully-functioning society could be mostly comprised of such units.[3]

Dawson in his book summarizes some of the most important

---

①    *Ibid*.
②    Global Ecovillage Network, GEN. In:https://ecovillage.org
③    Jonathan Dawson, *Ecovillages. New Frontiers for Sustainability*, Green Books, 2006, p. 14.

elements of the Eco-Villages in the following points[①]:

1. self-reliance among members of the community;

2. spirituality;

3. intentional communalism;

4. cohousing[②];

5. small-scale and egalitarian communities which follow the ecological principles, equal rights between genders and races;

6. the use of intermediate technologies[③];

7. creation of alternative educational movement which provides a strong opposition to the consumerism;

8. ecological sustainability;

9. the process of decision making, governance and community life can only be based on a bottom-up approach.

There are also other points which are very important for an Eco-Village which came from other sources:

---

① These points is the synthesis of some concept discussed in Jonathan Dawson, *Ecovillages. New Frontiers for Sustainability*, op. cit., pp. 14-18.

② Initially created in Denmark and after internationally spreading, which can be defined as a human-scale settlements with the intention to have a lower energy footprint on the Earth, and technically based on a cluster of houses around a common point.

③ In our discussion we call this issue Multi-Scale Approach and Appropriate Technologies.

10. Permaculture[①] design;

11. Buildings constructed from local, natural materials;

12. Reliance on own (off-grid) power supply;

13. Utilisation of renewable energy/alternative technology;

14. Self-sufficiency of food supply using sustainable agriculture;

15. Being of service to specific populations in need;

16. On-site cottage industries;

17. Participatory communal decision-making;

18. Established processes for conflict resolution;

19. Established process and communication skills for bonding and connecting the Eco-Village community.

In the Eco-Villages is very important the idea of *being local*. This idea can be applied for every form of production, industrial or agricultural. It could touch the management of the local resources, recycling, and even the decision making at local scale.

There is a famous sentence in the world of Ecology which became one of the most meaningful ideas in this field:Think globally, act locally.

It is one of the core philosophies in Ecology. It becomes a key idea

---

[①]    In short it can be defined as «integrated, evolving system of perennial or self-perpetuating plant and animal species useful to man» (Bill Mollison, David Holmgren, D. *Permaculture One*, Tagari Publications, 1978) and it is composed by the words permanent agriculture. Other publications are: David Holmgren, *Permaculture: Principles and Pathways beyond Sustainability*, Holmgren Design Services, 2002; Peter Bane and David Holmgren, *The Permaculture Handbook: Garden Farming for Town and Country*, New Society Publishers, 2012.

also in the Eco-Village philosophy. This sentence is attributed to Patrick Geddes, who was at the same time a biologist, a geographer, a sociologist and an important personality in the early urban planning of the green cities. What is the meaning of this important concept? It asserts that every form of correct governance and action has to touch simultaneously different scales, different levels, in a complex synthesis. To create an efficient plan and action, it is necessary to understand the problems at the global scale. To understand and solve the local problems, it is necessary to know the dynamic at global scale. Finally, the solution have to be local but linked with a bigger world.

Think globally, act locally could have many interpretations, but we need to consider at least three main perspective. The first one concerns the necessity to include the logic of Ecologist movement. The second is related on decision making in the Eco-Village communities. And the third have a special importance and it could be defined as Multi-Scale Approach (MSA).

## Idea, Decision Making and Approach

The first point is related to the idea of Ecology in the Eco-Village. It is so important that the very word "Eco-Village" include "Ecology". The living process in Eco-Village does not concern a *perfect system of life*. The Eco-Village denies with any form of large settlements (cities, megalopolis and similar). Eco-Villages propose small communities with limited numbers of individuals, based on ecology and sustainability, especially an *ecology of the mind*. According to experiences, Eco-Villages are never large. There are communities with only two people, others count 50 or 150 people. The number of 500 individuals seem to be the maximum limit to have a real sustainable community[①]. It is possible to find bigger communities up to 1.000 or even 2.000 people, but then other problems may come out especially related to the use of natural resources. We have to remember that one of the key points of the Eco-Village is to be a sustainable community, being in balance with the natural resources, recycling of the waste and close-cycle of all the processes of the community's life.

This means that the Eco-Village are in general very small. And this is not a negative point. A famous economist once assert: small is beautiful.[②] What is small is delicate and it does not consume too much energy. It is like a little boy or a little girl. They are beautiful exactly because they are small.

Concerning the second point, the decision making, the Eco-Village community adopt a very interesting process of discussion. In thc Eco-Village the decision making is mostly local, but respecting the regulation of the host country. In fact, the regulations are *more strict* than the law of the country. It has to respect at least three entity: the Country, the local community and, above all, the Nature. In many cases of Eco-Village the decision is taken once the whole community agree in totally freedom to a common and unique resolution which satisfied everyone. Every member of the community has freedom in the expression of their will. This

---

① Jonathan Dawson, *Ecovillages. New Frontiers for Sustainability*, Green Books, 2006, p. 15.
② Ernst Friedrich Schumacher, *Small Is Beautiful: A Study of Economics As If People Mattered*, Harper Perennial, 2010.

position does not create disorder, but on the contrary the full harmony in the community because everyone have to be listened in their opinion.

In the Eco-Village the strategy of decision making came by the experience. The community use a collaborative process of actions where all the different parts and expertise are coordinated together, and finally summarized into a decision. One of the advantages of this method is that the decision and actions came directly from the on-field experience. Another positive point is that in the Eco-Villages the final strategies will directly touch and benefit the local community. This is generated by a direct and better communication between the members of the system, creating a moral and ethical behavior. This happens because everyone is involved in the process, generating more responsible actions because the contribution of the single individual is listened and it may affects the lives of others. The weaknesses are also well known: this method need a lot of time to be processed.

The third point we need touch is related on a very complex issue: Multi-Scale Approach (MSA). Nowadays, there is a progressive trend toward the centralization, privatization, to copyright everything, including things that should be in public domain. On the contrary we propose the free sharing of knowledge. The main logic of this trend is that if I share my knowledge you become rich and I do not become poor. The spreading of the knowledge is the "contamination of the idea". Artists work on this concept. They unify cultures and create beauty thanks to the logic of sharing knowledge. The privatization is a way to avoid progress because the secret, the copyright, make all rigid and without the process of diffusion of the idea which was for thousand year the essence of the human progress. And in fact Nature work exactly in the direction of contamination. In the history, the logic of sharing knowledge was one of the fundamental basis of the civilization. The history is made by contamination of information (and gene). If a single person or group has the ownership of an idea or of a patent, finally this element has no possible evolution because it is strictly limited in its diffusion (and evolution).

There is the opposite philosophy which is the Open Source ethic.

Open source is a term that originally referred to open source software (OSS). Open source software is code that is designed to be publicly accessible—anyone can see, modify, and distribute the code as they see fit.

Open source software is developed in a decentralized and collaborative way, relying on peer review and community production. Open source software is often cheaper, more flexible, and has more longevity than its proprietary peers because it is developed by communities rather than a single author or company. Open source has become a movement and a way of working that reaches beyond software production. The open source movement uses the values and decentralized production model of open source software to find new ways to solve problems in their communities and industries.[①]

In the case of Open Source Software movement, everything is free, there is no control, no Top-Down decision making, there is no regulation,

① Source: Red Hat. (Obviously no author), *What is open source?*, *Overview*, access 2022-01-17. In: https://www.redhat.com/en/topics/open-source/what-is-open-source

no business intentions, no any form of control. And this is extremely important in Eco-Village strategy. It has to be global, non-profit, based on absolute freedom, against every form of control or imposition. This is the essence of Open Source Knowledge and the direct application in the field of construction concerns appropriate technologies.

Open Source means generosity to the world. What a single person knows is shared over internet without any expectation to be rewarded. The good results, the intention to help people who need, and the mutual support, they are only reasons to donate our own skill, knowledge and time to people who need. We do not know who they are and why they need information, but we give simply for a sense of humanity.

There is a terms that summarize very well this concept which is a keyword in all this discussion: "ubuntu". This is a word which came from the Xhosa/Zulu culture language. It is composed by the root "-ntu" which means "human", in the sense of "Humanity" in its highest sense. The complete phrase in Nguni language of Xhosa, Zulu, or Ndebele is:Umuntu ngumuntu ngabantu.[1]The deep meaning is:

I am because you are.[2]

Or  A person is a person through other persons.[3]

The Open Source philosophy has a great advantage compared with

① Quoted in Claire E. Oppenheim, *Nelson Mandela and the Power of Ubuntu*, Religions 2012, n. 3, pp. 369–388; doi:10.3390/rel3020369

② We thanks one of our students who, back in 2007, explain this topic to us. We intentionally do not mention his name because the idea of ubuntu is exactly the common knowledge, the donation of our own life to others without any regards to our self. He learned this concept from others and donate to us. This is Open Source.

③ Quoted in Claire E. Oppenheim, *Nelson Mandela and the Power of Ubuntu,* Religions 2012, n. 3, pp. 369–388; doi:10.3390/rel3020369 all other positions: it does not exists any *personal knowledge*, but only *sharing knowledge*. It is the obligation of person who knows to share what he acquire. There are no any personal discover. Every form of knowledge is based on other person's knowledge and the contribution of a single individual is inside a much larger intellectual system. Even science works in this way. Every discover is based on what is called research background, which is not the work of the single but the work of the whole community. Every minimum of innovation in the work of the single individual is possible only thanks to the education that he or she get from the community. In fact, every discovery is not a product of a person, but it is simply what the nature possess and we human being can only find what already exist. Find a rule in physics does not mean invent it; it only means to have a better intellect to recognize what is already there.

## ▌ Appropriate Technology, Appropedia.org

A very important topic in this regards is Appropriate and Sustainable Technology. The discussion about Appropriate Technology for the architecture in the Eco-Village touches a very difficult topic which is called cost-effectiveness in the management and the appropriate investments. This difficult terms simply means how a certain goal can be achieved using the right resources without waste of money and materials. In the area of Eco-Village there is a very famous Open Source website dedicated on solving technical problem in architecture and daily life. We are talking about *Appropedia*.

Appropedia.org is a sort of Wiki-like project dedicated to

appropriate technologies. We consider one of the major contribution in the recent years in the logic of Multi-Scale Approach (MSA), Open Source Knowledge (OSK), sharing information. This source helps people who need to find suitable solutions according with local economy and conditions. Everyone can edit and modify the information in this website using very simple commands. The intention of *Appropedia* is clearly declared in the website itself:

Appropedia is the site to develop and share collaborative solutions in sustainability, poverty reduction and international development through the use of sound principles and appropriate technology, original research and project information.[1]

The logic of this website is to share information primarily directed to developing areas and poverty alleviation. For this reason, most of the solutions proposed are extremely simple, self-buildable, low cost. In this regards, the logic of this project is very similar to Eco-Village philosophy, low-cost and low-tech. Actually, Appropedia is much bigger project related to help people to have a dignified life.

What is interesting in this website (and we admire very much) is that they publish not only solutions which work well, but also failure. In most of the cases, the articles published concern technologies, applications and solutions to solve practical problem in poverty alleviation, sustainability, Low-Scale Approach, participatory approach and similar. On the contrary of the Middle- and High-Tech, here there are no big corporations involved. Because the solutions mostly concern Low-Tech, they are very

---

[1]　Source: Appropedia.org. *Appropedia: About*, access 2022-01-22. In: https://www.appropedia.org/Appropedia:About#What_Appropedia_is

simple and the performance quite humble. This seems a weakness, but in the logic of Eco-Villages they are big advantages because it is easy to build and very low-cost.

*Appropedia* as well as all the Wiki project is constantly under development. It is what in Open Source Software is called "rolling release", which means there are no major update, but it is a project implemented every day by the community.

To conclude. Usually to copy is a very bad process. It is criticised by professors and scientists. Reverse engineering is also a criminal act in our perspective. But there are cases where copy is good and the logic of *Appropedia* is exactly this. *Appropedia* intend to propose some Open Source Knowledge and push people to copy. This is inherent the logic of Open Source. But there is a higher lesson here: copy is useful to implement. Every copy is not a passive act. Copying means also acquire some knowledge and eventually change according with our necessities. Copying means to change some notion according with our own necessity and the final product is not the same as the original one. To copy means to ask for implementation. Some notions, correct or wrong, are put into the public debate and the community itself copy, review, and finally improve.

## About the Author

Paolo Vincenzo Genovese is an architect, Ph.D. and professor. He is graduated at Politecnico di Milano. Since 2021 he has been Distinguished Professor and Ph.D. tutor in the College of Civil Engineering and Architecture at Zhejiang University; he is also Visiting Professor in School of Architecture in Tianjin University. From 2004 to 2021 he was full

professor at the School of Architecture of Tianjin University in China, where he was also Deputy Director of the International Exchange Office. He is the founder and director of the Lab of Bionic Architecture & Planning Research Center. He has published ten monographs, thirteen collaborative books, over four hundred articles and a novel. He has tutored over 60 PhD and Master's theses in China and abroad. His team is composed by students from over 34 different countries. He created more than twenty collaboration agreements between Chinese institutes and other faculties in different countries around the world. He was the author and responsible for three double degree agreements: Master between the Faculty of Architecture of Tianjin University and the Department of Architecture of the University of Sassari, Master and Ph.D. with Politecnico di Milano. He is advisory consultant of

China-Arab International Joint Laboratory on Featured Resources and Environmental Governance in Arid Regions, QS world university rankings Asia-Europe rankings, SCI and SSCI journals review experts.

His study, research and expertise concern design of architecture, bionic approach in the architecture planning, urban planning, restoration of traditional building and villages, history of modern architecture, metaphysics of ancient architecture, sustainable architecture, eco-villages, artificial intelligence applied in architecture. Since 2005, he has directed, developed and completed two National Natural Science Foundation projects named "Comparative Analysis between western and Chinese Eco-village" and "Research on MSA Strategy for Zero Emission Building in Chinese Eco-village–A Comprehensive Strategy for Affordable Guideline"; another research about new standard green residential areas named "New Standard for New Green Residential District" for the Tianjin Science and Technology Commission. He is actively involved in the planning for poverty village alleviation in China. He is also involved in the planning for "Toilet revolution" in China. In 2017 and 2018, he participated in a program for rural development for poverty villages alleviation in Taijiang County (Guizhou), Shijiazhuang County (Hebei) and Lindian County (Heilongjiang).

He is registered architect in Italy and also has been working as chief and consultant architect in several Chinese and International companies in the field of design of architecture and urban design in various projects. In 2004 he was responsible in China for the technologies and implementation of the project "Sino Italian Environmental Energy saving Building–SIEEB" in cooperation between Ministry of Environment and Territory Protection of Italy, Politecnico di Milano and Tsinghua University. In 2005-2006 he was the head of the cooperation between School of Architecture of Tianjin University, the Municipality of Tianjin and Politecnico di Milano as director of technologies of restoration, investigation and teaching plan for the technologies of restoration of Jing Yuan, the former residence in Tianjin of the Last Emperor Puyi. In 2010 he won the "Haihe Friendship Award" in Tianjin for his cultural contribution in China. He is member of the prestigious Aspen Institute in Italy.

He organized several workshops in China and other countries concerning the investigation of tangible and intangible heritage and self-construction building.

He is professional photographer. He is an advocate of free software, GNU/Linux.

# 计算机编程概论

文 / 开恩 [ 委内瑞拉 ]

译 / 林汉英

计算机方便了我们的生活，能够解决问题，并帮助我们高效地完成工作。那么人类也可以被当作电脑或是一台机器吗？按照逻辑答案是否定的，但如果我们换个角度来看，我们人类不也在按指令工作，处理信息，汲取经验么？我们的大脑可否被看作主板，心脏作为我们的动力源，而整个身体作为机器，可以接收数据，处理信息，并输出结果？

实际上人类比机器更复杂，我们可以自己思考，我们有感情，我们会学习，我们有思想，我们可以自由地做我们想做的事，我们有血有肉，还有更多显而易见的差异，尽管这种差异在遥远的未来可能会有所不同。

## ▎ 计算机

根据《牛津英语词典》，计算机的确切定义是"一种根据可变程序给出的指令存储和处理数据的电子设备，通常是二进制形式的数据"。

让我们将这个定义重新表述为：计算机以获得的信息或指令作为输入，并以高速进行数学和逻辑运算产生的结果作为输出。它会对你的命令做出回应。计算机由被称为硬件和软件的两个主要部分组成，一个离不开另一个，反之亦然，两者结合起来共同作用就给机器带来了生命。硬件是指计算机中你可以接触到的部分，也就是构成计算机主体的所有电路和组件。而软件是我们无法直接触及的东西，我们可以通过计算机外设来与软件进行交互。

如今，我们把硬件理解为计算机的主体，而把软件理解为使用物理组件的所有应用程序和操作系统。软件会和硬件对话并给出指令，硬件也会做出相应的回应和反应，就像在对话一样。所有这些指令都被分解成机器语言，这样机器就能理解更高层次的语言并在其能力范围内执行命令。

## ▎ 计算机能理解什么？

计算机的核心是一个处理器，它只能理解0和1。计算机由大量的交换机组成，每个交换机都可以打开或关闭，每个序列根据状态具有给定的功能，所有这些都有一个定义的操作来完成。计算机程序是构成算法的代码行，我们用这些代码行作为指令来说明这些开关的状态是如何确定的。但是，如果没有经过训练，人类很难只根据0和1来思考和创建代码，我们就需要找到一种方法来促进人和机器之间的交流，这种方法就是通过程序员提供一个封装好的程序来帮助我们和机器建立联系并互相理解。

人类的语言是一种通过说话、写作或他人能理解的信号进行交流的系统。我们通过一种共同的语言进行交流，这种方法也适用于计算机。世界上有7117种正在使用的人类口语语言（Ethnologue，2022），但其中三分之一因现代化而面临消亡（Michaels，2022）。另一方面，有700种人机语言，其中大约50种语言是最受欢迎和最常用的语言（Fowler，2022）。对于这些类型的语言，我们将通过"编程语言"来识别它们。

在计算机程序设计中，人们使用编程语言来为计算机编写一系列易于理解的指令，以完成一个确定的目标。

## ▍ 什么是计算机程序？

程序是控制机器操作的一系列编码指令（软件）。所有这些指令都可以用于机器编译。简单来说就是，所有的代码都被翻译了，以便机器能够理解软件需要做什么。

我们将"程序员""计算机程序员"或"软件开发人员"称为编写计算机软件（计算机程序）的人，这些软件（计算机程序）的形式包括算法、指令和按时执行的任务。

创建一个计算机程序就像我们去作曲、进行艺术创作或设计一个问题的解决方案。工程推进和思维方式并不严格依赖于一般人类认知的逻辑，我们需要对机器的结构、体系结构和行为有一些了解，才能创造出能够满足需要的软件。

程序员设计、编写和实现代码，创建针对特定需求或功能的软件应用程序。在设计出一个计算机程序后，程序员利用代码，将设计转换为一组计算机可以遵循和执行的指令。所有的设计最初都会有缺陷，因此需要一个测试阶段来寻找错误，并通过不断修复这些错误或调整变量以获得正确的结果及更好的性能，人们需要重复这些阶段直到没有错误且性能令人满意为止。程序员还会维护和评估当前使用的程序，根据需要进行更新和修正。

我们学习"编程语言"是为了与机器交流并下达指令。

## ▎ 编程语言

我们可以使用许多编程语言，最著名的有C/C++、Fortran、Pascal、Python、Java、Ruby、Assembler、JavaScript相关语言、类型脚本语言等。每种编程语言都可以归入特定的类别，这取决于该语言在句法上与人类语言的接近程度，或者与人类语言的差距，以及与机器理解指令方式的接近程度。

编程语言的分类描述如下：

```
L0:   MOV    R1, #a        ; Address of a
      MOV    R2, #b        ; in R1, of b in R2

L1:   LD     R3, (R1)      ; Inport bits in R3
      CMP    R3, #0        ; IF-condition
      BNE    L3            ;

L2:   MOV    R4, #1        ; IF-branch
      JMP    L4            ;

L3:   MOV    R4, #0        ; ELSE-branch

L4:   ST     (R2), R4      ;
      JMP    L1            ;
```

低级："接近机器语言"
几乎用机器语言说话的程序。例如：机器语言，汇编程序。

```cpp
#include <iostream>
#include <string>
using namespace std;

int main()
(

    string yourName;

    cout << "Enter your name: ";
    cin  >> yourName;
    cout << "Hello " + yourName << endl;

    return 0;
)
```

中级：可理解的
在不影响性能和效率的情况下，人类可以理解的。例如：C, C++。

```python
def print_hi(name):
    # Use a breakpoint in the code line below
    # Press Ctrl+F8 to toggle the breakpoint.
    print(f'\nHi, {name}')


# Press the green button in the gutter to run
if __name__ == '__main__':
    print_hi('Welcome to programming\n')
```

高级："更接近人类语言"
在编写程序时不太考虑程序应该如何翻译给机器。例如：Python, Ruby, Java。

## ▊ 编程环境

在我们的日常生活中，当我们学习任何东西时，我们需要有一个场所、材料和一个良好的学习环境，这个过程也适用于我们学习编程语言，我们需要一个环境来创建、开发、发现错误、解决问题和评估我们的代码。

编程环境就提供了这样一个平台，在这个平台上我们可以开发、解决和评估我们所创建的任何程序。不是所有的编程环境都支持所有的语言，有些编程环境特定于一种或一组语言和技术，有些编程环境更通用，但总的来说，它们为代码开发提供了空间和工具。

高级开发人员甚至可以在没有任何编程环境的情况下，只在文本文件中创建程序，虽然由此带来了缺点和限制，但这也显示了在任何地方创建任何程序的灵活性。

在本文中，我们将介绍两种类型的环境，第一种是集成开发环境（IDE）和可视化编程环境（VPE）。

根据EDUCBA，一个集成开发环境（IDE）为代码开发、测试和调试提供了用户界面。这样有助于组织代码，提供方便开发的工具，并根据所选择的编程语言进行规范化。机器无法理解代码本身，这就是为什么IDE也具有为机器翻译代码的功能（EDUCBA，2022）。

IDE帮助程序员开发新的软件、应用程序、网页、网页应用程序、小程序、计算机程序、移动应用程序、服务、游戏等。最流行和常用的环境是Microsoft Visual Studio、Microsoft Visual Studio Code、NetBeans、PyCharm、IntelliJ IDEA、Android Studio、Komodo和XCode。

它的主要目标是帮助开发人员编写机器能够理解的快速无误的代码。下面我们可以看看PyCharm，它是一个帮助我们更好地组织项目和文件的接口。还允许编译、执行和调试。这个IDE专门用于运行Python代码，如图1所示。

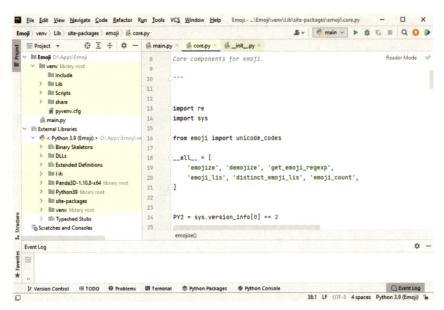

图1. PyCharm集成开发环境

另一方面，可视化编程环境（VPE）使用图形化模块，其中包含已定义的代码模块，可以像乐高积木一样使用该代码模块来构造程序。换句话说，常用的代码被分割成更小的组件，因此它们就像拼图碎片一样，通过一定的逻辑连接在一起就能创建一个新的程序，这是一种Block编程语言。

常规编程必须考虑如何编写机器能够理解的代码，而VPE允许你使用常规逻辑思考所需的指令，而不必深入了解每个模块背后的代码应该如何运行。有很多可视化编程环境使用可视化的编程语言，有代表性的是Scratch和Blockly（GeeksforGeeks，2022）。

Scratch是由Mitchel Resnick携手美国麻省理工学院（MIT）提出的，它被广泛用于教孩子们学习如何在不写任何代码的情况下开发一个程序，从而呈现了一种交互式编写程序的方法，并抓住了对该领域感兴趣的人的注意力。

从图2中我们可以观察到Scratch的可视化编程。

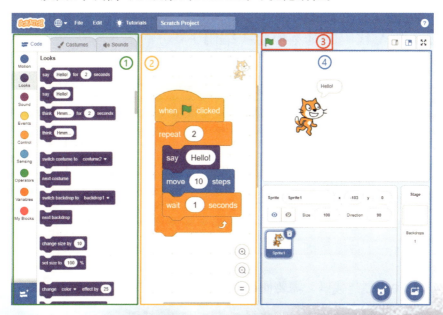

图2. Scratch可视化编程

在图2中，我们可以从左侧面板①中选择组件和预定义的函数，并将它们拖拽到中心空间②中，在那里我们可以构建将对角色生效的指令模块。一旦代码准备好了，我们可以在③处运行或停止代码的执行，我们将注意到右边面板④上的结果，那里的小猫将按照指示做相应的动作。

给出的代码示例有一个事件动作，后面跟着一个重复动作循环，其中包含一个指令模块，直到满足条件才会停止。这个事件动作是一个"点击"动作，点击开始程序，角色（小猫）将显示一条消息说："你好！"并继续移动10步，然后等待一秒钟，接着再次执行相同的过程，如此往复两次即为完成程序，因为没有更多的指令要执行了。

## 编写代码的基本概念（编码）

像任何语言一样，我们需要共同的规则来理解它，解释它，并正确使用它。在本节中，我们从基本数据类型开始来讲解，描述编码的基本组件。我们将了解什么是数据类型、变量、操作符、语句和函数，这些概念对于理解如何创建代码非常重要。为了保持代码的一致性，我们使用Python语法来创建和解释代码。

### （一）数据类型

为了创建代码，需要使用明确的数据类型来声明对象。它是一个属性，用于指示如何与数据交互以及确定处理代码和执行程序需要多少内存。它们可以是数字、字母等。下面，我们介绍一些基本数据类型。

### 文本

· 字符（char）：定义单个字符。例如, a，~，!，o。

· 字符串（str）：定义一个长字符串，换句话说，就是一个字符序列。例如，"Hello" "World！"。

### 数字

· 整数（int）：定义整数，不认任何其间的小数。根据编程语言的不同，它的覆盖范围从负值算起。例如，82，2，0，48985。

· 十进制数（单精度，float）：定义一个小数，一个带有单一精度的浮点数。允许小数点后最多7位。例如，5.425，7566.77。

· 十进制数（双精度，double）：定义一个小数，一个带有双精度的浮点数。允许小数点后最多15位。例如，56.989889489E+22，98.8888060032。

### 逻辑

· 布尔表达式（bool）：在代码中显示逻辑，它有两种状态，真或假。用于创建条件语句（真/假语句）。根据条件的状态，代码将执行相应的操作。布尔表达式使用运算符AND、OR、NOT。

· 零（Nothing）

意味着代码没有数据，没有值。可能是缺少代码或逻辑问题。

它也被称为"可空类型"。例如，null，NaN。

数据类型告诉我们如何与数据交互；因此，我们需要引入变量作为数据的容器。

## （二）变量

变量可以根据程序中使用的信息而改变。它们可以存储你在整个程序或多个程序中使用的信息。这种方式加快了代码的编写，更容易阅读，这有助于代码的进一步更新。声明变量很简单。我们首先指出数据类型，然后是变量的描述性名称，最后是我们想要存储在变量中的数据。在这里，我们介绍按数据类型分类的变量的基本示例。

### 文本变量

· charcharacter（字符）："H"

· str word（字符串）："Hello,World（你好，世界）！"

### 数值变量

· int number（整数）：23

· float temperature（温度）：36.5

### 逻辑变量

· bool have money（有钱）：False（假）

每种编程语言都有自己的变量类型，这些变量有不同的声明和用法。为了在程序中使用这些变量，我们需要运算符来给出变量、语句和函数之间的关系。

### （三）运算符

由特定符号表示，表明它必须执行的进程类型。这些操作可以是数学的、关系的或逻辑的（Coding，2022）。

#### 算法

算术计算，如加（+）、减（−）、乘（*）、除（/）、模数（%）等。取模运算返回除法运算的余数。

#### 比较

比较操作数两边的值并确定它们之间的关系，也被称为关系操作符。最常见的比较操作符有：

- 相等（=）：值= 值

- 小于（<）：值<值

- 小于等于（<=）：值<= 值

- 大于（>）：值>值

- 大于等于（>=）：值>= 值

- 不相等（!=）：值 != 值

## 赋值

赋值两个相等的东西（＝）。将运算符右边的值赋给左边的值。

还有一些组合运算符，在相同的指令下进行算术运算和赋值。操作符可能会根据编程语言的不同而改变，但功能保持不变。我们可以在下面观察到与这个类别最相关的操作符。

· 加法（+=）：将运算符右侧的值加到当前变量上。

· 减法（−=）：将运算符右侧的值减去当前的变量。

· 乘法运算（*=）：运算符右边的值乘以当前的变量。

· 除法（/=）：将运算符右侧的值除以当前的变量。

## 逻辑

常见的逻辑操作符有与（AND）、或（OR）和非（NOT）。它可以与比较运算符一起使用来获得一个布尔值结果。

· AND运算符（&&）：如果两个操作数（左边和右边）都是真实的，则返回TRUE。

· OR运算符（||）：如果操作数（左边或右边）有一个是真实的，则返回TRUE。

· NOT 运算符（!）：如果操作数是假的，则返回TRUE。它可以添加到布尔变量和比较器中来反转当前值。

在表1中，我们可以观察到常用的操作符。

表1. 操作符汇总

| Type | Operators |
|------|-----------|
| Arithmetical | a. Addition → int add = valueA + valueB<br>b. Subtraction → float subtract = valueA - valueB<br>c. Modulo → int remainder = valueA % valueB |
| Comparison | a. Equal to → 56 == 589<br>b. Less than → 8599 < 8829<br>c. Greater or equal → 988 >= 988 |
| Assignment | a. Normal → valueA = ValueB<br>b. Addition → add = add + valueA :: add += valueA<br>c. Subtraction → subtract = subtract - valueA :: subtract -= valueA |
| Logical | a. AND → (a == 0 && b == 5)<br>b. OR → (a == 4 \|\| b == 3)<br>c. NOT → (a != 0) |

## （四）语句

运算符与语句结合起来执行指令块。我们将讨论以下语句：
条件语句或决策语句（if-else语句和switch-case语句）、迭代语句
（for语句、while语句和do-while语句）和跳转语句（break语句、
continue语句和return语句）。这些语句是控制程序流的基本语句。

### 条件语句

决策语句需要满足一个条件才能执行一组指令。这些语句使用
操作符来设置条件并确定它们的关系。

"if-else"语句：如果满足给定条件，将允许执行一个指令
块，否则，它将跳过指令块。决策语句可能有也可能没有"else"
部分，它指示在条件未满足时执行块的该部分。还可以在条件语句
中嵌套条件语句。它的语法很简单，就像伪代码（伪代码，其中呈
现了一系列人类可以理解的动作和指令）。

215

```
thousand: int = 10000          # Variable
million: int = 8800000         # Variable

if thousand < million:
    # Block of instructions if the condition was met
    print ("Indeed, a thousand is less than a million")
else: # Block of instructions if the condition was not met
    print ("Wow! There must be a mistake")

# Output: Indeed, a thousand is less than a million
```

"switchcase"语句：是if-else case的组合，但更直接，因为它不会所有的条件，而是直接到达和它匹配的。当一个变量有一组值，并且每个状态将执行一组单独的指令时，它就变得很有用。Switch-case将运行每一个case，直到它遇到暂停或完成相应的指令。该语句还有一种不履行的情况，如果呈现的情形都不满足条件，它将被执行，尽管这是一个可选的情况。

请考虑每种语言的语法和结构是不同的，尽管它们的逻辑与下面我们可以观察到的伪代码相同。

```
switch(keywordPress)
    case 1:
        print("HIGH")
        break
    case 2:
        print("LOW")
        break
    # More cases can go in here...
    default:
        print("FORWARD")

# Input: keywordPress = 5
# Output: FORWARD
```

## 迭代语句

在许多情况下，我们需要反复重复指令。因此，迭代语句（也称为循环）的存在是为了提高效率，不需要再重复代码（Kumar，

2022）。

"for"语句：此循环将用于顺序的情况，在这种情况下，我们知道何时开始和何时结束迭代。伪代码的基本语法如下所示，它将以字符串形式打印迭代软件的数据索引。

```
accumulated: str = "" # Variable

for number in range (10):
    # Concatenate accumulated values in a string with the new
one
    accumulated = f'{accumulated} {number}'
print(accumulated)

# Output: 0 1 2 3 4 5 6 7 8 9
```

"while"循环：如果与"for"循环相同，但在这种情况下，我们不知道确切的迭代必须终止的时间。换句话说，循环将继续运行，直到条件变为"伪"。在某些情况下，如果没有任何停止条件，我们需要在循环内部添加断点，否则，循环将无限地进行下去，或者等它自己停止。

```
index: int = 0
cars: int = 5

while index <= cars:
    print(index)
    index += 1       # Increment index by one

# Output: 1 2 3 4 5
```

"do-while"循环：与"while"循环相似，不同的是循环将在核查条件之前，至少执行一次指令块。语法也类似于我们可以观察到的伪代码。

```
do
    # Execute a block of code
    # Increment / decrement
while condition
```

## 跳转语句

这些语句旨在满足条件时终止循环，或不终止一个无限的循环，而是帮助将程序的控制转移给另一个程序，并跳过循环内的指令块。

"break"语句：用于中断交换机和回路。一旦遇到此语句，就终止循环的执行，在切换的情况下，它将忽略和跳过其余的情况。

```
accumulated: str = "" # Variable

for number in range (10):
    # Concatenate accumulated values in a string with the new
one
    accumulated = f'{accumulated} {number}'
    if number == 5:
        break;

print(accumulated)

# Output: 0 1 2 3 4 5
```

"continue"语句：必须在跳过循环中的当前迭代时使用。一旦遇到，我们就跳过循环中的其余语句，并在同一个循环中执行下面的迭代。在下一个示例中，如果索引的模块除以2等于0，我们将不打印任何内容。

```
accumulated: str = ""

for number in range (10):
    if number % 2 == 0:
        continue
    accumulated = f'{accumulated} {number}'

print(accumulated)

# Output: 1 3 5 7 9
```

"return"语句：该关键字将控制权传递给调用它的方法。主要方法将执行一个算术操作，该操作将调用方法"add"，这是一个算术函数，它接受两个参数，并返回一个整数作为操作的结果。

```python
# Public addition function def
add (a: int, b: int) -> int:
    result: int = a + b
    print (f" Sum of {a} + {b} = {result}")
    return result # Main
method if __name__ ==
'__main__':    x: int = 5
# Variable
    y: int = 10    # Variable      sum:
int = add (x, y)

# Output: Sum of 5 + 10 = 15
```

## （五）函数

在一些特定情况下，我们想要重复使用代码块，而且还想要动态地改变变量和条件。这时，就需要使用到函数。通过使用函数，我们可以对代码块进行分组，并在需要的时间和条件下调用它。当我们将它们分开时，我们也可以多次调用它们，换句话说，我们可以重用代码，改进程序以获得更好的性能和状态，并最小化代码中的冗余。代码优化和函数的变量可以根据需要进行调整。

通过这种方式，函数将其功能扩展到更动态的状态，而不是将其固定在一个唯一的目的上。由于其灵活性，对于不同的输入数据，函数将返回不同的结果。像下面的例子，我们可以多次调用一个带有不同参数或变量的函数并返回正确的结果。

219

```
def subtract (a: int, b: int) -> int:          # Public function
    result: int = a - b
    print (f" Results of {a} - {b} = {result}")
    return result

if __name__ == '__main__':
    sub: int = subtract (10, 12)

# Output: Results of 10 - 12 = -2
```

所有这些概念都将帮助您轻松编写代码，当然这并不容易，不过一旦你掌握了概念和逻辑，编程就会变得容易。

这是一个编程的概要图，类似的图还有更多，理解概要图会是编程学习的一个好的开始。

图3. 编程的概要图

而且无论你如何开始，只要你有愿望去学习，你最终会通过努力与勤奋掌握它。

●参考引用

https：//www.guru99.com/computer-programming-tutorial.html

https：//www.fullstackacademy.com/blog/what-is-coding-part-1

https：//www.educba.com/coding-vs-programming/

**作者简介**

开恩（Lo Leung Mimia Hoi Yan），委内瑞拉籍，硕士毕业于南开大学软件工程专业，目前在天津国际生物医学联合研究院从事脑机接口（BCI）应用开发、技术支持和与部门研究配套的软件开发等工作。在她的职业生涯中，曾在创业公司、咨询公司和研究领域从事各种项目。她的座右铭是：享受你的工作，寻求新的挑战，每天成长为一个更好的人。作为专业人士，她期望学习和培养自身的技能，并将知识传递给年轻一代，因为错误将由他们来删除，未来等着他们改写。

# Introduction to Computer Programming

By Lo Leung Mimia Hoi Yan (Venezuela)

Computers are made to facilitate our life, solve problems, and provide efficiency in what we need to accomplish. Have humans also been considered a computer? A machine? The logical answer is no, but if we see it from another perspective, don't we humans also work on instructions? Process information? Learn from experiences? Can our brain be considered as the motherboard, the heart as our power source, and the whole body as the machine that can receive an input, process information, and give an output?

We are more complex than a machine. We can think by ourselves. We have feelings. We learn. We have a philosophy. We are free to do what we want. We are flesh, and more, so the differences are clear to the eye. Although, in the far future, things might be different.

## Computer

According to *The Oxford English Dictionary*, the exact definition of a computer is "An electronic device for storing and processing data, typically in binary form, according to instructions given to it in a variable program".

Let us rephrase this definition like this: A computer gets information/instructions as input and does mathematical and logical operations at high speed to produce a result, which is the output. It gives you an answer to your commands. A computer consists of two main parts, and one cannot function without the other and vice versa. These two parts are called Hardware and Software, and the combination of both functioning together brings life to the machine. Hardware is the part where you can touch physically the computer. It refers to all the circuits and components that form its body. Software is what we cannot physically touch. Instead we can interact through the computer peripherals.

Nowadays, we understand hardware as the body of the computer and the software as all the applications and Operating System that uses the physical components. The software talks and gives instructions to the hardware and vice versa, just like having a conversation. All these instructions are broken down into the machine language as a way for the machine to understand a higher level of language and execute what it is requested within its abilities.

## What does a Computer Understand?

The core of the computer is a processor which can only understand zero's (0) and one's (1). A computer is made up of a large number of switches. Each switch can either be turned on or off, each sequence with a given function depending on the state, and all with a defined action to accomplish. The computer programs are lines of codes that form algorithms; we are writing instructions as to how these switches' states are going to be under certain variables. Hence,It is hard for humans to think and create code based on zero's and one's (1) without training; that is why we need a way to facilitate the communication between humans and machines. Providing a layer of abstraction from the programmer will help to encapsulate what we cannot understand from the machine and what the machine cannot understand from humans.

Language is a system of communication by speaking, writing, or by signals that can be understood by others. We communicate with each other through a common language.This method also applies to the computer. There are 7,117 spoken human languages in the world (Ethnologue, 2022), but a third of them face the risk of extinction due to modernization (Michaels, 2022). On the other hand, there are seven hundred human-computer languages, of which around fifty (50) languages are the most popular and commonly used ones (Fowler, 2022). For these types of languages, we will identify them by "programming languages".

In computer programming, a programming language is used by a person who writes a sequence of instructions for computers understandably to accomplish a defined goal.

## ▌ What is a Computer Program?

A program is a series of coded instructions (software) to control an operation on a machine. All these instructions can be compiled by a machine. A straightforward way to say this is that all the code is translated for the machine to be able to understand what is needed from the software.

We will label "programmer", "computer programmer" or "software developer" to the person that writes any software (computer programs) for a computer in the form of algorithms, instructions, and jobs to be executed on schedule.

Creating a computer program can be like composing music, creating art, or designing a solution for a problem. The way of engineering and thinking does not rely strictly on common logic. We need to understand a bit about the machine's structure, architecture, and behavior to be able to create software adequate to what is desired.

A programmer designs, write, and implement the code, creating software applications directed to a particular need or function. After designing a computer program, the programmer writes code that converts the design into a set of instructions a computer can follow and execute. All designs at the begging will have flaws, and therefore a testing phase is needed to look for errors, rewrite for better performance, and fix those errors or adjust variables for a correct outcome. These phases are repeated until are error-free and satisfactory in their performance. A programmer also maintains and evaluates programs that are in current use, making updates and fixes as needed.

We learn "Programming languages" to communicate and indicate instructions to a machine.

# Programming Language

We can use many programming languages, the most famous ones are C/C++, Fortran, Pascal, Python, Java, Ruby, Assembler, JavaScript-related languages, Type Scripting languages, and more. Each programming language can be classified in a specific category depending on how close the language is to a human language in syntax or further away from it and closer to how the machine understands instructions.

The classification of programming languages is described as follows:

```
L0:  MOV   R1, #a        ; Address of a
     MOV   R2, #b        ; in R1, of b in R2

L1:  LD    R3, (R1)      ; Inport bits in R3
     CMP   R3, #0        ; IF-condition
     BNE   L3            ;

L2:  MOV   R4, #1        ; IF-branch
     JMP   L4            ;

L3:  MOV   R4, #0        ; ELSE-branch

L4:  ST    (R2), R4      ;
     JMP   L1            ;
```

**Low-level: "Close to machine language"**
*Program that talks almost in the machine language.*
i.e.: Machine Language, Assembler.

```
#include <iostream>
#include <string>
using namespace std;

int main()
{
    string yourName;

    cout << "Enter your name: ";
    cin  >> yourName;
    cout << "Hello " + yourName << endl;

    return 0;
}
```

**Mid-level: Understandable**
*Which is understandable for humans without affecting performance and efficiency.*
i.e.: C, C++

```
def print_hi(name):
    # Use a breakpoint in the code line below
    # Press Ctrl+F8 to toggle the breakpoint.
    print(f'\nHi, {name}')


# Press the green button in the gutter to run
if __name__ == '__main__':
    print_hi('Welcome to programming\n')
```

**High-level: "Closer to human language."**
*Abstraction in writing a program without taking much care of how it should be translated to the machine.*
i.e.: Python, Ruby, Java

# ▌ Programming Environment

In our daily life, when we learn anything, we need to have a place, material, and a good environment for our study. This process also applies when we learn programming languages. We need an environment to create, develop, find errors, resolve problems, and assess our code.

A Programming environment offers a platform where we can develop, resolve, and evaluate any program that we create. Not all environments support all languages. Some are specific to one or a group of languages and technologies, and some are more generic, but overall, they provide the space and tools for code development.

Advanced developers can even create a program in a text file without any programming environment; this brings disadvantages and limitations, but then this shows the flexibility of creating any program anywhere.

In this article we are going to introduce two types of environments.

227

The first one is an Integrated Development Environment (IDE) and a Visual Programming Environment (VPE).

According to EDUCBA, an Integrated Development Environment (IDE) provides the user interface for code development, testing, and debugging. It helps to organize the code, provides tools for easy development, and is standardized depending upon the chosen programming language. Code alone cannot be understood by the machine, which is why IDEs also have functionalities that translate the code for the machine (EDUCBA, 2022).

IDE helps programmers to develop new software, applications, webpages, web apps, mini-programs, programs for the computer, mobile apps, services, games, and more. The most popular and used environments are Microsoft Visual Studio, Microsoft Visual Studio Code, NetBeans, PyCharm, IntelliJ IDEA, Android Studio, Komodo, and XCode.

Its main objective is to help developers to write fast and error-free code that a machine can understand. Bellow we can see the IDE PyCharm, an interface that helps us to better organize our project and files. Also allows for compilation, execution, and debugging. This IDE is especially for running Python code as we can see in Figure 1.

On the other hand, a Visual Programming Environment (VPE) uses a graphical block where it contains a defined block of code where it can be used like Lego blocks to construct a program. In other words, commonly used code is separated into smaller components. Therefore they can be used as puzzle pieces to create a new program by joining the pieces together logically. A Block programming language.

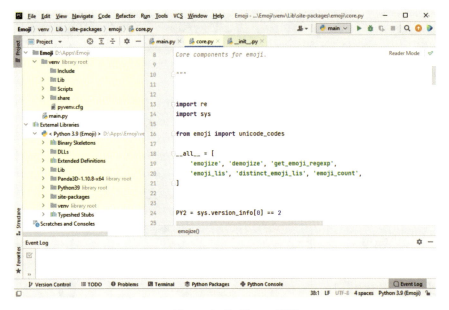

Figure 1. PyCharm IDE

Whereas regular programming must think of how to write a code that the machine can understand, the VPE allows you to think in common logic the instructions that are required without going deep into the details of how the code behind each block should be. There is a lot of visual programming environment that uses their visual programming language. A few of the visual programming languages are Scratch and Blockly (GeeksforGeeks, 2022).

Scratch was Introduced by Mitchel Resnick with the MIT and is widely used to also teach kids to learn how to develop a program without writing any line of code. This presents a way to write a program interactively, which captures the attention of anyone interested in this field.

As we can observe in Figure 2 the structure of the program Scratch.

Figure 2. Visual Programming in Scratch

In Figure 2. Visual Programming in Scratch.Figure 2, we can select components and pre-defined functions from the left side panel (1) and drag them into the center space (2) where we can construct a block of instructions that will take effect on the character. Once the code is ready, we can run or stop the execution of the code at pleasing (3) and we will notice the outcome on the right panel (4), where the cat is going to perform what has been instructed.

The presented code example has an event action followed by a repetition loop where it contains a block of instructions to be performed till the stop condition is fulfilled. This event action is a "clicking" action, where it will start the program with a click. Then the character (kitten) will display a message saying "Hello!" and will continue a loop of repetition that will move the cat 10 steps and wait a second before doing the same process again twice to later finalize the program because there are no more instructions to execute.

## ▌ Base Concepts for Writing Code (Coding)

Like any language, we need common rules for understanding the language, interpreting it, and using it properly. In this section we are going to describe the base components for coding, starting with the base types of data. For this section, we will have a grasp of what are data types, variables, operators, statements, and functions. These concepts arc important for understanding how we can start creating code. To maintain coherence in the code, we are using Python syntax to create and explain code.

### Data Types

For creating code, it is needed to declare objects with a clear type of data. It is an attribute to indicate how to interact with the data; it also will determine how much memory is needed to process the code and execute a program. They can be numeric, alphanumeric, etc. Next, it is described the base types of data we can use when creating instructions and algorithms.

### Text

• Character (char): Defines a single character. i.e., a, ~, !, o.

• String (str): Defines a long string, in other words, a sequence of characters. i.e., "Hello", "World!".

## Numeric

- Integer (int): Define whole numbers. Do not acknowledge any fractional number in between. Depending on the programming language, its coverage goes from negative values. i.e., 82, 2, 0, 48985.

- Decimal Number (float): Define a fractional number, a floating-point number with single precision. Allows up to seven points after a decimal. i.e., 5.425, 7566.77.

- Decimal Number (double): Define a fractional number, a floating-point number with double precision. Allows up to fifteen (15) points after a decimal. i.e., 56.989889489E+22, 98.8888060032.

## Logical

Boolean (bool): Show logic in code, it has two states, true or false. Used for creating conditional statements (true/false statements). Depending on the state of the condition, the code will perform the corresponding action. Boolean expressions use the operators AND, OR, and NOT.

## Nothing

Indicates that a code has no data, no value. Might be a missing code or problems in the logic. It is also called the "nullable type". i.e., null, NaN.

Data types are used to indicate how we can interact with the data; therefore, we need to introduce variables as the container of the data.

## Variables

Variables can change depending on the information used in a program. Those can store information that you might use throughout the program or across multiply programs. This way speeds up the writing of the code and is easier to read, which helps with further updates on the code. It is simple to declare variables. We first indicate the data type, followed by a descriptive name of what is the variable for, and lastly, the data that we want to store in the variable. Here we can appreciate base examples of the variables classified by their data type.

- **Text variables**

  - char character : 'H'

  - str word : "Hello, World!"

- **Numeric variables**

  - int number : 23

  - float temperature : 36.5

- **Logical variables**

  - bool have money :False

Each programming language has its types of variables that have different declaration and use. As a way to use these variables in a program, we need operators to give a relationship among variables, statements, and functions.

## Operators

Represented by a specific symbol, indicating what type of process it must perform. These operations can be mathematical, relational, or logical (Coding, 2022).

### *Arithmetical*

Arithmetic calculations like addition (+), subtraction (-), multiplication (*), division (/), modulo (%), and more. Modulo operation returns the remainder value from a division.

### *Comparison*

Compares the values on either side of the operand and determines the relation between them. It is also referred to as relational operators. Most common comparison operators in are:

- equal to (==): value == value

- less than (<): value < value

- less than or equal to (<=): value <= value

- greater than (>): value > value

- greater than or equal to (>=): value >= value

- different/distinct than (!=): value != value

### *Assignment*

Assigning two things equal (=). Assign what is on the right side of the operator to the left side of the operator.

There are combined operators where it does arithmetical operations and assignments at the same instructions. The operators might change depending on the programming language, but the functionality remains the same. We can observe below the most relevant operators for this category.

- Addition (+=): The value on the right side of the operator is added to the current variable.

- Subtraction (-=): The value on the right side of the operator is subtracted from the current variable.

- Multiplication (*=): The value on the right side of the operator is multiplied by the current variable.

- Division (/=): The value on the right side of the operator is divided by the current variable.

*Logical*

Common logical operators are AND, OR, and NOT. It can be used with a comparison operator to get a single Boolean result.

- AND operator (&&): It returns TRUE if both the operands (right side and left side) are true.

- OR operator (‖): It returns TRUE if either of the operand (right side or left side) is true.

- NOT operator (!): It returns TRUE if the operand is false. It can be added to Boolean variables and comparators to reverse their current value.

In Table 1, we can observe common useful operators.

Table 1. Summary of the operators.

| Type | Operators |
|---|---|
| Arithmetical | a. Addition → int add = valueA + valueB |
| | b. Subtraction → float subtract = valueA - valueB |
| | c. Modulo → int remainder = valueA % valueB |
| Comparison | a. Equal to → 56 == 589 |
| | b. Less than → 8599 < 8829 |
| | c. Greater or equal → 988 >= 988 |
| Assignment | a. Normal → valueA = ValueB |
| | b. Addition → add = add + valueA :: add += valueA |
| | c. Subtraction → subtract = subtract - valueA :: subtract -= valueA |
| Logical | a. AND → (a == 0 && b == 5) |
| | b. OR → (a == 4 \|\| b == 3) |
| | c. NOT → (a != 0) |

## Statements

Operators work combined with statements to perform a block of instructions. We are going to cover the following statements: Conditional or decision statements (if-else statements and switch-case statements), Iteration statements (for statements, while statements, and do-while statements), and Jump statements (break statement, continue statement, and return statement). These statements are basic to control the flow of the program.

### Conditional statements

Decision statements require a condition to be met to execute a set of instructions. These statements use operators to set the conditions and determine their relation.

The "if-else" statement: Will allow the execution of a block if the given condition is satisfied, otherwise, it will skip the block of instructions. The decision statement might and might not have an "else" section, which indicates the execution of that section of the block if the condition was not fulfilled. You can also have nested conditionals within conditional statements. The syntax is simple as below as pseudocode (fake code in which you represent a sequence of actions and instructions understandable for humans):

```
thousand: int = 10000          # Variable
million: int = 8800000         # Variable

if thousand < million:
    # Block of instructions if the condition was met
    print ("Indeed, a thousand is less than a million")
else: # Block of instructions if the condition was not met
    print ("Wow! There must be a mistake")

# Output: Indeed, a thousand is less than a million
```

The "switch-case" statement: Is a combination of if-else cases but is more straightforward because it will not go through all the conditions, and will go directly to its match instead. It is useful when a variable has a set of values, and each state will perform a separate set of instructions. The switch-case will run every case till it meets a break or finishes the corresponding instructions. The switch-case also has a default case where it will be executed if none of the presented cases meets the condition, although this is an optional case.

Consider that each language's syntax and structure are different, although is the same logic as we can observe below as pseudocode:

```
switch(keywordPress)
    case 1:
        print("HIGH")
        break
    case 2:
        print("LOW")
        break
    # More cases can go in here...
    default:
        print("FORWARD")

# Input: keywordPress = 5
# Output: FORWARD
```

*Iteration statements*

There are many instances where we need to repeat instructions repeatedly. That is why the iteration statements, also known as loops exist for efficiency. There will not be a need for code repetition (Kumar, 2022).

The "for" statements: This loop will be used in a sequential case where we are aware of when to start and when to end the iteration. The base syntax as pseudocode can be seen as follows with an example where it will print the iteration index as a string of characters:

```python
accumulated: str = "" # Variable

for number in range (10):
    # Concatenate accumulated values in a string with the new one
    accumulated = f'{accumulated} {number}'
print (accumulated)

# Output: 0 1 2 3 4 5 6 7 8 9
```

The "while" loop: If the same as the "for" loop but in this case, we do not know exactly when our iteration must be terminated. In other words, the loop will continue to run till the condition changes to false. At some point we need to add a breaking point inside the loop if there are not any stopping conditions, otherwise, the loop will go indefinitely or when the program halts.

```python
index: int = 0
cars: int = 5

while index <= cars:
    print (index)
    index += 1          # Increment index by one

# Output: 1 2 3 4 5
```

The "do-while" loop: Working similar to the while loop, the difference is that the loop will execute at least once the block of instructions before checking with the condition. The syntax is also similar as we can observe as pseudocode:

```
do
    # Execute a block of code
    # Increment / decrement

while condition
```

## *Jump statements*

These statements are meant to discontinue a loop whereas a condition was met or not to end an endless loop; help to transfer the control of the program to another and skip a block of instructions inside the loop.

The "break" statement: Used to interrupt switch cases and loops. Once encountered, it terminates the execution of the loop. In the case of the switch, it will ignore and skip the remaining cases.

```
accumulated: str = "" # Variable

for number in range (10):
    # Concatenate accumulated values in a string with the new
one
    accumulated = f'{accumulated} {number}'
    if number == 5:
        break;

print (accumulated)

# Output: 0 1 2 3 4 5
```

The "continue" statement: Used when the current iteration inside the loop must be skipped. Once encountered, we skip the remaining statements inside the loop and execute the following iteration in the same loop. In the next example, we will not print anything if the module of the index divided by two (2) is equal to zero (0).

```python
accumulated: str = ""

for number in range (10):
    if number % 2 == 0:
        continue
    accumulated = f'{accumulated} {number}'

print(accumulated)

# Output: 1 3 5 7 9
```

The "return" statement: This keyword transfers the control to the method who called it. The main method will perform an arithmetical operation which will call the method "add", which is an arithmetical function that takes two parameters and returns an integer as the result of the operation.

```python
# Public addition function def
add (a: int, b: int) -> int:
    result: int = a + b
    print (f" Sum of {a} + {b} = {result}")
    return result # Main
method if __name__ ==
'__main__':      x: int = 5
# Variable
    y: int = 10     # Variable    sum:
int = add (x, y)

# Output: Sum of 5 + 10 = 15
```

## Functions

We want to reuse the blocks of codes and we will want to change the variables and conditions dynamically, right? Here is where functions come in handy. We can group a block of code and call it when and with the conditions we want it to. When we keep them separate, we can also call them more than once.In other terms, we can reuse the code, Improving the program to better performance and maintenance, and minimizes redundancy in the code. Simpler for code optimization and the variables for the function can be adapted depending on what is needed.

With this, the function expands its functionality to a more dynamic state rather than having it fixed for a sole purpose. Due to its flexibility, the function will return different results upon different input data. Like the following example, where we can call many times a function with different arguments/parameters and returns a proper result:

```python
def subtract (a: int, b: int) -> int:        # Public function
    result: int = a - b
    print (f" Results of {a} - {b} = {result}")
    return result

if __name__ == '__main__':
    sub: int = subtract (10, 12)

# Output: Results of 10 - 12 = -2
```

All these concepts will help you ease into coding. It would not be easy, but it will be better once you grasp the concepts and the logic. Here is a summary graph of programming, there is more but this is a good beginning.

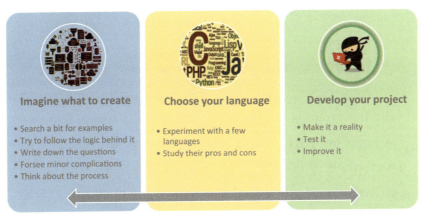

**Imagine what to create**

• Search a bit for examples
• Try to follow the logic behind it
• Write down the questions
• Forsee minor complications
• Think about the process

**Choose your language**

• Experiment with a few languages
• Study their pros and cons

**Develop your project**

• Make it a reality
• Test it
• Improve it

Figure 3.  A summary graph of programming

No matter how you start, you will eventually get hold of it with effort and dedication.

## Extra References

https://www.guru99.com/computer-programming-tutorial.html

https://www.fullstackacademy.com/blog/what-is-coding-part-1

https://www.educba.com/coding-vs-programming/

## About the Author

Mimia Lo acquired her master's degree as a Software Engineer at Nankai University and currently working at Tianjin International Joint Academy of Biomedicine in developing Brain-Computer Interface (BCI) applications, technical support, and development of software adequate for the department's research. She has worked on a variety of projects throughout her career with startup companies, consultancy companies, and in the research field. Her motto is to enjoy what you do for a living, find new challenges to overcome and grow as a better person each day. As a professional, it is expected to learn and nurture her skills and to pass her knowledge to younger generations because they are going to improve what is next and remove what is faulty.

# CHAPTER 3 第三章

## 科技前沿

### Frontier of Science and Technology

# 神奇的聚变能量

文 / 李飞 [法]

核工业西物院"人造太阳"博士科普团

译 / 吴庭

## 钢铁侠的神奇力量：核聚变能

能源危机是当今社会面临的一个重要问题。科学家为了寻求更可靠、高效、清洁的能源而殚精竭虑、苦心钻研，文学创作者在科幻小说和电影中也以能源问题为题材，极力发挥自己的奇思妙想，著名电影《钢铁侠》就是其中之一。如果你看过这部电影，或许你会发出这样的疑问：为什么钢铁侠可以持续战斗，好像拥有无限能量呢？其实，钢铁侠强大力量的关键所在，就是他发明的一项黑科技——铠甲胸口处的迷你核聚变反

图1. 《钢铁侠》中的核聚变反应堆

应堆，它可以源源不断地释放能量。

　　而钢铁侠的这项发明与其说是小说中的幻想，倒不如说像是一次科学实验。自1934年在实验室首次实现核聚变反应以来，全世界的科学家前赴后继，为以此获取核聚变能源接续奋斗。想象一下，未来，人类可以像钢铁侠一样，利用核聚变来获得用之不竭的能源，为我们的家庭供电，为汽车和飞机等交通工具提供动力。相信这一天很快就会到来！

## ▌ 什么是核聚变？

　　核聚变和核裂变都是利用原子核进行反应产生巨大能量的形式，两者都可以用来发电。但不同的是，核裂变反应，是由较重的原子核分裂成两个或多个较轻的原子核；核聚变反应，是由两个较轻的原子核发生聚合反应生成新的较重的原子核。

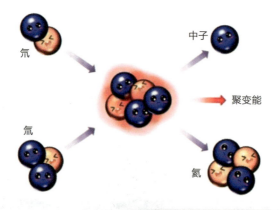

图2. 核聚变反应示意

很多恒星内部都存在这种类似的反应过程，如太阳。氢原子在太阳内部受到1500万度高温加热时，被电离成为氢等离子体（等离子体是气体被电离后形成的气体状物质，它由正负离子组成，是不同于气体、液体、固体的物质的第四种状态），在2500亿个大气压的高压环境下，这些氢等离子体的原子核互相碰撞，发生着核聚变反应。

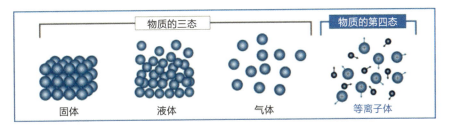

图3. 等离子体示意

在这种核聚变反应过程中生成物的总质量略小于反应物的总质量，亏损的质量转化为能量释放出来。根据著名的爱因斯坦质能方程$E=mc^2$：其释放的能量E等于亏损的物质质量m乘以光速c的平方。由于光速c的平方是一个极为庞大的数字，所以即便很小的质量亏损，与其相乘也会得到巨大的能量。

理论上，核聚变能可以为涡轮机提供动力来发电，其原理与当前的裂变核电站相同。详细而言，不论是聚变还是裂变，产生的热量首先加热初级冷却水回路，然后继续加热二级冷却水回路，进而产生蒸汽，推动涡轮旋转，最终达到让交流发电机发电的目的。

## ▋ 核聚变的优势

核聚变能可以说是一种近乎完美的能源：其原料在自然界储量丰富且易于获取，从海水中便可提取氘等氢的同位素；反应放能效率极高，世界上只有正反物质湮灭的放能效率比核聚变反应高；产物无污染，无温室气体排放。

举例而言，一座100万千瓦的大型烧煤电站，每年需烧煤150万~200万吨，二氧化碳排放量400~540吨；同功率的核裂变电站，一年耗铀燃料约30吨，无二氧化碳排放；而核聚变电站，每年仅需消耗150公斤水和锂即可产生与100万千瓦电站同样的能量，且无二氧化碳排放。

同时，核聚变反应也更加安全，如果有任何一个参数使其不满足聚变"点火"条件，聚变反应就会停止，不会再产生其他连锁反应。如果人类能够掌握可控磁约束核聚变反应技术，以海水作为燃料，则更是取之不尽，用之方便。

## ▋ 从理论到实践：核聚变发电面临的挑战

尽管核聚变在理论上具有很多优势，可在技术上仍然极具挑战性：等离子体温度、密度、能量约束时间，这三个参数的乘积（"聚变三乘积"）必须达到一定值，才能实现聚变"点火"。所以想在地球上"复刻"一个类似太阳的核聚变装置，需要满足极其苛刻的条件：

1）燃料达到极高的温度——上亿摄氏度；

2）长时间约束等离子体运行；

3）等离子体有足够高的密度。

图4. 核聚变装置中的等离子体

此外，要实现核聚变，需要先产生并约束等离子体。目前，主要有两种方法：惯性约束和磁约束。

第一种方法，惯性约束。主要是通过激光束提供的巨大能量（约3000000亿瓦），加热一个含氘和氚元素的两毫米大的金属"胶囊"，受到能量冲击的"胶囊"外壳变成等离子体，再被压缩，最终发生核聚变并产生能量。

第二种方法，磁约束，是目前的主流方式。一般是用通电导体周围的磁场使带电粒子（超高温等离子体）受洛伦兹力的作用，被约束在有限的体积内，从而发生核聚变反应。由此，一种最具代表性之一的磁约束核聚变装置——托卡马克（Tokamak）应运而生。

# ▌ ITER：实现聚变之路

国际热核聚变实验堆（ITER）计划中就利用了托卡马克来实现核聚变。有趣的是，在拉丁语中"ITER"有着"之路"的意思，在实现聚变之路上，ITER是当今世界最具雄心壮志的能源项目之一。

法国南部，35个国家正在合作建造世界上最大的磁约束核聚变托卡马克装置，旨在验证核聚变能和平利用的科学可行性。可见，ITER计划中的实验项目对于促进聚变科学和未来聚变反应堆发展至关重要。

自20世纪50年代以来，世界各地已经建造了200多个托卡马克装置，例如JET（Joint European Torus）、中国环流器二号A（HL-2A）、EAST（Experimental Advanced Superconducting Tokamak）、KSTAR（Korea Superconducting Tokamak Advanced Research）、新一代"人造太阳"（HL-2M）、WEST（Wolfram Environment in Steady-state Tokamak）等，它们为国际项目"ITER"计划提供了丰富的理论支撑及实践经验。

自1985年ITER计划提出以后，数千名工程师和科学家潜心钻研，协力奉献。目前ITER成员包括欧盟、中国、印度、日本、韩国、俄罗斯和美国，正在进行为期35年的合作来建造和运行ITER实验装置，携手发展聚变实验研究，为未来设计示范聚变反应堆奠定基础。

## ITER 概述

ITER主要装置的体积为800m³，是迄今为止最大的托卡马克。该装置工程庞大，技术复杂，部件繁多，其中主要有真空室、磁体、包层、偏滤器、杜瓦/低温恒温器。

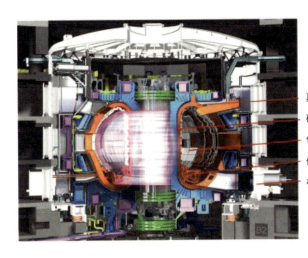

真空室腔体

磁体

包层

偏滤器

杜瓦/低温恒温器

图5. ITER托卡马克装置结构示意

1. 真空室：真空室是一个大型密封的环形真空容器，腔体由厚厚的钢材料制成，ITER实验的聚变反应就在这里进行。同时它也是聚变反应的第一层安全屏障，将等离子体粒子约束在内。真空室为等离子体提供高真空的运行环境，同时提高辐射屏蔽性能以及等离子体稳定性。它不仅是放射性物质的主要屏障，还是内部件（如包层和偏滤器等）的结构支撑。

在托卡马克装置中，真空室容积越大，约束等离子体的时间就越长，就越容易达到较高的聚变输出功率。ITER真空室的直径为19.4米（外径），高11.4米，重约5200吨，容积为1400立方米，所含的等离子体比目前已运行的最大的托卡马克装置内的还高十倍。

2. 磁体：ITER的磁体系统是有史以来规模最大、集成度最高的超导磁体系统，由一万多吨磁铁构成，其磁能储存量达5.1万兆焦耳，用于产生磁场，从而激发和约束等离子体。磁铁由铌锡（Nb3Sn）或铌钛（Nb-Ti）制成，通过零下269℃的氦冷却后，就会变为超导磁体。超导磁体能够携带比传统磁体更高的电流并产生更强的磁场，且能耗低，操作方便……这些优势使得超导磁体技术成为ITER大型磁体系统的不二选择。

3. 包层：它由440个包层模块组成，将真空室内壁完全覆盖。它可以保护内部钢结构以及超导环形磁体，使其免受聚变反应产生的热量和高能中子辐照的影响。当中子辐照到包层时，会在包层中迅速减速，这时中子的动能就会转化为热能，然后被水冷却剂吸收，这些热能也可转换成电能用于未来的聚变发电工程。

包层模块共有180多种（取决于真空室内模块的位置），每个包层的尺寸为1×1.5米，重达4.6吨。它们都具有可拆卸的表面，称为第一壁，还有专门用于屏蔽中子的屏蔽块，并且为诊断观察系统和等离子加热等功能系统预留了窗口。ITER包层表面积为600平方米，第一壁要直接面对等离子体并吸收等离子体带来的热负荷，这是ITER装置中最具技术挑战性的关键部件之一。铍元素由于其低等离子体污染、低燃料保留的物理特性被用于制造第一壁，而包层模块的其余部分由高强度铜和不锈钢制成。ITER通过在4MPa和70℃下注入冷却水来降低高达736MW的辐射热能，是第一个使用主动冷却包层运行的聚变装置。

4.偏滤器：偏滤器位于真空室底部，用于过滤聚变反应产生的热量和废尘，可最大限度地减少等离子体污染，降低热负荷和中子负荷对附近第一壁的影响。ITER偏滤器由54个10吨的"盒式组件"构成，每个组件都有一个不锈钢支撑结构和三个直接面向等离子体的部件——内外部垂直靶和圆顶。组件内还有许多用于等离子体控制和物理评估及优化的诊断部件。内外部垂直靶位于磁感线的交叉处，在ITER装置运行时，粒子轰击十分强烈，当高能等离子体撞击垂直靶材时，其动能转化为热能，并通过主动水冷系统进行冷却。ITER偏滤器垂直靶材持续的热通量约为$10MWm^2$（稳态）和$20MWm^2$（暂态），这对材料的热负荷要求极高。各国科学家们为此苦心孤诣、潜精研思，不断进行模型测试，终于获得了振奋人心的实验结果，于是所有金属中熔点最高的"钨"，被选为该"装甲"材料。ITER偏滤器组件通过远程操作安装和更换以保证其使用期内的可靠性。

5. 杜瓦（低温恒温器）：ITER的杜瓦是目前世界最大的不锈钢高真空压力室（1.6万立方米），可为ITER真空室和超导磁体提供高真空、超低温环境。它的尺寸取决于其周围最大部件（两个最大的极向场线圈）的尺寸，宽和高近30米，内径28米，重3850吨。其基座部分重达1250吨，是ITER托卡马克最大载荷的组件。杜瓦中有23个用于设备维护的贯穿组件，以及200多个用于冷却系统、磁体进料器、辅助加热、诊断以及偏滤器包层部件拆装的贯穿组件，其中一些组件尺寸可达4米。杜瓦和真空室之间用大型波纹管连接，用来补偿不同温度下运行时的结构收缩和膨胀导致的相对位移。

如果能够将上述5个主要部件成功研制并组装，那么ITER仅使用50MW的输入功率即可产生500MW的聚变输出功率，达到Q值（输出功率与输入功率之比）≥10将指日可待，未来的聚变发电工程也必将成功实现。

## ▎后 ITER 时代

在ITER等离子体实验研究的技术经验基础上，将建造一座聚变示范电厂DEMO，将为其设计一套准稳态运行装置，以进行高效能源获取、大规模电力生产以及氚自持等方面的研究。DEMO一词描述的是一个阶段，而非一台机器，预计在21世纪30年代开始建设，40年代投入运营。

DEMO将解决聚变能量引入电网的技术问题，该阶段的主要目标是在准稳态运行条件下，研究聚变装置的有效能量捕获系统，实现Q值范围为30至50（与ITER的10不同）的功率输出，并在容器内产氚（称为氚增殖）。DEMO将比ITER更加简化，其诊断更少，设计更多面向能量捕获，而非等离子体研究。虽然ITER已在建设中，DEMO处于概念设计阶段，但DEMO同时在先进材料开发、氚自持和热耗尽等领域进行着其他不同特性指标装置的补充研发。例如，在日本，国际聚变材料辐照装置（IFMIF）项目的工程验证阶段已经开始，该装置将进行全尺寸聚变电站所需先进材料的测试认证。

除DEMO外，生产聚变能还有最后一步——建造一个原型反应堆，该反应堆经过全面优化，可进行更具商业优势的发电。这一聚变能源发展阶段预计在21世纪中叶达到。

### 作者简介

李飞，目前在核工业西南物理研究院聚变反应堆包层工程技术中心工作，担任机械设计负责人，来中国工作之前在ITER国际组织担任机械设计师。主要成就：五年托卡马克装置屏蔽块及测试包层主要机械设计师，三年托卡马克装置第一壁主要机械设计师。负责ITER 国际计划参与方国家（欧盟、中国、俄罗斯及韩国）承担的 ITER 部件技术指导与设计协调工作。

# What is Nuclear Fusion

By Rafael Nieto [France]

SWIP Science Popularization Group

## ▌ The Power of Iron-man: Fusion Energy

The energy is at the heart of our modern society. Scientist around the world spend a lot of resources trying to find new ways to produce energy, which are more reliable, efficient and environmentally friendly. Difficulty of making energy is an interesting topic not only for scientists but also for writers to creative science fiction books or movies, which are full of innovative ideas. Iron-Man, the famous film, is one of them. If you have seen this movie, you may ask the question: Why can Iron- Man continue to fight, as if he is filled with unlimited energy? In fact, the key to Iron-Man's power is a high-tech he invented, the mini nuclear fusion reactor at the chest of armor, which can continuously release energy.

His invention could be more science than fiction. Since the first fusion reaction realized in a laboratory in 1934, scientists of the world are trying to make fusion reaction a viable source of energy. Could you imagine that one day, we could master the power of fusion energy, just like the Iron-man who has nearly unlimited source of energy, to power our homes, planes and cars. Well, this day may come soon!

Figure 1. Nuclear fusion in Iron-Man

# ▌ What is Nuclear Fusion?

Nuclear fusion and fission, are both processes to produce a huge thermal energy by nuclear reaction with the goal to produce electricity. But the difference is that, the nuclear fission reaction is the splitting of a heavier nucleus into two or more lighter nuclei; Nuclear fusion reaction is the polymerization of two lighter nuclei to produce a new heavier nucleus.

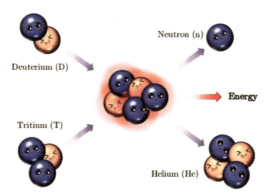

Figure 2. Schematic diagram of nuclear fusion reaction

It's the same reaction which can be found in stellar interior like our sun. When the hydrogen atom is heated by 15 million degrees high temperature in the sun, it is ionized into a hydrogen plasma. Plasma is a gas-like substance formed after the ionization of gas, which is composed of positive and negative ions, and is the fourth state of matter different from gas, liquid and solid. Under the high pressure environment of 250 billion atmospheric pressure, the atomic nuclei of these hydrogen plasma collide with each other, and nuclear fusion reaction occurs.

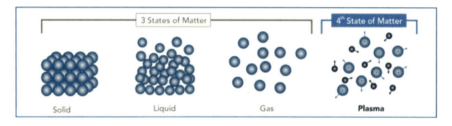

Figure 3. Schematic diagram of plasma

The mass loses during this fusion. Loss of mass produces energy. It's the famous Einstein equation, $E=mc^2$: Energy is equal mass multiply by square light speed, an extremely large number. Therefore, the loss of mass, even tiny, will produce an unbelievable quantity of energy.

Theoretically nuclear fusion is possible on earth to power a turbine and produce a lot of electricity, on the same principle as current fission nuclear plant. With fusion or fission, the heat produced increases the temperature of a primary water circuit, which then heats a secondary water circuit. The resulting steam makes a turbine rotate, generating electricity using an alternator.

## ▎ Advantage of Fusion

Nuclear fusion energy is an almost perfect energy source: its raw materials are abundant in nature and easy to obtain. Tritium and other hydrogen isotopes can be extracted from seawater. The energy release efficiency of the reaction is extremely high, second only to that of the annihilation of positive and negative matter. The product has no pollution and produces no greenhouse gas.

For example, a large coal-burning power station with a capacity of 1 million kilowatts needs to burn 1.5 to 2 million tons of coal each year, with a carbon dioxide emission of 400-540 tons. The nuclear fission substation of the same power consumes about 30 tons of uranium fuel a year and has no carbon dioxide emission. While a nuclear fusion power station generate the same energy with no carbon dioxide emissions by consuming only 150 kg of heavy water and lithium every year.

At the same time, nuclear fusion reaction is also very safe. It will stop and no other chain reaction will occur, if any parameter makes it fail to meet the fusion "ignition" condition. If human beings have mastered the controllable magnetic confinement nuclear fusion reaction technology and use seawater as fuel, the fusion energy will be inexhaustible.

## ▎ From Theory to Practice: Challenges of Producing Electricity from Fusion

Despite having many theoretical advantages, fusion remain a

technical utopia. Known as "fusion triple product", the product of three parameters, namely, the temperature, density and energy constraint time of plasma, must reach as certain value to realize fusion "ignition". So if we want to "reproduce" a nuclear fusion device which is similar to the Sun, we need to meet strict conditions:

·To be able to maintain a high temperature——hundreds of millions of degrees Celsius;

·To constrain plasma operation for a long time;

·Finally, to make the plasma density high enough.

Figure 4.  Plasma in a nuclear fusion device

To achieve nuclear fusion, it remains to generate the plasma. Currently, two techniques are mainly studied by scientists in order to produce plasma: inertial confinement and magnetic confinement.

The first method, inertial confinement,  consists in heating with the help of laser beams energy – 300,000 billion watts –a metal capsule about two millimeters large and containing the main resources for fusion – tritium and deuterium. Hit by the significant amount of energy, the envelope of the capsule will turn into plasma. Under the effect of pressure, the nuclei merge and produce energy.

The second method, magnetic confinement, the main method at present, The magnetic field around the electrified conductor makes the charged particles (ultrahigh temperature plasma) constrained in a limited volume by the Lorentz force, then nuclear fusion reaction occurs. Thus, Tokamak, one of the most representative magnetic confinement fusion devices, came into being.

## ▌ ITER - the Way of Fusion

Tokamak thereby have been chosen by the project ITER as the most suitable way of making fusion. From Latin "The Way", ITER is one of the most ambitious energy projects in the world today on the way of fusion.

In southern France, 35 nations are collaborating to build the world's largest tokamak, a magnetic fusion device that has been designed to prove the feasibility of fusion as a large-scale and carbon-free source of energy.

It can be seen that, the experimental campaign that will be carried out at ITER is crucial to advancing fusion science and preparing the way for the fusion power plants of tomorrow.

Since the 1950s, more than 200 tokamaks have been built around the world, such as JET (Joint European Torus), HL-2A, EAST (Experimental Advanced Superconducting Tokamak), KSTAR (Korea Superconducting Tokamak Advanced Research), the new generation of "artificial sun"(HL-2M), WEST (Wolfram Environment in Steady-state Tokamak) ,etc. These different projects provide knowledge to the great international project "ITER" (International Thermonuclear Experimental Reactor).

Thousands of engineers and scientists have contributed to the design of ITER since the idea for an international joint experiment in fusion was first launched in 1985. The ITER Members—China, the European Union, India, Japan, Korea, Russia and the United States—are now engaged in a 35-year collaboration to build and operate the ITER experimental device, and together bring fusion to the point where a demonstration fusion reactor can be designed.

## ITER in the Details

With a volume of $800m^3$, ITER is by far the biggest tokamak ever built. This incredibly complex machine relies on 5 main components. Those are Vacuum Vessel, Magnets, Blanket, Divertor, Cryostat.

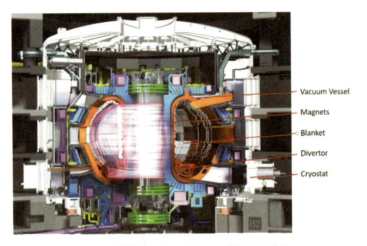

Figure 5. Schematic diagram of tokamak of ITER

1. Vacuum Vessel: Vacuum Vessel, a hermetically sealed thick steel

toroidal vacuum container that houses the fusion reactions of ITER and acts as a first safety containment barrier. The plasma is in its doughnut-shaped chamber, or torus, without touching the walls. The vacuum vessel provides a high-vacuum environment for the plasma, improves radiation shielding and plasma stability, acts as the primary confinement barrier for radioactivity, and provides support for in-vessel components such as the blanket and the divertor.

In a tokamak device, the larger the vacuum chamber volume, the easier it is to confine the plasma and achieve the type of high energy regime that will produce significant fusion power. The ITER vacuum vessel will measure 19.4 meters across (outer diameter), 11.4 meters high, and weigh approximately 5,200 tons. Its interior volume is 1,400 $m^3$. The volume of the plasma contained in the center of the vessel is fully ten times larger than that of the largest operating tokamak in the world today.

2. Magnets: The ITER magnet system will be the largest and most integrated superconducting magnet system ever built. Ten thousand tons of magnets, with a combined stored magnetic energy of 51 Gigajoules (GJ), will produce the magnetic fields that will initiate, confine, shape and control the ITER plasma. Manufactured from niobium-tin (Nb3Sn) or niobium-titanium (Nb-Ti), the magnets become superconducting when cooled with supercritical helium in the range of -269 °C. Superconducting magnets are able to carry higher current and produce stronger magnetic field than conventional counterparts. They also consume less power and are cheaper to operate ... making superconducting magnet technology the only option for ITER's huge magnet systems.

3. Blanket: The 440 blanket modules that completely cover the inner walls of the vacuum vessel protect the steel structure and the superconducting toroidal field magnets from the heat and high-energy neutrons produced by the fusion reactions. As the neutrons are slowed in the blanket, their kinetic energy is transformed into heat energy and collected by the water coolant. In a fusion power plant, this energy will be used for electrical power production.

Each blanket module measures 1 x 1.5 meters and weighs up to 4.6 tons. Over 180 design variants exist (related to the position of the modules in the vacuum vessel), but all have a detachable first wall, and a main shield block that is designed for neutron shielding. The blanket modules also provide passageways for diagnostic viewing systems and plasma heating systems. The ITER blanket, which covers a surface of 600 $m^2$, is one of the most critical and technically challenging components in ITER: it directly faces the hot plasma. Due to its unique physical properties (low plasma contamination, low fuel retention), beryllium has been chosen as the element to cover the first wall. The rest of the blanket modules will be made of high-strength copper and stainless steel. ITER will be the first fusion device to operate with an actively cooled blanket. The cooling water—injected at 4 MPa and 70 °C—is designed to remove up to 736 MW of thermal power.

4. Divertor: Situated at the bottom of the vacuum vessel, the divertor extracts heat and ash produced by the fusion reaction, minimizes plasma contamination, and protects the surrounding walls from thermal and neutronic loads. Each of the divertor's 54 ten-ton "cassette assemblies" has a supporting structure in stainless steel and three plasma-facing

components: the inner and outer vertical targets and the dome. The cassette assemblies also host a number of diagnostic components for plasma control and physics evaluation and optimization. The inner and outer vertical targets are positioned at the intersection of magnetic field lines where particle bombardment will be particularly intense in ITER. As the high-energy plasma particles strike the vertical targets, their kinetic energy is transformed into heat and the heat is removed by active water cooling.The heat flux sustained by the ITER divertor vertical targets is estimated at 10 $MWm^2$ (steady state) and 20 $MWm^2$(slow transients). It requires extremely high thermal load of materials. Tungsten, with the highest melting point of all the metals, has been chosen as the armor material following an international R&D effort, encouraging experimental results, and successful prototype testing. The cassette assemblies of the ITER divertor will be installed—and also replaced at least once during the machine's lifetime—by remote handling.

5. Cryostat: The ITER cryostat—the largest stainless steel high-vacuum pressure chamber ever built (16,000 $m^3$)—provides the high vacuum, ultra-cool environment for the ITER vacuum vessel and the superconducting magnets. Nearly 30 meters wide and as many in height, the internal diameter of the cryostat (28 meters) has been determined by the size of the largest components its surrounds: the two largest poloidal field coils. Manufactured from stainless steel, the cryostat weighs 3,850 tons. Its base section—1,250 tons—will be the single largest load of ITER Tokamak assembly. The cryostat has 23 penetrations to allow access for maintenance as well as over 200 penetrations—some as large as four meters in size—that provide access for cooling systems, magnet feeders,

auxiliary heating, diagnostics, and the removal of blanket sections and parts of the divertor. Large bellows situated between the cryostat and the vacuum vessel will allow for thermal contraction and expansion in the structures during operation.

If these 5 main components can be successfully manufacture and assemble all together, then ITER will be able to produce 500MW of fusion power using only 50MW of heating power, making a ratio of Q≥10, and demonstrating the viability of fusion energy.

## ▌ After ITER

For the demonstration power plant (DEMO), the knowledge and the know-how garnered during the exploration of ITER's hot plasmas will be used to conceive a machine that will explore continuous or near-continuous (steady-state) operation and test the large-scale production of electrical power and tritium fuel self-sufficiency. The term DEMO describes more of a phase than a single machine. Construction is foreseen to start in the 2030s, and operation in the 2040s.

DEMO will address the technological questions of bringing fusion energy to the electricity grid. The principal goals for the DEMO phase of fusion research are the exploration of continuous or near-continuous (steady-state) operation, the investigation of efficient energy capture systems, the achievement of a power output in the Q-value range of 30 to 50 (as opposed to ITER's 10), and the in-vessel production of tritium (called tritium breeding). DEMO would be a simpler machine than ITER, with fewer diagnostics and a design more targeted to the capture of energy than to the exploration of plasma regimes. While ITER is under construction and DEMO is in its conceptual phase, other installations with diverse characteristics and objectives are planned to conduct complementary research and development in the areas of advanced material development, tritium self-sufficiency, and heat exhaustion. In Japan, for example, the engineering validation phase for the International Fusion Materials Irradiation Facility (IFMIF) program has begun. This installation will test and qualify the advanced materials needed for a full-scale fusion plant.

Beyond DEMO, the final step to produceg fusion energy would be the construction of a prototype reactor, fully optimized to produce electricity competitively. Most forecasts place this phase of fusion energy development at the middle of the century.

### About the author

Rafael Nieto, currently working in the Fusion Reactor Blanket Engineering Technology Center of the Southwestern Institute of Physics. He served as the head of mechanical design in the technical center, and worked as a mechanical designer in the ITER International Organization before coming to China. The main

achievements are: five years as the main mechanical designer of shield blocks and test blanket for tokamak devices, three years as the main mechanical designer of the first wall of tokamak devices. Responsible for coordinating the technical guidance and design coordination of ITER components undertaken by the participating countries of the ITER international program (EU, China, Russia and South Korea).

# 无处不在的AI

文 / 郑子斌 [新加坡]

今天我们的生活中人工智能无处不在，我们身边的手机、平板、电脑、智能音箱等各类智能设备和服务后面隐藏着各种先进的人工智能算法。虽然人类文明上下五千年，但近几十年科技发展更加迅速。尤其是在人工智能领域，科技有了突破性的进展。我们回顾一下人类科技的历史，这能帮助我们从一个更广泛的角度去感受人工智能的诞生及发展。

最早在公元前11000年至公元前8000年，人类社会的第一次跟科技相关的革命——第一次农业革命在整个地球的各个族群、各个地区不约而同地发生了。人类成功驯化了牲畜、种植了谷物、发明了石器。在这次革命中，人类完成了向农耕文明的转化。

> **有趣小知识**　经过历史考证，农业革命——又名新石器革命最早发生的地点是中东的一个地区。这个地区有多条河流，土地十分肥沃，形状又像月牙一样，所以又名新月沃土（The Fertile Crescent）。

直到公元后1760年，人类社会的第二次跟科技相关的革命——第一次工业革命迈开了它的脚步。在这次革命中，人类利用蒸汽动力和水动力完成了从手工生产向机器生产的转变，影响了人们生活的方方面面，如纺织品和化工产品的大规模生产，复杂机械制品，水泥，等等。

之后的科技发展节奏越来越快。随着电气的广泛应用，以电灯为代表的第二次工业革命在1870年展开；1969年人类首次登上了月球；20世纪90年代，互联网被广泛应用；2002年SpaceX航空航天器制造公司成立，提供商用太空运输服务。

当我们回顾人类科技发展的历史时，会注意到有一个有趣的现象，就是人类的科技发展是不断在加速的。科技发展从早期手工作坊，转向了机器时代，直到今天数字时代。人类的创造能力被逐步地释放出来，科幻小说中的各种场景正在变成现实。我们可以借鉴一下哲学家里奇塔（Radovan Richta）的理论，"人类科技最终将向自动化全面转变"。未来人类文明将走向何方呢？在科学业界有一种普遍的认知，为了解决人类发展的限制，人类文明最终将走向宇宙，成为真正的星际文明。今天有的企业家正在将这个梦想变成现实。当我们激动地畅想未来生活的时候，毫无疑问人工智能将是这些未来场景后面最重要的基石之一。

**有趣小知识** 为什么技术发展会逐步加速？因为科技发展类似进化过程，而进化是加速发展的。库兹韦尔（Kurzweil）在

2001年解释道：“技术发展实质上是一种进化行为，而进化行为会对积极的反馈做出响应，更多积极反馈会被传递到下一个阶段。”这最终导致进化的加速。

## 什么是人工智能呢？

现在人工智能比较被广泛接受的定义是，通过机器模拟的人类认知能力——解决问题的能力和做决定的能力。

经历了几十年的发展，人工智能领域并不是一帆风顺的，其间经历了几次起起伏伏。大致上可以分为三个阶段：人工智能的兴起、机器学习的萌芽，以及今天的人工智能的再次腾飞。

## 人工智能的兴起

20世纪50年代，科学家、数学家和哲学家都在探讨人工智能的基本概念。其中最著名的是英国数学家图灵（Alan Turing）。图灵指出机器也能像人类一样，利用有效的信息作为理性的原因，去解决问题并做出决定。1950年，图灵发表了一个逻辑框架论文，讨论如何构建一个智能机器，以及如何去测试这台机器的智能。

**有趣小知识** 图灵测试是机器是否跟人类的表现一致的测试。图灵假设有一位人类评估者，事先知道他要面对一台机器或一位人类进行文字沟通，但不知道具体哪个是机器哪一个是人类。经过评估者跟两个对象分别沟通后，如果评估者无法区分哪一个是机器哪一个是人类，那就说明机器通过了图灵测试。

1956年，在英国达特茅斯（Dartmouth）举办了一个学术研讨会，在这个为期八周的会议上，"人工智能"这个领域词被正式提出，人工智能的可能性被大家认同，研究方向被广泛讨论。约有20位数学家和科学家共同讨论了人工智能领域的各种可能性，涉及方方面面，例如神经网络、符号学、早期的专家系统等等。这次会议被广泛视为人工智能领域的开创会议。

**有趣小知识** 1955年，约翰·麦卡锡（John McCarthy）为这个领域挑选了一个名字：人工智能（Artificial Intelligence），之前人工智能还有另外一个名字：思想机器（Thinking Machine）。对比这个老名字，人工智能更被大家认可。从这点看如果你能够选个好名字，你也会被历史铭记。

1964年，首台聊天机器人ELIZA诞生了，使用了脚本方式来模拟心理治疗。尽管它的创建者坚持它远没有智能，但是部分使用者发现，在与它对话中的某些时刻，会有跟真人对话的感觉。

之后，几份重要的人工智能领域的研究报告，引发了人工智能领域的冬天。分别是1966年美国的自动语言处理顾问协会（ALPAC）和1973年英国数学家詹姆斯·赖特希尔（James Lighthill）的研究报告。ALPAC的报告反映了公众对于人工智能领域的发展速度的失望。而赖特希尔的报告直接给出悲观的预测："人工智能领域的任何研究都无法做出之前承诺过的重要突破。"这些严厉的批评和质疑导致各个国家对人工智能领域的研究经费大幅削减。

## ▌ 机器学习的萌芽

1980年，专家系统成为人工智能研究的焦点，并被积极商业化。美国卡耐基梅隆大学（CMU）为DEC公司开发了XCON专家系统，在1986年为公司节约了4000万美元左右的费用，特别是在决策方面能提供有价值的辅助。

1987年，Apple和IBM生产的个人台式电脑机的性能已经超过了Symbolics（一家从麻省理工学院人工智能实验室分拆出的电脑公司）和其他厂家生产的昂贵的专家系统机，专家系统产品失去了存在的理由。到1991年，人们发现十年前日本人宏伟的"第五代工程"并没有实现；1993年，大量的公司倒闭，一夜之间人工智能的第一次商业化浪潮结束了。

## ▌ 人工智能的再次腾飞

1997年，IBM公司的国际象棋电脑深蓝（DeepBlue）战胜了国际象棋世界冠军卡斯帕罗夫（Garry Kasparov），它的运算速度为每秒2亿步棋，并存有70万份大师对战的棋局数据。

2011年，IBM开发的人工智能程序"沃森"（Watson）参加了一档智力问答节目并战胜了两位人类冠军。沃森存储了2亿页数据，能够将与问题相关的关键词从看似相关的答案中抽取出来。这一人工智能程序已被IBM广泛应用于医疗诊断领域。

2016年，阿尔法狗（AlphaGo）战胜欧洲围棋冠军，开启了与人类的不断挑战并均获胜。AlphaGo，具有自我学习能力。它能够收集大量围棋对弈数据和名人棋谱，学习并模仿人类下棋。与此同时，无人驾驶路面测试在越来越多的国家和地区获得许可。

尽管经历了几十年的发展，人工智能领域的研究有了长足进步，但对于哲学家，现在的人工智能能力仍然非常原始。哲学家约翰·赛尔（John Searle）提出了对人工智能的分类：强人工智能和弱人工智能。

这个分类的定义来源于赛尔在1984年提出的一个著名的思想实验：中文房间问题。这个实验是为了驳斥一个广泛存在的理解：机器可以拥有思想，人工智能等同于意识。最终业界普遍认同现在的人工智能研究都属于弱人工智能，弱人工智能不能产生意识：在特定领域，人工智能系统表现得好像有意识，但实际上并不拥有；而强人工智能是指人工智能系统拥有像人类一样的意识，也是科幻小说中经常提到的有自主意识的机器人。

有趣小知识 弱人工智能和强人工智能也许没有本质区别，弱人工智能发展到一定程度就变为了强人工智能。现在仍然有很多计算机科学的专家是同意这个观点的。如果换个有意思的角度：模拟的意识能变为真实的意识，那么真实的意识可能并不存在，只是一种错觉。

在今天，我们现在常见的人工智能系统仍然都属于弱人工智能，如视觉识别、语音识别以及推荐系统。

现在我们讲一讲人工智能的实际案例。我们先讲一个关于人工智能识别小猫小狗的案例。在这个例子里我们将阐述一下人工智能的工作流程。首先我们要准备一组小猫小狗的图片和一个人工智能的模型。我们使用这组图片来训练我们的人工智能模型。在这组小猫小狗的图片里，我们明确知道哪些图片是小猫，哪些图片是小狗。这样我们就能够开始训练模型：通过输入这些图片，并告诉人工智能模型程序识别的结果是否正确，让模型进行自我修正。经过反复多次的训练，人工智能模型就能够比较准确地识别结果了。通常识别的正确概率并不是100%，而是例如92%，95%甚至97%。经过调整和反复训练，人工智能模型的准确率会不断提高。当达到一个满意结果，如97%，人工智能模型就可以让大家正式使用了。

不知道大家有没有用过小度音箱、天猫精灵？在这些智能设备里，使用了人工智能语音识别的功能。那么人工智能语音识别怎样运行的呢？将语音变为文字大致分为三个步骤：音频预处理，数据通过模型识别结果，文字和识别结果匹配。首先我们需要将音频数据处理为广谱图像，然后建立人工智能模型通过训练识别光谱图像的特征。当我们取得这些特征后，我们会通过一种叫做CTC的方法，将图像与文字进行最优化的匹配。最终我们就得到了音频与文字匹配的识别结果。

在我们的日常数字生活里，无论买东西，看视频，都会涉及一个幕后隐藏的系统：推荐系统。推荐系统会在幕后默默工作，它会根据你的喜好，向你推荐你可能感兴趣的内容和物品，简化查找的过程。基于人工智能的推荐系统也是人工智能技术最成功应用的领域之一。在推荐系统的模型中，模型会利用你的浏览历史记录、相似行为的用户或好友，以及你自己的特征标签，来进行预测，排列出跟这些信息最匹配的物品或内容。

在今天这个大数据时代，人工智能在很多地方都取得了成功，人工智能的科技创新正在潜移默化地对我们生活的方方面面产生重要的影响。通过人工智能的优势，我们轻易解决了很多之前很难解决甚至无法解决的问题。当人工智能在更多的地方取得成功，我们未来的生活会变得更美好。

**有趣小知识** 什么是科技创新呢？科技创新不仅是发明新的科学理论，而是应用新的科学理论，在生活中发明新的事物，为人类社会创造新的价值。

## 作者简介

郑子斌，毕业于美国加州伯克利大学和美国斯坦福大学，分别获得计算机科学及人工智能学学士学位与硕士学位。

自2021年7月1日起，郑子斌加入宾理，负责人工智能及软件战略，基于强大的算力能力和云基础架构平台，通过领先的AI算法能力打造宾理辅助系统，为用户提供全感知、全响应、全触达的智能服务。

加入宾理之前，从2019年7月1日起郑子斌担任VIPKID首席技术官，负责公司整体教研、产品及技术战略，推动AI前沿技术与在线教育场景的深度融合与应用，打造教育市场行业标杆。

此前，郑子斌担任百度搜索公司CTO，负责百度搜索和信息流等核心业务的技术战略布局，同时全面负责百度大商业体系，包括搜索广告、信息流广告、联盟广告等核心业务板块，用产品技术驱动公司营收高速发展，9年时间实现业绩20倍增长。2011年创办百度美国硅谷研发公司，并兼任总经理，吸引硅谷高端人才，打造世界一流AI研发团队。郑子斌有深厚的国际化背景、丰富的研发和管理经验，曾在Google总部、阿里巴巴、Oracle等知名企业担任重要技术和管理岗位。

# AI Is Everywhere

By Alex Cheng (Singapore)

Artificial Intelligence is everywhere in our lives today. Various advanced Artificial Intelligence algorithms are hidden behind mobile phones, tablets, computers, smart speakers, various smart devices and services around us. After 10,000 years of human civilization, science and technology evolve more rapidly in recent decades than ever before, especially in the field of Artificial Intelligence (AI). Let us review the history of technology revolutions to help us understand the evolution of Artificial Intelligence from a broader perspective.

As early as 11,000 BC to 8,000 BC, the first technology-related revolution happened in human history-the first agricultural revolution occurred in all ethnic groups and regions on this blue planet. Humans had successfully domesticated various animal species, farmed grains, and invented stone tools. This transition was associated with subsequent series of changes from largelya nomadic hunter-gatherer way of life to a more settled, agrarian one, laying the foundation for the further development of civilizations.

> **Tidbit:** *Archaeological data indicates that the earliest location of the First Agricultural Revolution was in the Middle East - also known as the Neolithic Revolution. This region was alongside several rivers and marshlands. The shape of the land is like a crescent moon, thus it is called The Fertile Crescent.*

From 1760, the second technology-related revolution in human history-the first industrial revolution took its footsteps. In this revolution, the increasing use of steam power and water power led to the transition from manual methods to new machinaries, new chemical manufacturing and pro production processes. Various new technological inventions have deeply affected all aspects of our lives, such as mass production of textiles and chemical products, complex machinery products, cement, etc.

Since then, the pace of technological development has become faster and faster. With the widespread application of electricity, the second industrial revolution represented by electric lights began in 1870; in 1969, humans set foot on the Moon for the first time; in the 1990s, the use of Internet exploded; in 2002, SpaceX was established, an aerospace manufacturing company providing space transportation services.

As we review the history of science and technology evolution, we will notice an interesting phenomenon that the development of human science and technology is constantly accelerating. The innovative ability of human beings has been continuously released, turning many science fictions into reality. Where is the technology evolution heading? We can learn from the theory of a philosopher Radovan Richta: the transition is destined for fully automation. Then where will human civilization lead to? There is a general perception among scholars that in order to solve the limitations of our planet, human civilization will eventually go to the universe and become a true galactic civilization. Today, some entrepreneurs are turning this dream into reality. As we passionately imagine the future life, there is no doubt that AI will be one of the most important cornerstones behind these future scenarios.

*Tidbit: Why does technological evolution gradually accelerate? This will be a very interesting topic if discussed in depth. Kurzweil wrote in 2001: "Evolution applies positive feedback. The more capable methods resulting from one stage of evolutionary progress are used to create the next stage." The behavior of this evolutionary transmission will eventually lead to the acceleration of evolution.*

## ▌ What is Artificial Intelligence?

The more widely accepted definition of AI is that Artificial Intelligence leverages machines to mimic the problem-solving and decision-making capabilities of the human mind.

After decades of development, the field of Artificial Intelligence has not always been smooth sailing, and has experienced several ups and downs. It can be roughly divided into three stages: the rise of Artificial Intelligence, the blooming of machine learning, and the revival of today's

Artificial Intelligence.

## ▌ The Rising of Artificial Intelligence

In the 1950s, a generation of scientists, mathematicians, and philosophers had explored the basic concept of AI. Alan Turing, a famous British mathematician, is one of such persons. Turing suggested that machines could behave, just like humans, in using available information to reason, solve problems and make decisions. This was the logical framework of his 1950 paper, in which he discussed how to build intelligent machines and how to test the intelligence of this machine.

> *Tidbit:* *The Turing test is a test of a machine's ability to exhibit intelligent behavior equivalent to a human. Turing proposed that a human evaluator would judge natural language conversations between a human and a machine. The evaluator would be aware that one of the two partners is a machine. If the evaluator cannot reliably tell the machine from the human, the machine is said to have passed the test.*

In 1956, The Dartmouth Workshop was organized lasting approximately six to eight weeks, in which the field called 'Artificial Intelligence' was formally introduced and widely accepted. About 20 mathematicians and scientists attended this workshop covering every aspect of intelligence that be done with machines, such as neural networks, symbolic methods, early expert systems, and so on. This workshop marked the founding event of Artificial Intelligence as a field of research.

> **Tidbit:** *In 1955, John McCarthy picked a name for the field: Artificial Intelligence. Before this, there was old name: Thinking Machine. Compared to the old name, Artificial Intelligence is more popular. From this point of view, if you could pick a good name, you will be remembered in history.*

In 1964, the first chatbot, ELIZA, was born which could simulate a psychologist therapy based on a scripted approach. Despite its creator's insistence that ELIZA could not truly understand, some users discovered the feeling of talking to a real human being at certain moments of conversations.

In the 1970s, several infamous reports in the field of Artificial Intelligence triggered the AI winter, particularly the American Automatic Language Processing Consultants Association (ALPAC) report for U.S. Government in 1966 and the Lighthill report for British government in 1973. ALPAC's report echoed the disappointments felt by the public and pointed out the researchers still need much more basic study. The Lighthill report directly gave a pessimistic prediction: "In no part of the field have discoveries made so far produced the major impact that was then promised." These reports had the deadly effect of cutting research funding in this field across many countries.

## ▮ The Blooming of Machine Learning

In 1980, the expert system became the focus of AI research and was actively commercialized. XCON an expert system was developed at Carnegie Mellon University (CMU) for DEC, which saved the company about 40 million dollars by 1986, especially by reducing errors made by technicians and speeding the assembly process.

In 1987, personal desktop computers from Apple and IBM had become more powerful than the expensive expert system machines from Symbolics and others. By 1991, it was found that the goals of Japan's "Fifth Generation Project" did not materialize after ten years. In 1993, an entire industry was demolished overnight, effectively ending the first commercial wave of AI.

## ▮ The Revival of Artificial Intelligence

In 1997, DeepBlue, the chess-playing computer, defeated world chess champion Garry Kasparov. It was capable of processing 200 million moves per second, and stored the games data of over 700,000 grandmasters.

In 2011, IBM's other Artificial Intelligence system "Watson" participated in a quiz show and defeated the two greatest human champions. Watson stores 200 million pages of content and is able to extract relevant keywords from questions from relevant answers. This question-answering AI skills has been widely used by IBM in the field of medical diagnosis.

In 2016, AlphaGo defeated the European Go champion and started a constant challenge with humans to win. AlphaGo, with self-learning ability. It can collect a large amount of Go game data and famous records, learn and imitate how humans play. On the other side, AI based self-driving testing on public road is licensed in a number of countries.

The field of Artificial Intelligence has made tremendous progress after decades of development, but in the eyes of philosophers the capabilities of Artificial Intelligence today are still very primitive. Philosopher John Searle proposed a classification of Artificial Antelligence: strong Artificial Intelligence and weak Artificial Intelligence.

The definition of this classification came from a famous thought experiment proposed by Searle in 1984: the Chinese room argument. The experiment was designed to refute a widely held point that machines can have understanding and that artificial intelligence could rise to consciousness. In the end, the industry generally agrees that the current Artificial Intelligence research belongs to weak Artificial Intelligence, and weak Artificial Intelligence may seem to have consciousness, but they do not actually possess them. While strong Artificial Intelligence means the systems have human-like consciousness, just like the self-conscious robots often mentioned in science fictions.

**Tidbit:** *There could be no essential difference between weak AI and strong AI. While weak AI develops in a certain level, it might become strong AI automatically. Today there are many computer scientists who agree with this. But you might express it in another way: if simulated consciousness could become real consciousness, real consciousness may not exist indeed, just be an illusion.*

Today, most Artificial Intelligence systems are still weak AI, such as visual recognition, speech recognition, and recommendation systems.

Let's explain a practical case of AI visual recognition program. We will illustrate the process of this AI program by classifying photos of cats and dogs. First, we need to prepare a set of photos of cats or dogs with classified marks, then set up an AI model. With these photos, we clearly know which ones are cats and which ones are dogs. We then use these photos to train the AI model by telling it if it works correctly and letting it correct itself. Through repeating previous process, the AI model will become more accurate to identify the results. Usually the accuracy of classification is not 100%, but perhaps 92%, 95% or even 97%. After adjustment and repeated training, the accuracy of the AI model will continue to improve. After reaching a satisfied result, such as 97%, the AI model will be ready for everyone to use.

Do you ever use Xiaodu smart speakers and Tmall Genie? These smart devices use AI technology for speech recognition. How does AI speech recognition operate? In a nutshell, transforming speech into words involves three steps: audio pre-processing, data transform into symbolic features, and words matching the features. First, speech audio data are transformed into a broad-spectrum image, and then use an AI model to recognize the symbolic features of the image. With these symbolic features result, we can use a method called CTC to match the most appropriate set of words with these features. Finally, we get the text result matching the audio of the speech.

In our daily digital life, whether buying things or watching videos, there is often a hidden system behind the scenes: a recommender system. The recommender system tries to understand your interests and what you like, automatically suggests content and items based on your preferences, thereby simplifying the process of searching. Recommender system is also one of the most successful applications of AI technology. Within the recommender system, an AI model uses your browsing history, behavioral data of people similar to you or your friends, as well as your own attribute tags to make predictions and rank the most matching items or content for you.

Today in the age of big data, AI is successfully applied in many aspects of our lives, making significant impacts in the way we live. With the advantages of AI, we can easily solve many problems that are difficult or even impossible to solve before. As AI become even more successful in everywhere, our future will become even better.

*Tidbit:* *What is technological innovation? Technological innovation is not the invention of new scientific theories, but the application of new scientific theories to implement new things and create new value for human society.*

**About the Author**

Alex Cheng graduated from Stanford University and received his Master's degree in Computer Science (Artificial Intelligence). He has over 20 years of managerial and product development experience in US & Chinese high-tech companies. He devoted to internet marketing technology innovation more than a decade, and he also is a senior practitioner of Artificial Intelligence and big data field.

Since July 1st 2021, Alex Cheng joined BeyonCa, responsible for artificial intelligence and software strategy. Alex is working on building BeyonCa Assistant through leading AI algorithm capability, to provide users an intelligent service with total sensing, total responding and total reach.

Before that, Alex served VIPKID from July 1st, 2019. As the CTO of the company, he took great measures in planning, composing and execution of both company's overall product and technology strategy. He also stressed considerable emphasis on the development of Artificial Intelligence as well as the integration of cutting-edge technology into online education scenarios, so as to maintain the leading status of the company's product in education industry.

Prior to joining VIPKID, Alex served as the CTO of Baidu Search, responsible for the technical strategic layout of Baidu search、Feeds and other core businesses, he was also fully responsible for Baidu's large business system, including search business, Feeds advertising, alliance advertising and other core business sectors. He has helped achieving a 20-fold increase in performance growth in 9 years. In 2011, he founded Baidu USA in Silicon Valley and served as general manager to attract high-end talents from Silicon Valley and build a world-class AI R&D team.

Prior to Baidu, he held senior engineering management roles in Google and Alibaba. With his leadership search-advertising revenue has seen a significant growth by technology innovations in digital marketing and advanced AI in consumer intent prediction and insights since 2010.

# 纳米科技：改变我们对物质的认识

文 / 穆罕默德·沙法 [ 巴基斯坦 ]

译 / 王受信

我们为什么应该关注纳米科技？因为它将改变我们的生活，改变我们对物质的认知。1999年由美国国家科学基金会召集的顶级科学家曾说："纳米科技对21世纪人类健康、财富和生活水平的影响，至少可以与20世纪发展的微电子、医学成像、计算机辅助工程和人造聚合物的综合影响一样重要。"

想要了解纳米科技，我们首先得明白什么是纳米。纳米和米一样，都是长度单位，1纳米等于$10^{-9}$米。这是什么概念呢？把一个1纳米的物体放到乒乓球上，就像把乒乓球放到地球上一样。在1—100纳米范围里研究物质的特性和相互作用包括对原子、分子的操纵叫做纳米科技。纳米科技是一个多学科领域，不仅聚焦于材料、物理、化学，还有生物学、工程学和计算科学等，正是由于它的多学科性，纳米科技需要我们去关注不同领域的知识。

## ▋ 纳米科技的起源

1959年12月，物理学家Richard Feynman在加利福尼亚理工学院召开的美国物理学学会上发表了一篇名为《底部还有很大空间》的著名演讲，描述了未来科学家能够操纵和控制单个原子和分子的过程。他的这一预言被科学界称为纳米科技萌芽的标志。纳米科技一词则由日本学者谷口纪男在1974年开始使用。直到1981年，扫描隧道显微镜的发展让科学家看到了单个原子，现代纳米科技才开始发展起来。

## ▋ 物质在纳米尺度三大效应

### 1. 表面效应

球形颗粒的表面积与直径的平方成正比，其体积与直径的立方成正比，故其比表面积（表面积/体积）与直径成反比。随着颗粒直径的变小，比表面积将会显著地增加，颗粒表面原子数相对增多，从而使这些表面原子具有很高的活性且极不稳定，致使颗粒表现出不一样的特性，这就是表面效应。比如1克5纳米氧化铝的总表面积相当于一个标准篮球场面积那么大。

### 2. 小尺寸效应

当颗粒的尺寸与光波波长、德布罗意波长以及超导态的相干长度或透射深度等物理特征尺寸相当或更小时，晶体周期性的边界条件将被破坏，非晶态纳米粒子的颗粒表面层附近的原子密度减少，导致声、光、电、磁、热、力等特性呈现新的物理性质的变化，这称为小尺寸效应。常见的金子是黄色的，而在纳米尺度下，不同纳米的"金"则表现为不同的颜色。事实上，所有的金属在超微颗粒状态都呈现为黑色。尺寸越小，颜色越黑。

### 3. 量子隧道效应

当粒子尺寸下降到某一值时，金属费米能级附近的电子能级由准连续变成离散能级的现象称为量子尺寸效应。物质在纳米尺度下表现出隧道效应，可穿透平常物质不能穿透的壁垒。

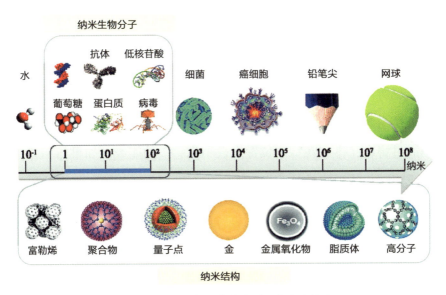

图1. 用纳米来衡量你的生活：多小才算小

## ▌ 如何构建纳米结构？

碳纳米管是最近创造的结构，并且具有许多新奇性能。它非常轻且坚固，可以添加到各种材料中以增加强度而不会增加太多重量。与此同时它也有许多有趣的电导（电学）特性。碳巴基球（足球烯）是一种非常坚固的基于其交错"足球"形状的结构。它有一个独特的性能，能够携带一些东西穿透细胞壁，然后把东西送到细胞内。一般来说，身体对此没有反应，所以你的身体不会试图攻击它，它可以很容易地随着血液流动。

构建纳米结构。我们如何构建如此小的东西呢？目前主要有三种方法。首先，扫描探针显微镜的尖端可以与它们所扫描的材料的原子成键并移动原子。1990年，IBM用这种方法操作氙原子制作出了有史以来最小的商标。其次，科学家可以从表面凿出材料，直到出现所需的结构。这是计算机工业用来制造集成电路的过程。最后，自组装是分子构件自然"组装"形成有用产品的过程。分子试图通过将自己排列在特定位置来最小化它们的能级。如果与相邻的分子成键能达到较低的能量状态，则会键合。我们可以在自然界的许多地方看到这种情况。例如，球形的气泡或雪花的形状是分子最小化其能级的结果。

晶体的自组装。晶体生长是一种特殊的自组装类型。这种技术被用来"生长"纳米管。在这种方法中，"种子"晶体被放置在某些表面，引入一些其他原子或分子，这些粒子模仿了"种子"晶体的模式。例如，制造纳米管的一种方法是在硅之类的材料上制造一组铁纳米粉颗粒阵列，把这些阵列放在一个腔室中，然后往腔室中加入一些含碳的天然气。碳与铁发生反应，并使其过饱和，形成碳沉淀，随后析出。通过这种方式，可以使纳米管像树一样生长！

自然界中的生物纳米机器。在我们的生物世界中存在着许多天然的纳米级器件。生命始于纳米！例如，在所有细胞内部，各种大小的分子和粒子都必须四处移动。一些分子可以通过扩散而移动，但离子和其他带电粒子必须在细胞周围和细胞膜之间进行特异性运输。生物学中有大量蛋白质可以自行组装成纳米级结构。

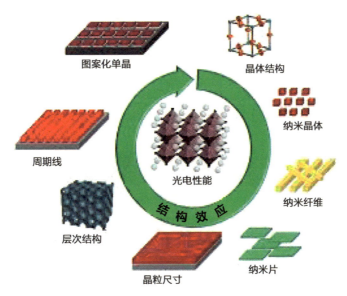

图2. 控制纳米结构生长：从纳米晶体到图案化单晶

## ▋ 如何来看纳米结构？（显微镜的发展）

科学中的一个重要思想是，创造工具或仪器来提高我们收集数据的能力，这个过程往往伴随着新的科学理解。科学是动态的。科学仪器的创新伴随着对科学的更好理解，并与创造创新的技术应用相关联。传统的光学显微镜（用光来看到你想要看到的）在许多与生物学相关的应用中仍然非常有用，因为使用该工具可以很容易地看到细胞和细菌等。它们也相当便宜，易于安装。

光学显微镜。纳米有多大？你可以用肉眼看到大约1000微米，而生物课上使用的典型显微镜可以让你看到大约10微米。更先进的显微镜，如扫描电子显微镜，可以获得相当好的分辨率（1微米）范围。更新的技术（在过去20年左右）允许我们"看到"100纳米到1纳米范围。

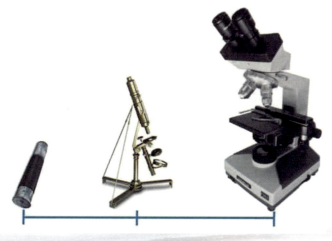

图3. 光学显微镜

电子显微镜。扫描电子显微镜和标准光学显微镜的区别在于，从被观察物体的表面"反弹"的是电子而不是各种波长的光，由于电子体积小，所以可以获得更高的分辨率。打一个比方，你可以在一个表面上拍沙滩球来确定其表面是否平坦（球向各个不同方向散射）。

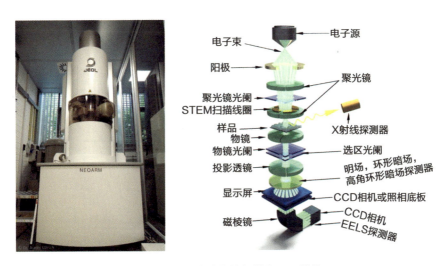

图4. 显示纳米结构的扫描电子显微镜

原子力显微镜（AFM）。原子力显微镜利用针尖与样品表面原子发生相互作用，从而探测样品表面信息，具有原子级的分辨率。人们能做到的最小的针尖必须由原子制成。针尖与要观测的材质表面会相互作用，因此针尖越小，分辨率越高。但是因为针尖是由原子组成的，它不可能比你看到的原子小。针尖由多种材料制成，如硅、钨，甚至碳纳米管。

原子力显微镜和扫描隧道显微镜（STM）之间的区别在于AFM

依靠原子间电磁力引起的运动显像，而STM则依靠针尖和表面之间的电流显像。需要注意的是AFM正是为了克服STM的基本缺点（它只能用来测量导体，因为它依赖于针尖和表面之间电流的产生）而发明的。AFM依靠实际接触而不是电流，因此它可以用来探测几乎任何类型的材料，包括聚合物、玻璃和生物样品。人们利用这些仪器的信号（力或电流）来推断原子的图像。针尖的波动被记录下来并输入计算机模型中，计算机模型根据数据生成图像。这些图像给我们提供了原子尺度的大致情况。

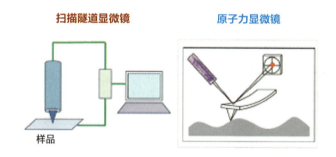

图5. 扫描隧道显微镜和原子力显微镜

纳米科学的特殊之处在于，在如此小的尺度下，不同于宏观世界的物理定律占据主导地位，材料的性质也会发生变化。

## 作者简介

材料科学家的最终目标是生产出具有理想物理、化学和机械性能的材料，用于实际应用。穆罕默德·沙法喜欢探索未知的世界，特别是原子间的相互作用如何影响材料的性能，如带隙修改，以及揭示异质结间的电荷转移机制。虽然他并没有直接将他的研究应用到现实世界中，但他的工作为具有优异性

穆罕默德·沙法
（巴基斯坦）

能的材料结构设计提供了指导，例如，用于汽车和航空工业中的传感器，其材料非常坚固且轻量化。穆罕默德·沙法的目标是找出具有最好的化学和物理性质的结构，并搞清楚形成这些性质的原子机制。他从2013年开始在这个领域工作，在中国电子科技大学攻读博士学位，并获得了中国国家留学基金委的奖学金，在完成博士学业后，他获得了阿联酋大学的博士后奖学金，那里有最先进的研究设备用于显微镜检查、微分析以及传感器设备制造，使他的研究保持在他所在领域的前沿。目前他在西安交通大学（潘毅教授组）通过物理/化学汽相沉积法、水热法、电化学蚀刻等方法进行薄膜生长研究，并且通过电化学阻抗谱EIS、TGA/DSC、AFM和STM、HR-XRD、FE-

SEM、EDS、HR-TEM和SAED、AFM、拉曼光谱、FTIR、霍尔测量、J-V测量–低温系统提供的数据进行产品描述。他研究的最终目标是制造新颖的以2D和0D材料为基础的材料器件以制造气体和生物传感器。

# Nanotechnology: Changing our Understanding of Matter

By Muhammad Shafa (Pakistan)

Why should we care about nanotechnology? It will change our lives and change our understanding of matter. In 1999, a group of leading scientists gathered by the National Science Foundation said, "The effect of nanotechnology on the health, wealth and standard of living for people in this century could be at least as significant as the combined influences of microelectronics, medical imaging, computer-aided engineering and man-made polymers developed in the past century."

To understand nanotechnology, we first have to understand what a nanometer is. A nanometer, like a meter, is a unit of length, with one nanometer equal to $10^{-9}$ meters. What is this concept? Putting a one-nanometer object on a Ping-Pang ball is like putting a Ping-Pang ball on the Earth. The study of properties and interactions of matter, including the manipulation of atoms and molecules, on the scale of 1-100 nanometers is called nanotechnology. Nanotechnology is a multidisciplinary field and draws not only on the material, physics, chemistry, but also biology, engineering and computer science, etc. Because of its multi-disciplinary nature, nanotechnology may require us to focus on the knowledge of different fields.

## The Origin of Nanotechnology

In December 1959, physicist Richard Feynman gave a famous lecture- "There's Plenty of Room at the Bottom" at the California Institute of Technology, describing the process by which scientists would be able to manipulate and control individual atoms and molecules in the future. This prediction has been called a sign of the budding of nanotechnology by the scientific community. The term nanotechnology was first used by the Japanese scholar Norio Taniguchi in 1974. It wasn't until 1981 when the development of scanning tunneling microscope allowed scientists to see individual atoms, that modern nanotechnology began to develop.

## Three Major Effects at the Nanoscale

### I Surface effect

The surface area of a spherical particle is proportional to the square of its diameter, and its volume is proportional to the diameter cube, so its specific surface area (surface area/volume)is inversely proportional to its diameter. With the decrease of particle diameter, the specific surface area will increase significantly, and the relative number of atoms on the particle surface will increase, so that the surface atoms have high activity and extreme instability, resulting in different characteristics of particles, which is called the surface effect. For example, the total surface area of one gram of 5 nanometer alumina is equivalent to the area of a standard basketball court.

## II Small size effect

When the particle size is equivalent to or smaller than the physical characteristics such as the wavelength of light, the wavelength of de Broglie and the coherence or transmission depth of the superconducting state, the boundary condition of periodicity of the crystal will be destroyed, the atomic density of amorphous nanoparticle near the surface area will decrease, resulting in a change in the physical properties of sound, light, electricity, magnetism, heat, and mechanics, which is called small size effect. The gold is yellow in common, however, at the nanoscale, different size of gold shows different colors. All metals appear black in the ultrafine particle state. The smaller the size, the darker the color.

## III Quantum tunneling effect

When the particle size drops to a certain value, the phenomenon that the electron energy level near the Fermi level changes from the quasi-continuous to discrete is called the quantum size effect. Substances exhibit a tunneling effect at the nanoscale, penetrating barriers that ordinary substances cannot penetrate.

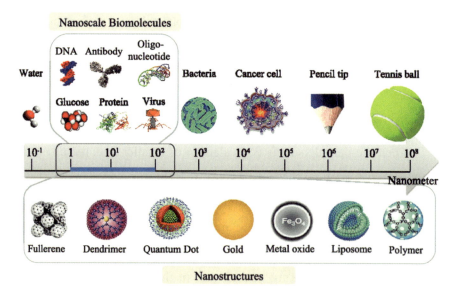

Figure 1. Measure your life in nano: how small is small

# How to Build Nanostructures?

Carbon Nanotubes: This describes a recently-created structure that has some amazing properties. Nanotubes are very light and strong, and can be added to various materials to give them added strength without adding much weight. Nanotubes also have interesting conductance (electrical) properties. Carbon Buckyballs: Buckyballs are another very strong structure based on their interlaced "soccer ball" shape. It has the unique property of being able to carry something inside of it, penetrate a cell wall, and then deliver the package into the cell (not sure how you "open" the buckyball!). It is also non-reactive in general the body, so your body will not try to attack it and it can travel easily in the bloodstream.

Building Nanostructures: How do we build things that are so small?

Three main methods are used to make nanoscale structures. First, the tips of scanning probe microscopes can form bonds with the atoms of the material they are scanning and move the atoms. Using this method with xenon atoms, IBM created the tiniest logo ever in 1990. Alternately, scientists can chisel out material from the surface until the desired structure emerges. This is the process that the computer industry uses to make integrated circuits. Finally, self-assembly is the process by which molecular building blocks "assemble" naturally to form useful products. Molecules try to minimize their energy levels by aligning themselves in particular positions. If bonding to an adjacent molecule allows for a lower energy state, then the bonding will occur. We see this happening in many places in nature. For example, the spherical shape of a bubble or the shape of a snowflake is a result of molecules minimizing their energy levels.

Self-Assembly by Crystal Growth: One particular type of self-assembly is crystal growth. This technique is used to "grow" nanotubes. In this approach, "seed" crystals are placed on some surface, some other atoms or molecules are introduced, and these particles mimic the pattern of the small seed crystal. For example, one way to make nanotubes is to create an array of iron nanopowder particles on some material like silicon, put this array in a chamber, and add some natural gas with carbon to the chamber. The carbon reacts with the iron and supersaturates it, forming a precipitate of carbon that then grows up and out. In this manner, you can grow nanotubes like trees!

Biological Nanomachines in Nature: Many natural nanoscale devices exist in our biological world. Life begins at the nanoscale! For example, inside all cells, molecules, and particles of various sizes have to move around. Some molecules can move by diffusion, but ions and other charged particles have to be specifically transported around cells and across membranes. Biology has an enormous number of proteins that self-assemble into nanoscale structures.

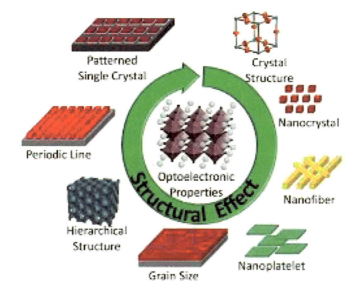

Figure 2. Control growth of nanostructures: from nano-crystal to pattern single crystals

## ▌ How to See Nanostructures?(The Evolution of Microscopes)

One of the big ideas in science is that the creation of tools or instruments that improve our ability to collect data is often accompanied by new scientific understandings. Science is dynamic. Innovation in scientific instruments is followed by a better understanding of science and is associated with creating innovative technological applications. Using Light to See You may want to point out that traditional light microscopes are still very useful in many biology-related applications since things like cells and bacteria can readily be seen with this tool. They are also fairly inexpensive and are easy to set up.

Optical Microscope: How Big is a Nanometer? You can see down to about 1000 microns with the naked eye, and a typical microscope as used in biology class will get you down to about 10 microns. More advanced microscopes, such as scanning electron microscopes can get you a pretty good resolution (1 micron) range. Newer technologies (within the last 20 years or so) allow us to "see" in the range of 100 nanometers to 1 nanometer.

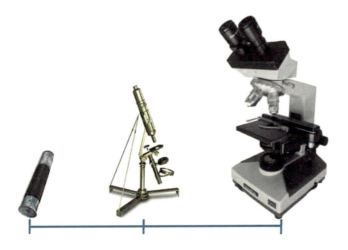

Figure 3. Optical Microscope

Electron Microscope: The difference between the standard light microscope and the scanning electron microscope is that electrons, instead of various wavelengths of light, are "bounced" off the surface of the object being viewed and that electrons allow for a higher resolution because of their small size. You can use the analogy of bouncing a beach ball on a surface to find out if it is uneven (beach ball scattering in all different directions.)

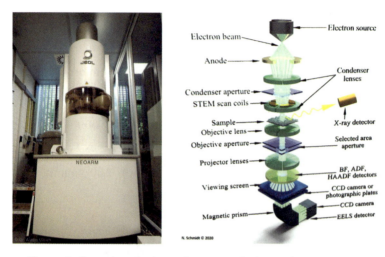

Figure 4. Scanning electron microscope that reveal nanostructures

Atomic Force Microscope: The atomic force microscope uses the tip to interact with the atoms on the surface of the sample to detect information with atomic resolution. The smallest tip you can make has to be made from atoms. The tip interacts with the surface of the material you want to look at, so the smaller the tip, the better the resolution. But because the tip is made from atoms, it can't be smaller than the atoms you are looking at. Tips are made from a variety of materials, such as silicon, tungsten, and even carbon nanotubes.

The difference between the Atomic Force Microscope (AFM) and the Scanning tunneling microscope (STM) is that the AFM relies on movement due to the electromagnetic forces between atoms, and the STM relies on electrical current between the tip and the surface. Mention that the AFM was invented to overcome the STM's basic drawback: it can only be used to sense the nature of materials that conduct electricity since it relies on the creation of a current between the tip and the surface. The AFM relies on actual contact rather than a current flow, so it can be used to probe almost any type of material, including polymers, glass, and biological samples. Point out that the signals (forces or currents) from these instruments are used to infer an image of the atoms. The tip's fluctuations are recorded and fed into computer models that generate images based on the data. These images give us a rough picture of the atomic landscape.

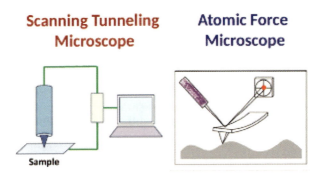

Figure 5. Scanning tunnelling microscopy and Atomic force microscopy

What makes the science at the nanoscale special is that at such a small scale, different physical laws dominate and properties of materials change.

## About the Author

The ultimate goal of a materials scientist is to produce materials with desirable physical, chemical, and mechanical properties for practical applications. Muhammad Shafa enjoys exploring the unknown world, especially how atomic interactions affect the properties of materials such as band gap modifications and to reveal the charge transfer mechanism among hetero junction. Although he doesn't

Muhammad Shafa
(Pakistan)

work directly on the real-world applications of his research, his work provides guidance for the structural design of materials with superior properties, such as very strong and lightweight materials for use in the automobile and aviation industries as sensors. His goal is to determine the structures that provide the best Chemical and physical properties, and to understand the atomic mechanisms responsible for those properties. He has been working in this field since 2013. He won scholarship from CSC China for PhD at the University of Electronics Science and Technology of China. After completion of PhD, he won Postdoc fellowship at United Arab Emirates University where the state-of-the-art research facilities for Microscopy and Microanalysis as well as sensor device fabrication enable me to keep his research at the forefront of his field. Here at Xian Jiaotong University (Group of Prof. Pan Yi), Muhammad Shafa is working on thin film growth through Physical/chemical Vapor deposition System, as well hydrothermal, electrochemical etching, and characterization through Electrochemical Impedance Spectroscopy EIS, TGA/DSC, AFM and STM, HR-XRD, FE-SEM, EDS, HR-TEM & SAED, AFM, Raman Spectroscopy, FTIR, Hall Measurement, J-V measurements–Cryogenic System. The ultimate goal of his research is to fabricate novel 2D and 0D materials-based devices for the fabrication of Gas and biological Sensor.

# 分子机器和马达的作用：从生物学到化学

文 / 让-皮埃尔·索维奇 [法]

译 / 张晓

在讨论复杂的分子系统之前，我们先来了解什么是分子，并看几个简单的例子。首先，分子由通过化学键相互连接的原子组成。化学键有几种类型，但本文主要关注 "共价键"，它很强，很难断裂。

## ▌ 简单的分子与有机合成

我们先从一些简单的化学结构开始。来看看两个非常简单的分子，苯（benzene）和环己烷（cyclohexane）。这两个分子的结构对化学家来说非常初级，对法国高中生来说则是必备知识。苯，化学式是$C_6H_6$，结构是一个六边形，由六个碳原子构成一个六边形，每个碳原子连接一个氢原子。环己烷并不完全相同。它有六个亚甲基（$CH_2$），彼此间以环状方式相连接，但它不是平面的，与苯相反（见图1）。

310

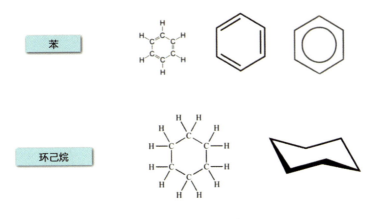

图1. 苯和环己烷

现在我们来看另一个相对简单的分子富勒烯（fullerene）。它的发现很偶然，完全是一个意外。发现富勒烯项目的最初目标可以说与富勒烯南辕北辙。这个分子的发现令人兴奋，它接近于一个球体，与足球非常相似。富勒烯引出了许多新发现，其本身无论是电化学还是光化学特性都非常奇妙，是一项意义重大的发现。

我们已经看过了一些简单分子，现在来谈谈有机合成。合成是化学的一个重要部分，至少对分子化学来说是如此。B型短裸甲藻毒素是与红潮现象有关的海洋神经毒素，它拥有大量碳原子，数量多得让人难以置信，而且结构非常复杂。K.C.尼古劳（K.C. Nicolaou）团队1995年成功合成这种分子。2004年又发表了一种大幅改进后的合成法，包含90个独立的化学步骤。这不得不说是一次了不起的壮举，化学家居然能够创造出一个如此复杂的分子（见图2）。

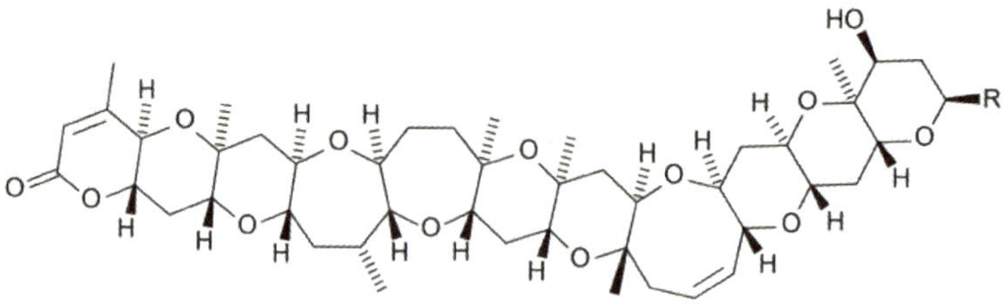

图 2．B型短裸甲藻毒素

## 索烃的合成

让我们来看一下分子机器。分子机器有两类，一类是人工合成的，另一类存在于生物界。大体来讲，合成分子被认为是静态的，它们不移动，或者移动时是随机的。物理学家会说这是随机运动，它们振动、伸长、收缩，但这些运动不受控制。但在生物领域，事情就不一样了。恰恰相反，在生物体内，分子系统的运动方式是受严格限定的。这些分子系统非常重要，其中大多数被称为"马达蛋白"，能够实现极其重要的功能。比如旋转马达、线性马达和步行马达（分子就像是在路上走），还有可以收缩、伸展的蛋白，也就是分子压缩机，等等。这些马达蛋白可以说无处不在，且至关重要。

让我们来看两个例子：三磷酸腺苷合酶（ATP 合酶）是一个旋转马达；驱动蛋白（kinesin）则能够在微管上沿直线轴行走。ATP合酶负责将ADP和无机磷酸盐合成ATP，而ATP是生命的燃料，地球上的任何生命、任何有机体都有赖于ATP。就在此刻，在你我的身体里有数以亿计的ATP合酶在运动。他们做着旋转运动，非常快，特定条件下一分钟旋转1万次，几乎是F1方程式的速度。驱动蛋白则是沿着微管行走，它们存在于所有细胞里。在细胞里，驱动蛋白在行走时携带一个非常大的袋子，即细胞器。驱动蛋白可以携带蛋白质、核苷酸、激素等。正如ATP合酶一样，驱动蛋白的运动速度也非常快（见图3）。

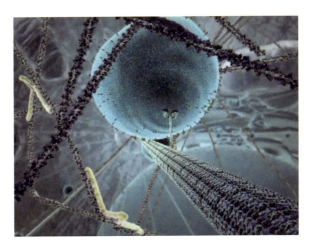

图3. 在细胞内，驱动蛋白可以在微管上行走并携带一个很大的袋子（细胞器），他们也可以携带蛋白质、核苷酸、激素等。

现在让我们通过人工合成的化合物走进分子运动的领域。首先，我们来看索烃和轮烷。索烃由两个或几个互锁的环组成。索烃和轮烷令化学家着迷了一个多世纪，但它们是如此难以制备，以至于在某种程度上，学界又对这些分子感到沮丧万分。因为太难以生产，在20世纪60年代，这些分子只能以非常小的规模产出，因此大多数化学家变得对它们不那么感兴趣。

实际上，我研究索烃、轮烷是始于一个完全不同的研究领域，利用太阳能研究光催化分解水。水的分解是一个非常令人兴奋的研究领域，如果你能利用光能，特别是太阳能将水分子分解成氢气和氧气，这将形成一个非常有用的系统。氢气是一种理想的燃料，燃烧氢气会产生水，而不是像传统能源产生二氧化碳，很多团队都在研究水的光化学分解。这很难，目前也仍在研究中，但我相信某天会取得成功。当我们开始研究时，很多人都在使用$Ru(bipy)_3^{2+}$作为光催化剂。这种钌络合物有特别棒的属性，可以吸收太阳光谱中的大部分。它是一种深红色的复合物，当被光激发时会变成一种非常强的还原剂或者氧化剂，这一特性使它在水的裂解上特别有前景。事实上，因为要分解水分子，你需要一种强氧化剂来生成氧气，需要一种强还原剂来生成氢气。但问题在于，钌非常昂贵且罕见，就像金或铂一样，时至今日这都是一个非常严重的问题。

所以在某个阶段，我们决定完全改变思路，尝试用其他金属代替钌。特别是，我们与美国朋友、普渡大学（美国印第安纳州）的大卫·麦克米林教授一起，决定使用铜研究铜络合物，尝试将其用于水的裂解。大卫·麦克米林是一位光物理学家，而我们团队主要是化学家。大卫·麦克米林决定来法国斯特拉斯堡休假，这真是个好主意！当他抵达时，我们决定合作。我们正在制造新的含铜分子，而他与他的美国团队正在研究这些分子。

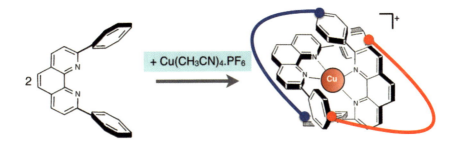

图4. 拥有两个配体的铜（Ⅰ）络合物

我们携手制成了这个化合物（如图4）。看到这个铜（Ⅰ）络合物分子时，大卫·麦克米林非常兴奋。两个新月形的结构相互交织着，以非常有效的方式保护着金属，这似乎与它的光化学性质有关且非常重要。大卫·麦克米林告诉我们，我们必须制造这种化合物，他对这种化合物的光化学性质非常期待。于是，我们制备了这种化合物，这很容易；麦克米林的小组研究了它的光化学性质。实话实说，从光化学的角度来看，它令人激动。它的光化学性质类似于Ru(bipy)$_3^{2+}$，但是它更便宜，因为铜非常便宜且丰富。

但是，它还有另一个更有趣的特性，这是我们开始这个项目时完全没有意料到的。让我们来看看这个分子的形状，两个有机碎片相互交织在铜（Ⅰ）的周围，这意味着它在分子拓扑学、索烃相关方面值得期待。让我们仔细看看配体的端点以及将它们互联的方式。两种配体的端点分别以蓝色和红色表示。现在，让我们来想一想，如果把两个蓝点互连，并将两个红点互连，可以得到什么？很显然，我们可以得到两个环。令人兴奋的是，这两个环是互锁的，这是一个索烃。简单来说，我们可以用一个非常简单的铜络合物制造一个索烃，而这本来是用于水分解的。我们小组内部进行了讨论，是要继续在一个非常成熟的无机光化学领域进行研究，这对于我们来说比较舒适，还是去探索一些不同的东西，跳入几乎未知的索烃和轮烷领域。于是我们决定跳入索烃的未知领域，该研究在当时并不热门（活跃）。

几个月后，得益于我的好朋友、同事、出色的合成化学家克里斯蒂安·迪特里希–布切克博士的帮助，我们在1983年发表了我们关于索烃合成的第一篇论文。我们可以通过三个化学步骤制备索烃，并以相对较大的量（克）获得这种化合物。

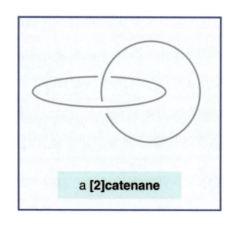

图5. 索烃

这就是开始。我认为，这项成果完全改变了化学家对索烃的看法，索烃变成了一种方便获得的分子。在此之前，它被认为是几乎不可能合成的。1964年，Schill和Lüttringhaus发表了索烃的合成，尽管这项开创性的工作很漂亮，但没有人尝试重复它，因为它太难

了（超过20个单独的化学步骤）。在我们的第一篇论文发表（1983
年）几年后，其他几个研究团队也以高效的方式合成了索烃。弗雷
泽·斯托达特和他的团队在1989年发表了一篇文章，另外两个团队
在20世纪90年代初发表了文章。应该说，从1995年开始，这个领域
出现了爆发式的发展，许多非常有创造力的团队都投身于此。在中
国，也有几个团队做了出色的工作。

## ▌ 分子机器

在开始讨论第一个分子机器之前，我想先介绍一下拓扑学。拓
扑学是数学的一个领域，而化学拓扑学则是把数学概念应用于分子
领域。所以我们制作了新的拓扑结构，特别是三叶结，它是一个打
结的环，结构非常有趣；或者是双重交错的索烃结构，也叫所罗

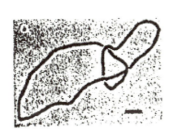 

（a）三叶结 （b）八连环

图6. 经旋转酶产生的DNA索烃和结在电子显微镜下的成像

门环。生物学中也存在有大量的索烃和结。化学家对此可能感到惊讶。有证据表明，1%的蛋白质是结状的。用显微镜可以观察到DNA形成的许多索烃。尤其是，环状双链DNA在复制时形成索烃。生物领域存在大量有趣的拓扑结构，这也是学界研究新分子拓扑学的一个动机所在。

现在，我们来讨论分子机器的概念。先问一个非常简单的问题：为什么索烃和轮烷在分子机器领域这么吸引人？答案很简单。索烃和轮烷是两个非常简单的系统，你可以想象这些分子正在运动之中。轮烷是一个线性马达，类似于在气缸中运动的活塞。索烃是一个旋转系统，像一个旋转马达。这当然是非常令人兴奋的。所以好几个团队都开始致力于分子机器的研究。

现在，让我解释一下以2-索烃（2-catanane）为基础的第一个分子机器的原理。我们在1983—1984年制作的第一个索烃中引入了三个吡啶（三个氮原子）即三联吡啶（terpyridine）。其中的三个氮原子"非常乐意"与过渡金属（本例中为铜）相互作用。我们从1价铜开始，它乐于同4个氮原子配位，尤其是当这4个氮原子按四面体（三棱锥）结构排列时。我们从化合物中抽取一个电子，然后产生2价铜，系统重新排列，形成分子的五配位形式，结构非常稳定。现在，你再加入电子，重新变回1价铜，结构依然稳定。其美妙之处在于其稳定性。你可以通过多次注入电子或空穴（指共价键上流失一个电子留下空位的现象）来重新排列化合物，该分子永远不会降解。所以从化学意义上讲，这个系统非常完美。必须说明一下，这还不是一个旋转马达，因为我们还不能控制其运动的方向性。也就是说，一个环在另一个环内的运动可以顺时针或逆时针。想要控制方向，还要等到本·费林加（Ben Feringa）和他的团队在1999年发表成果之后了。

随后，我们花了大概12到15年的时间来提炼其中的概念、改进整个系统。尤其是，我们做了一些作旋转或摇摆运动的轮烷。这种化合物包含一个可以在两个位置之间旋转的环。现在，这些旋转机器的响应速度比我们在1994年做的索烃快得多。我们现在处于微秒级时间尺度。这与我们的第一个系统相比提升很大。

1994年，就是我们团队发现旋转索烃的同一年，我的好朋友斯托达特和凯弗教授团队也发表了一项成果，描述了一个分子穿梭机的概念。分子穿梭机的原理比较简单，一个轮烷上面有一个圆环，可以从绿点滑行到红点然后再回到绿点。这就是第一个分子穿梭机，一个令人振奋的系统，当然也是一个非常美妙的结构。通过长期富有成效的合作，斯托达特与吉姆·希斯（Jim Heath）发表了一种使用分子来存储、处理信息的新方法，这令人振奋。2007年，他们发表了一种新的分子电子存储装置，该装置基于长而规则的轮烷，其端点连接到纳米电极上。

1999年，本·费林加团队首次发表了一种光化学驱动的旋转分子，该分子具有完美的方向性控制。在该系统中，旋转仅沿一个方向进行。光子信号产生必须重新排列的激发态。在一系列过程（两次光驱动重排和两次热控制过程）中，它以完全受控的方式进行旋转。本·费林加团队还在网上发了一个漂亮的视频，建议大家观看。

让我向你们介绍一些最新的进展。许多人热衷于尝试制造可以随意收缩或延伸的分子系统。我们在2000年发表了第一个我们称之为"人工分子肌肉"的系统。随后，几个小组在人工分子肌肉领域做了有趣的工作。他们甚至可以制造微米长的纤维等材料，通过改变pH值或其他信号使其拉长、收缩。

如今，全世界有许多分子机器的例子，也有大量的研究团队在这个领域开展工作。比如回旋索烃（pirouetting catenane）和分子穿梭机（molecular shuttle）是该领域最早设计、制备和研究的系统之一。从1999年起，本·费林加团队发表的光驱动旋转马达甚至纳米汽车，也是受控分子运动领域的里程碑。然后，斯托达特教授的分子肌肉、压缩机、分子泵等，是过去几十年中发表的最引人注目的系统之一。

总之，应该强调的是，在分子机器出现之前，合成分子大多被认为是静止的（即运动较少或进行随机运动）。分子系统进行大幅运动的情况非常罕见。科学家研发的这些分子机器，或许改变了化学家看待分子的方式。如今，许多分子机器和分子马达已经被研究出来。许多团体正在这一令人兴奋的研究领域开展工作。

我认为现在谈论其应用还不太现实。据我所知，轮烷在智能材料领域仅有一个商业应用，比如材料能对刺激作出反应。其他的应用方面，可以想到的有信息存储、处理。但长期来看，也许生物活性物质的矢量化最值得期待。当然，如果我们能够用于靶向入侵物和细菌、癌细胞和肿瘤细胞的活体检测，那就太棒了。

当然，我们必须重视应用对未来的重要性，但事实上，我们不知道真正重要的应用需要多长时间才会出现。我们今天一直在使用的一些技术其实根植于，或者说起源于基础研究，这些基础研究的历史可能非常漫长。当你想到计算机时，它始于晶体管，晶体管始于半导体，关于半导体的研究是在19世纪进行的。

如果某一天你想成为科学家，请记住好奇心是最重要的。与他人互动也是非常重要的，不要把一切都保密，试着与许多人互动。从一个你非常熟悉的领域跳到另一个领域也会非常有益。还有，别忘了偶然性。（楼玉娇协助审核本文专业内容，在此表示感谢。）

### 作者简介

让-皮埃尔·索维奇，法国化学家，1944年10月21日生于巴黎。1971年在路易斯·巴斯德大学（现为斯特拉斯堡大学的一部分）获得博士学位。1979年至2009年，他担任法国国家科学研究中心（CNRS）研究主任。他因与苏格兰裔美国化学家詹姆斯·弗雷

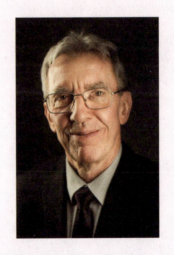

泽·斯托达特爵士和荷兰化学家本·费林加在分子机器方面的工作而获得2016年诺贝尔化学奖。他现在是斯特拉斯堡大学名誉教授。

索维奇教授和他的研究团队致力于以下领域的研究：（1）配位光化学和太阳能转换；（2）二氧化碳电催化还原；（3）化学拓扑学：索烃、结和轮烷；（4）用于光诱导电荷分离的多功能钌和铱络合物；（5）作为光合反应中心模型的多功能卟啉；（6）分子开关和分子机器原型，如"摇摆索烃""分子肌肉"或"分子压缩机"。

# Molecular Machines and Motors in Action: from Biology to Chemistry

By Jean-Pierre Sauvage (France)

Before discussing complex molecular systems, it could be useful to remind you what a molecule is and to show you a few simple examples. First, a molecule consists of atoms connected to one another by chemical bonds. There are several types of bonds but, we will mostly be concerned with "covalent bonds", which are very strong and difficult to cleave.

## ▌ Simple Molecules and Organic Synthesis

I would like to start with very simple structures. Let's look at two very simple molecules, benzene and cyclohexane. I know that for chemists it's very naive and totally useless, but for high school kids in France, it will be very useful. Benzene, whose chemical formula is C6H6, is a hexagon made up of six carbon atoms, each of which being connected to a hydrogen atom. Cyclohexane is not exactly the same. It has six CH2 groups connected to one another in a cyclic way, but it is not planar, contrary to benzene. (Figure 1)

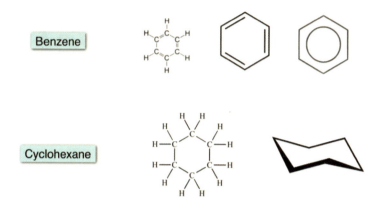

Figure 1. Benzene and Cyclohexane

Another relatively simple molecule is fullerene, which was found totally due to serendipity, meaning discovery by accident. And this molecule is very exciting. Of course, it's close to a sphere. It is also very similar to a soccer ball. And it led to many new discoveries, and it has wonderful properties, either electrochemical or photochemical properties. And it is considered as a major discovery.

Now, we have seen very simple molecules, let's talk about organic synthesis. Synthesis is a very important component of chemistry, at least of molecular chemistry. Brevetoxin B, a marine neurotoxin most commonly associated with Red Tide, which has an incredible number of carbon atoms, is one of the records in terms of complexity. The synthesis of this molecule was successfully achieved by K. C. Nicolaou in 1995 in California and in 2004, they published an improved synthesis. This second strategy represents 90 individual chemical steps. This is really a "tour de force", and it is really amazing that chemists can achieve that (making such a complex molecule). (Figure 2)

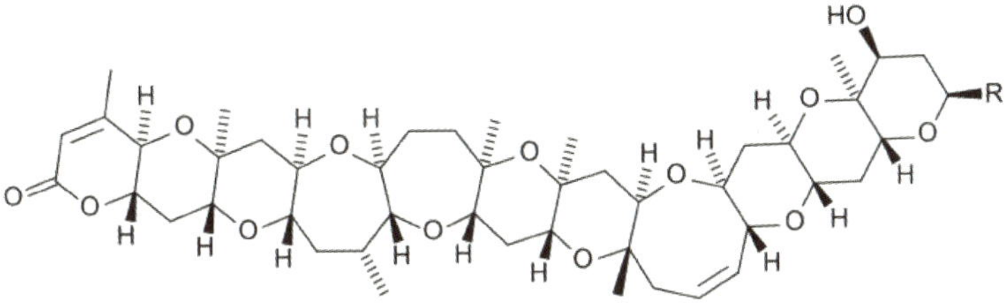

Figure 2. Brevetoxin B

## ▮ The Synthesis of a Catenane

Now let's move on and talk about molecular machines. Basically, there are two families of molecular machines: one is that of synthetic systems, and the other one belongs to the biological world. Synthetic molecules are considered as static objects. They do not move or if they move, they do not move in a controlled fashion. They move at random. Physicists would say that they undergo motion in a stochastic manner. They can vibrate, elongate, contract, etc. but their motions are not controlled. In biology, it is totally different. By contrast, in biology molecular systems move in a very strictly controlled fashion. And these systems are extremely important. Most of them are called "Motor proteins". And these motor proteins fulfil incredibly important functions. We will find rotary motors, linear motors, even walkers, molecules which can walk, on the path, and systems that can be contracted, or extended, molecular compressors, etc. So, these motor proteins are everywhere and at the same time, they are essential.

Now, let's look at two examples, ATP synthase, which is a rotary motor, and kinesin, which is a walker being able to walk on a microtubule along a linear axis. ATP synthase is responsible for the synthesis of ATP from ADP and inorganic phosphate. ATP is the fuel of life. Anything which lives on earth, any organism relies on ATP. Everybody uses ATP, and for the moment in your body, in my body, there are billions and billions of ATP synthase enzymes in motion. And they are rotary motors. In fact, it is very fast. Under certain circumstances, it can rotate at a rate of about 10,000 rounds per minute, which is about the speed of a Formula One engine, extremely fast. the kinesin enzyme walks on the microtubules. In all cells you have those kinesins, and they can walk and carry a very big cargo, an organelle, within the cell. They can carry proteins, nucleotides, hormones, etc. And it walks very fast like ATP synthase rotates very fast. (Figure 3).

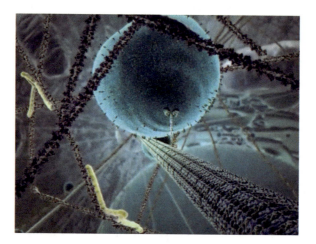

Figure 3. Kinesin can walk on the microtubules while carrying a very big bag (an organelle) within the cell, and they can carry proteins, nucleotides, hormones, etc.

Now we will enter the field of molecular motion using synthetic compounds or synthetic assemblies. At first, we will talk of catenanes and rotaxanes. Catenanes are molecular systems consisting of two or several interlocking rings. Chemists have been fascinated by these molecules for more than a century, but the synthesis of these compounds seemed to be exceedingly difficult, which discouraged the community. These molecules, which could be obtained in very tiny quantities in the 60s, did not appear as particularly attractive to most of the chemists, mostly because they were considered as too difficult to be produced.

In fact, I entered the field of catenanes and rotaxanes from a field of research which was very far away from catenanes. I was particularly interested in a very important research project related to photochemical "water splitting" using solar energy. Water splitting is a very exciting field of research, because if one can cleave the water molecule to $H_2$ and $O_2$ using light energy and, in particular solar energy, it will be a fantastic system. Everybody agrees that $H_2$ is the ideal fuel. $H_2$ is not a polluting fuel because when one burns it, it generates water instead $CO_2$ when a classical fuel is burnt. There are many groups all around the world which have been working on the photochemical cleavage of water. This reaction is very difficult to realise. The water splitting research is still actively going on today and I am quite confident that someday this project will be met with success. When we started in this field, many people were using $Ru(bipy)_3^{2+}$ as photoactive species. This ruthenium complex has fantastic properties. It is able to absorb a relatively large fraction of the solar spectrum due to the fact that it is a deep red complex and, when it is excited by light, it becomes a strong reductant or a very strong oxidant. This property makes this complex a particularly promising photoactive compounds for splitting the water molecule. Indeed, because if one wants to split the water molecule, one needs a strong oxidant to generate $O_2$ and a strong reductant to make $H_2$. There was and still is a very serious problem linked to the fact that one would have to use ruthenium, a noble metal. The problem was that ruthenium is very, very expensive and it is very rare, like gold or platinum.

Thus, at some stage, we decided to change completely and to try to replace ruthenium for other metals. In particular, with an American friend, Professor David McMillin at Purdue University (Indiana), we decided to use copper and to investigate copper complexes and possibly use them in relation to water splitting. David McMillin was mostly a photophysicist and in my group we were chemists. David McMillin decided at some stage to take his sabbatical leave in Strasbourg, which was a great idea! When he arrived in Strasbourg, we decided to join our efforts. We were making new copper-containing molecules, and he was studying them, mostly in his group in the US.

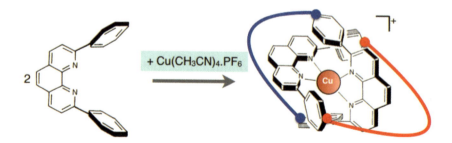

Figure 4. the very special copper(I) complex which led to the copper-containing [2]catenane

We prepared the compound shown in Figure 4 and David McMillin was very excited when he saw the molecule. The two crescent shaped organic components which were intertwined with one another were protecting the metal in a very efficient way, which seemed to be important in relation with the photochemical properties of the copper(I) complex. Dave McMillin told us that we had to make this compound and that he was expecting highly photochemical properties for this compound. So, we prepared the complex, which was quite easy, and McMillin's group studied the photochemical properties. Honestly, it turned out to be a very exciting complex from a photochemical view. Its photochemical properties were like those of $Ru(bipy)_3^{2+}$ but, of course, this copper(I) complex was much cheaper because copper very cheap and abundant.

But the other property, which was totally unexpected when we started the project on copper(I)-based photoactive species, was, probably even more interesting. While observing the shape of this molecule, which is just consisting of two organic fragments intertwined with one another around copper(I), which noticed something very exciting in relation to molecular topology and catenanes. Let us carefully look at the endpoints of the ligands and at the way we can interconnect them. These end points are indicated in blue and in red for both ligands respectively. Now you may ask yourself the question: What it the figure I will generate if I interconnect the two blue points and, separately, if I interlink the two red points. Clearly, I will obtain two rings. The exciting observation is that these two rings are interlocked and the result is simply a [2]catenane (i.e. a molecular system consisting of two interlocking rings). In principle, we can make a catenane using a very simple copper complex, which was prepared mostly for water splitting. We had to discuss in our group in order to decide whether we will continue to work in a very well-established field of inorganic photochemistry, in which we felt very comfortable, or to jump into something very different which was the field of catenane and rotaxanes. As you probably know, we decided to jump into the field of catenanes which, at the time, was not very active.

After a couple of months, thanks to my good friend and co-worker Dr Christiane Dietrich-Buchecker, who was a fantastic synthetic chemist, we could publish our first paper on the first practical synthesis of a [2] catenane in 1983. So, we could make a catenane in three chemical steps and obtain this compound in relatively large amounts (gramme quantities).

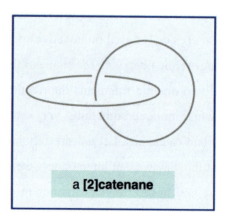

Figure 5. Catenanes

This was the very beginning. Suddenly, it changed completely the view that chemists had on catenanes because catenanes became accessible molecules. As I said before, before our work, catenanes were considered as molecules whose synthesis was almost impossible. The synthesis of catenanes had been reported in 1964 by Schill and Lüttringhaus but, although this pioneering piece of work was beautiful, nobody tried to repeat it because it was too difficult (more than 20 individual chemical steps). A few years after our first paper (1983) our team was followed by a few other research groups also able to make catenanes in an efficient way. Fraser Stoddard and his co-workers published a very efficient synthesis in 1989. Two other groups in the UK and in Germany published pioneering work on catenanes at the beginning of the 90s. And I should say that from 1995 on the field basically blew up. Many very creative groups became interested in catenanes. And in China there were also several groups that did novel work.

## Molecular Machines

Before we start to discuss the first molecular machines, I would like to introduce topology. Topology is a field of mathematics, but chemical topology uses the concept of mathematics, applied to molecules. So, we could create novel topologies, and in particular the trefoil knot, which is a knotted ring, a very exciting species, or a doubly interlocking catenane which is also called the Solomon rings. In biology, there are lots of catenanes and knots. (Figure 4) This is perhaps surprising to chemists. It has been shown that 1% of the proteins are knotted. Lots of catenanes formed with DNA have been characterized by microscopy. In particular, circular duplex DNA forms catenanes when it replicates. Knowing that topologically interesting species were very abundant in biology was another motivation for us to prepare new molecular topology.

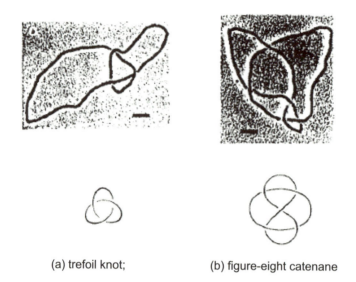

(a) trefoil knot;                    (b) figure-eight catenane

Figure 6. Electron micrographs of gyrase-produced DNA catenanes and knots

Let us now discuss the concept of molecular machines and ask ourselves the very simple question: Why are catenanes and rotaxanes so interesting in relation to the field of molecular machines? Very simple. Catenane and rotaxanes are just two very simple systems. You can imagine that these molecules can be set in motion. A [2]rotaxane can behave as a linear motor, very similarly to a piston moving in a cylinder. A [2]catenane can be a pirouetting system, and thus it on the way to rotary motors. This is of course very motivating and very exciting. And therefore, several groups embarked in the field of molecular machines.

Now, let me explain the principle of the first molecular machine built on a [2]catenane. We introduced 3 pyridines (3 nitrogen atoms) to the chemical structure of first catenane made in 1983-84 by our group. The added fragment is called "terpyridine". The three nitrogen atoms of the terpyridine "would be very happy" to interact with the transition metal (copper in this case). Let's start from here: Copper 1+ , classically called Cu(I), is very happy when it is coordinated with 4 nitrogen atoms, especially if the 4 nitrogen atoms are arranged as a tetrahedron. Now, let us abstract an electron to the compound. We generate copper 2+ (or, more simply, Cu(II). The system will start rearranging and after the rearrangement process is finished, we obtain the five-coordinate form of the molecule, a very stable species. Now you can inject back the electron and regenerate Cu(I), again a very stable compound. The beauty of the system is that it is perfectly stable. You can rearrange the compound by injecting an electron or a positive hole as many times as you like. The molecule does not degrade at all. The whole system never shows fatigue, so chemically speaking it is a perfect system. To be honest, I would like to make it clear that this system is not a rotary motor because we have no control over directionality. In other words, the rotation motion of one ring within the other one can be clockwise or counterclockwise. If you want to have control of directionality you have to wait for the work of Ben Feringa and his group published in 1999.

The system was very slow to move. And thus, we spent maybe 12 to 15 years generalizing the concepts and improving the system. We made some pirouetting or oscillating rotaxanes. Such compounds incorporate a ring which can pirouette between two positions. These pirouetting machines are now much faster to response than the machine we proposed in 1994, the pirouetting catenane. We are now in the microsecond time scale. And this is a big change compared to the very first system we have.

My good friends, Professors Stoddart and Kaifer, and their two co-workers, published a molecular shuttle in 1994, the same year as our swinging catenane. The principle of the molecular shuttle is relatively simple. We have rotaxane with a ring that can glide from the green station to the red station and go back to the green station. That was the first molecular shuttle, a very exciting and beautiful system. After some time and a very long and fruitful collaboration with the group of the Jim Heath in the US, Stoddart, Heath and their teams published a new way for storing and processing information using molecules. This was a very exciting and promising result. In 2007, they published a new molecular electronic memory device, based on long regular rotaxanes whose endpoints were attached to nano electrodes.

Ben Feringa and his group were the first in 1999 to publish a photochemically driven rotary molecule with perfect control of directionality. In this system, rotation proceeds in only one direction. Photonic signals generate excited states which have to rearrange. In a sequence of events (two light-driven rearrangements and two thermally controlled processes), the rotor of the molecular motor undergoes a complete rotation in a perfectly controlled fashion. Feringa and his team published a beautiful video on the web which I would recommend you look at.

So let me show some more recent work. Many people have been interested in trying to make molecular systems which can contract or extend at will. We published the first system of what we called "a synthetic molecular muscle" in 2000. Later on, several groups have done interesting work in this field of molecular muscles. They could even make materials such as micrometer long fibres, which can be elongated or contacted by changing pH or by using another signal to "speak" to the molecule and force it to elongate and contract.

Nowadays there are many examples of molecular machines as well as a large number of research teams working in this field all around the world. The pirouetting catenanes and the molecular shuttle were among the first systems designed, prepared and studied in the field. From 1999 on, the light driven rotary motors, and even the nano cars, reported by Ben Feringa and his group were also real landmarks in the area of molecular systems undergoing controlled molecular motion. Then molecular muscles, compressors, molecular pumps, another beautiful example of Professor Stoddard, are among the most remarkable systems published in the course of the last decades.

To conclude, it should be stressed that before the emergence of molecular machines, synthetic molecules were mostly considered as still objects (i.e., motion less or undergoing random movements). Molecular systems undergoing large amplitude motions were very rare. The work of the scientists who created these molecular machines probably changed the way chemists look at molecules. Nowadays, numerous molecular machines and molecular motors have been created and studied. In addition, many groups are now working in this exciting field of research.

I think it is very risky to talk about precise applications,today, as far as I know, there is only one commercial application of rotaxanes in the field of intelligent materials, i.e., materials which can react to stimuli. One can think of information storage and processing, and several other applications, but probably for a long term, perhaps long-term future vectorization of biologically active species, is the most exciting, the most spectacular. Potentially, of course, if we can target invaders and bacteria, biopsy of tumorous cells, malignant cells that can of course be very exciting.

Of course, we have to keep in mind that applications are very important for the future, but we don't know how long it will take before really important applications come out. And some technologies which we are using nowadays, come from or originate from the basic research, and these basic research works can be very old. When you think of computers, it started with transistors and transistors started with semiconductor, and research on semiconductors was carried out during the 19th century.

If you would like to become someday scientists, please keep in mind that novelty is the most important. And it's also very important to be ready to interact with the others. Don't keep everything secret. Try to interact with many people. Jumping from a field that you are very familiar with to another, can also be very beneficial. And don't forget serendipity.

## About the Author

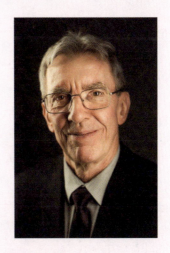

Jean-Pierre Sauvage, a French chemist, was born on October 21, 1944, Paris. He received his doctorate from the Louis Pasteur University (now part of the University of Strasbourg) in 1971. He served as director of research at the National Centre for Scientific Research (CNRS) from 1979 to 2009. He was awarded the 2016 Nobel Prize in Chemistry for his work on molecular machines with Scottish-American chemist Sir J. Fraser Stoddart and Dutch chemist Bernard Feringa. He now is Professor Emeritus of University of Strasbourg.

Sauvage and his wonderful research group have been interested in various fields including: (i) coordination photochemistry and solar energy conversion, (ii) $CO_2$ electrocatalytic reduction, (iii) chemical topology: catenanes, knots and rotaxanes, (iv) multifunctional ruthenium and iridium complexes for light-induced charge separation, (v) multifunctional porphyrins as models of the photosynthetic reaction centre as well as (vi) molecular switches and molecular machine prototypes such as a "swinging catenane", "muscles" or "compressors".

# 后　记

## 外国专家科学讲堂—— 一粒科学的种子

"外国专家科学讲堂"是科技部国外人才研究中心举办的公益性科普活动，旨在邀请外国专家、学者向中国青少年进行科普讲座与展示，促进中外科普交流，培养和提高青少年的科学兴趣和科学素养。

"科学讲堂"邀请外国专家针对公众关注的科技热点，面向青少年开展科普讲解、实验演示等活动。2019—2022年，科技部国外人才研究中心组织"外国专家科学讲堂"共51场，有来自英、美、法、德、日、意等20个国家的约40位专家作为主讲人参与，主题涉及人工智能、化学、物理、工程、航空、材料等领域。

### ▌高端外国专家讲授前沿科学知识

主讲外国专家大多为国内外高校和科研院所的教授、研究员，还有来自产业界的专家，具有较高的科研水平，包括两位诺贝尔奖获得者和多位中国政府友谊奖获得者。

讲座内容通常是外国专家的最新研究成果、本领域的研究热点等，比如中国科学技术大学教授储扎克讲解如何用光子的力量研究细胞，天津国际生物医药联合研究院研究员兰尼斯·梅里诺介绍脑机接口，西安交通大学助理教授穆罕默德讲解纳米技术的最新研究方向和应用。

外国专家在"科学讲堂"上重视学生体验、课堂互动，紧密围绕现实生活中的问题策划内容、设计课堂实验，引导学生探索现象背后的科学原理。中科院微电子所研究员亨利·阿达姆松以"为什么手机在过去几十年来变得越来越小"引导学生了解集成电路技术的发展。美国圣马丁大学教授帕克抛出问题"为什么救护车迎面而来时，警笛的声调越来越高，远离时声调越来越低"，以此解释多普勒效应，并设计课堂实验"发声网球"以帮助学生更好理解该理论。2021年5月邀请旅英华人高新科技商业协会会长张其军讲解病原微生物，科普新冠病毒。

高端专家结合当前全球科学热点把最前沿的科学知识、研究方法介绍给学生，深受学生喜爱欢迎，也推动了我国科普水平的提升。

## ▌ 在线授课便利全球科学家参与、惠及更多人群

为克服新冠疫情影响，"科学讲堂"积极探索在线授课新模式，不仅可以面向全球邀请科学家，也扩大了受众规模。

2021年5月全国科技活动周期间，两位诺贝尔奖获得者在线为我国青少年授课。2016年诺贝尔化学奖获得者让-皮埃尔·索维奇教授在线主讲"分子机器和马达的作用：从生物学到化学"，2016年诺贝尔物理学奖获得者迈克尔·克斯特里兹教授在线主讲"物理研究与诺奖之路"。为了这几场讲座，身在英国的张其军博士协助我们联系了英、美、法等国的多位诺贝尔奖获得者，我们和各位专家跨时空在线沟通，确定授课内容、在线技术细节等，成功促成了讲座的顺利举办。这几场讲座还进行了现场直播，约一万人通过直播观看让-皮埃尔·索维奇教授的讲座，这是"科学讲堂"的首次全程直播。

由于疫情防控需要，2021年原计划进入武汉两所小学的3场讲座，在湖北省对外科技交流中心、武昌区教育局的支持下提前半天由线下改为线上，武汉市14所小学的千余名小学生共同聆听专家授课，实现了更大规模的受众覆盖。

正如新加坡专家郑子斌在主讲"人工智能与未来学习"讲座时介绍的，人工智能前沿技术与在线教育的深度融合，提高了教育的可及性，让优质教育资源以更高效的方式惠及更广大的人群。

## ▌ 激发科学兴趣，助力提升青少年的科学素养

"科学讲堂"不仅激发了青少年的好奇心、想象力和对科学的浓厚兴趣，也有利于培育批判思维、创新意识和创新能力。

在井冈山小学，天津大学教授西格尔购买了大量荧光棒、液体暖宝，全体学生都能亲自体验化学反应中的发光发热现象，极大地激发了学生对科学的兴趣。北京亦庄实验中学学生黄明晋说，对分子马达"动起来"那堂课印象最深，这让他更加热爱化学。中国科技大学教授储扎克在安徽省岳西县柳畈小学做了关于成像的科学基础的讲授，令校长非常感慨，他说，短短的一节课激发了学生极大的求知欲，学生们从来没有像这样愿意去思考和分享科学问题。北京化工大学教授戴伟通过大量实验让学生了解到科学是要通过实验验证的，而不是人云亦云，要培养自己的独立思考能力和批判思维。

四年来，"外国专家科学讲堂"介绍了海豚、大熊猫、大象、岩鱼、兰花、无花果等独具特色的动植物。这些讲座让学生了解了这些动植物在生态系统中的独特作用，比如大象通过吃和排便促进种子的传播、无花果和榕小蜂的共生关系，也让学生认识人类生活给动植物带来的影响，比如很多兰花品种因为人类的过度采摘和栖息地丧失等被列入了中国红色濒危物种，引导学生从小拥有生态环境保护意识、热爱大自然。成都大熊猫繁育研究基地研究员、美国动物行为专家James Edward Ayala表示，希望孩子们知道人类发现

了自然界很多很有趣的规律，但还有更多有趣的现象和规律人类尚不清楚，需要年轻一代去探索和发现。

基于"科学讲堂"的优质内容，我们编写的《外国专家讲科普》（中英双语）于2021年在科技文献出版社出版，并于2022年3月入选国家新闻出版署《2022年农家书屋重点出版物推荐目录》。

本书是基于"科学讲堂"的第二本科普图书，各篇的主题更加具体，也更贴近日常生活。在向专家约稿时，各位专家都积极回应，表示对传播科学知识要全力支持。他们不辞劳苦在繁忙的教育和科研中挤出时间执笔撰写文章。特别感谢各位专家为"外国专家科学讲堂"项目和本书的辛苦付出。感谢你们为科学、为自然、为探索、为未来，种下一粒粒种子。


张　晓

科技部国外人才研究中心

《国际人才交流》执行主编

# Afterword

## Foreign Experts Science Class: A seed of Science

    Foreign Expert Science Class is a science popularization activity for public benefit held by Foreign Talent Research Center, Ministry of Science and Technology. It aims to invite foreign experts and scholars to give lectures and presentations on popular science to Chinese teenagers, promote exchanges between China and foreign countries in the field of science, develop teenagers' scientific interest and improve their scientific literacy.

    Foreign experts are invited to carry out popular science explanation, experimental demonstration and other activities for teenagers in view of the science and technology hot topics of public concern. From 2019 to 2022, Foreign Talent Research Center MOST of Ministry of Science and Technology organized 51 scientific lectures delivered by foreign experts, with about 40 foreign experts from 20 countries, including the UK, the US, France, Germany, Japan and Italy, participating as keynote speakers on topics ranging from artificial intelligence, chemistry, physics, engineering, aviation to materials and etc.

## ▌ High-end Foreign Experts Teach Cutting-edge Scientific Knowledge

Most of the foreign lecturers are professors and researchers from universities and research institutes at home and abroad. Experts from the industry are also invited. They have many academic achievements and have reached high research level.Two among them are Nobel Prize winners and others include several Chinese Government Friendship Award winners.

The content of the lecture is usually the latest research achievements of the foreign experts and research hotspots in the field. For example, Professor Chu Zak from the University of Science and Technology of China explained how to use the power of photons to study cells. Researcher Lannes Merino from Tianjin International Joint Research Institute of Biomedicine introduced brain-computer interface, and assistant professor Mohammed from Xi 'an Jiaotong University explained the latest research direction and application of nanotechnology.

Foreign experts attach importance to student experience and in-class interaction, plan content closely around problems in real life, and design classroom experiments, guiding students to explore the scientific principles behind phenomena. Henry Adamson, a researcher at the Institute of Microelectronics of the Chinese Academy of Sciences, guided students to understand the development of integrated circuit technology with a talk on "Why mobile phones have become smaller and smaller over the past decades." Parker, a professor at St. Martin's University in the United States, explained the Doppler effect by asking why siren tones get higher and higher when an ambulance is oncoming and lower when it is away. He even designed a classroom experiment called Vocal Tennis to help students better understand the theory. In May 2021, we invited Zhang Qijun, president of the Chinese Hi-tech Business Association in the UK, to explain pathogenic microorganisms and popularize the novel coronavirus.

The high-end experts introduce the most cutting-edge scientific knowledge and research methods to the students based on the current scientific hot spots in the world, which is welcomed by the students, but also help promote the popularization of science in our country

## ▎ Online Teaching Makes It Easier for Scientists around the World to Participate and Benefit More People

To overcome the impact of the COVID-19 pandemic, the Science Class has been actively exploring new online teaching modes. Not only have we been able to invite scientists from all over the world, but also to expand the audience.

During the National Science and Technology Week in May 2021, two Nobel Prize winners gave online lectures to our Chinese teenagers. Professor Jean-Pierre Sauvage, winner of the 2016 Nobel Prize in Chemistry, lectured on " Molecular Machines and Motors in Action From Biology to Chemistry ". Professor Michael Koesterz, winner of the 2016

Nobel Prize in Physics, lectured on "Research in Physics and the Path to the Nobel Prize". For these lectures, Dr. Zhang Qijun in the UK assisted us to contact a number of Nobel laureates from the UK, the US, France and other countries. We communicated with the experts online across time and space to determine the teaching content and online technical details, which successfully facilitated the smooth holding of the lectures. The lectures were also broadcast live, with about 10,000 people watching Jean-Pierre Sauvage's lectures, the first full live broadcast held by the Science Class.

In 2021, due to the need of epidemic prevention and control, the three lectures which were originally planned to be held in two primary schools in Wuhan, had to be delivered online with only half a day to get everything done. Thanks to the support of Hubei International Science and Technology Exchange Center and Education Bureau of Wuchang District, more than one thousand primary school students from 14 primary schools in Wuhan attended the lectures given by experts simultaneously, achieving a larger audience coverage.

As Zheng Zibin, an expert from Singapore, introduced in his lecture "Artificial Intelligence and Future Learning", the deep integration of cutting-edge artificial intelligence technologies and online education has improved the accessibility of education, allowing high-quality educational resources to benefit more people in a more efficient way.

# Stimulate the Interest in Science, and Help to Improve the Scientific Literacy of Young People

The Science Class not only stimulates the curiosity, imagination and keen interest in science among young people, but also helps cultivate critical thinking, innovative awareness and innovative ability.

In Jinggangshan Primary School, Segal, a professor from Tianjin University, bought a large number of glow sticks and liquid warmer, so that all students could experience the phenomenon of luminescence and heating in chemical reactions, which greatly aroused students' interest in science. Huang Mingjin, a student at Yizhuang Experimental High School in Beijing, said he was most impressed by the "moving molecular motors" lesson, which made him more interested in chemistry. The headmaster of Liufan Primary School in Yuexi county, Anhui province,once spoke highly of the class about the scientific basis of imaging given by Chu Zach, a professor at the University of Science and Technology of China. A short class, he said, inspired great thirst for knowledge and students had never been so willing to think about and discuss scientific problems. Dai Wei, a professor at Beijing University of Chemical Technology, demonstrated numbers of experiments and through which,taught his students that science should be verified by experiments rather than following others' opinions, and that they should cultivate their own independent thinking and critical thinking.

Over the past four years, foreign experts have introduced various animals and plants with unique characteristics, such as dolphins, giant pandas, elephants, rockfish, orchids, figs and etc. These lectures taught students about the unique roles of those animals and plants in ecosystems, like elephants promoting seed dispersal through eating and defecation, fig and fig wasp symbiosis, as well as the impact of human life on plants and animals. For example, in China many orchid species are listed as endangered species because of people's over-harvesting and habitat loss. The experts guided students to build the awareness of ecological environment protection and love to nature since childhood. James Edward Ayala, a researcher at the Chengdu Research Base of Giant Panda Breeding and an American expert on animal behavior, once mentioned that he expected children to know that humans have discovered many interesting laws of nature, but there are many more interesting phenomena and natural laws that are still unknown to humans and need to be explored and discovered by the younger generation.

Based on the good quality of the Science Class, Science Classes From Foreign Experts(bilingual in Chinese and English) compiled by us was published by Science and Technology Academic Press in 2021, and selected into the Recommended Catalogue of Key Publications of Rural Library in 2022 by the National Press and Publication Administration in March 2022 .

This is the second popular science book based on the Science Class, and the topics are more specific and more close to daily life. When being requested for their manuscripts, the experts all responded positively, expressing their full support for the dissemination of scientific knowledge. They take the trouble to find time in their busy education and research to write articles. Special thanks to all the experts for their hard work for the

Foreign Expert Science Class and this book. Thank you for planting seeds for science, for nature, for exploration and for the future.

Zhang Xiao

Executive Chiefeditor of International Talent,

Foreign Talent Research Center, MOST

(Translated by Lin Hanying)